Ecological and Soci

This book is an edited collection of essays by fourteen multicultural women (including a few Anglo women) who are doing work that crosses the boundaries of ecological and social healing. The women are prominent academics, writers and leaders spanning Native American, Indigenous, Asian, African, Latina, Jewish and multiracial backgrounds. The contributors express a myriad of ways that the relationship between the ecological and social has brought new understanding to their experiences and work in the world. Moreover, by working with these edges of awareness, they are identifying new forms of teaching, leading, healing and positive change.

Ecological and Social Healing is rooted in these ideas and speaks to an "edge awareness or consciousness." In essence, this speaks to the power of integrating multiple and often conflicting views and the transformations that result. As women working across the boundaries of the ecological and social, we have powerful experiences that are creating new forms of healing.

This book is rooted in academic theory as well as personal and professional experience, and highlights emerging models and insights. It will appeal to those working, teaching and learning in the fields of social justice, environmental issues, women's studies, spirituality, transformative/environmental/sustainability leadership and interdisciplinary/intersectionality studies.

Jeanine M. Canty, PhD, professor at Naropa University, intersects issues of social and ecological justice within the transformative learning process. Selected works have been featured in *The Wiley Handbook of Transpersonal Psychology*, *International Journal of Transpersonal Studies*, *Sustainability: The Journal of Record* and *World Futures: Journal of New Paradigm Research*.

"Jeanine Canty brings us one of those rare and priceless books that free us from conventional reality and, in so doing, illumine our own gifts for personal and collective healing. Like a clarion call to affirm the authority of our often-marginalized experience, Canty's powerful essay, along with the women's voices she has assembled here, thrill me with the challenge to see and act in new ways. The intellectual excitement as well as the emotional grounding that I find in this collection charge my life with a sense of truth and adventure."
Joanna Macy, author, *Coming Back to Life*

"*Ecological and Social Healing* is a transformative collection of women's voices whose pain, passion, and resilience are a representation of millions of women whose stories are powerful interventions that interrupt a master narrative and shape what it means to live in a diverse, inclusive, and ecological world. Their stories offer hope for ecological and social healing beginning with self, transformed into social praxis. A must read to further understand ourselves in a complex relationship with our natural and social environments."
Suzanne Benally, executive director, Cultural Survival

"*Ecological and Social Healing* is one of the most inspiring and beautifully conceived compendium of texts by formidable women writers and scholars on the most salient and urgent issues of our troubled Anthropocene. It is a clarion call, an imperative, a spiritual crossroads for understanding and appreciating our interconnectedness and indebtedness to one another and the 'more-than-human'. From explications of the profound spiritual traditions of Navajo and Filipino cultures, to talk of restructuring our global economy and so much more, this compelling book teems with antidotes to living in a dark, paralyzed, wounded time. Let us gather and absorb the gnosis here and act on it. Many kudos to editor Jeanine M. Canty for moving our century forward."
Anne Waldman, poet

"We often speak of books 'breaking' new ground. *Ecological and Social Healing* heals it. It asks us all to reconnect areas of life that have been falsely divided to (re)discover the wisdom necessary to bear witness to the pain of the societal disconnect that has led to the degradation of our collective habitat. Only from that place of honoring can true healing begin. It is more than just reclaiming the feminine and the indigenous. It is reclaiming the whole."
Rev. angel Kyodo williams, Sensei

Ecological and Social Healing

Multicultural Women's Voices

Edited by Jeanine M. Canty

Routledge
Taylor & Francis Group

NEW YORK AND LONDON

First published 2017
by Routledge
711 Third Avenue, New York, NY 10017

and by Routledge
2 Park Square, Milton Park, Abingdon, Oxon, OX14 4RN

Routledge is an imprint of the Taylor & Francis Group, an informa business

© 2017 Taylor & Francis

Library of Congress Cataloging in Publication Data
Names: Canty, Jeanine M., editor.
Title: Ecological and social healing : multicultural women's voices / edited by Jeanine M. Canty.
Description: New York, NY : Routledge, 2016. | Includes index.
Identifiers: LCCN 2016003530| ISBN 9781138193659 (hardback) | ISBN 9781138193666 (pbk.) | ISBN 9781315639239 (ebook)
Subjects: LCSH: Environmentalism--Social aspects--United States. | Environmental sociology--United States. | Environmental justice--United States. | Social justice--United States. | Women and the environment--United States. | Ecofeminism--United States. | Minority women--United States.
Classification: LCC GE197 .E26 2016 | DDC 304.2082/0973--dc23
LC record available at http://lccn.loc.gov/2016003530

ISBN: 978-1-138-19365-9 (hbk)
ISBN: 978-1-138-19366-6 (pbk)
ISBN: 978-1-31563-923-9 (ebk)

Typeset in Adobe Caslon Pro
by Sunrise Setting Ltd, Brixham, UK

To all the young women and gender fluid students of color I have worked with over the years and wished I had had a better text to share with you—Victoria, Chelsey, Jade, Rose Marie, Faridah, Piñar, Rhea, Sherry, Cassandra, Lynn, Isabelle and Kevin. May you see shards of your narratives reflected here. To all of the ancestors of the women who contributed to this book—you accompanied us on this journey and have inspired us toward healing and your presence was felt throughout this book's creation. To Mother Earth and all of her beings, thank you for your patience and love while we reconnect in right relationship.

CONTENTS

INTRODUCTION

Jeanine M. Canty

This book is a collection of a myriad of women's voices that speak to the intersections between our current ecological and social crises and the healing work that is emerging. The women are prominent academics, writers, leaders and embodied practitioners spanning Native American, Indigenous, Asian, African, Latina, Jewish, Anglo and multiracial backgrounds and yet all are, to some degree, living amidst the mainstream cultural paradigm of the United States. We span multiple generations of women—many who were on the frontlines of the movements of the 1960s and 1970s and many who were born during and after and were shaped by them. The contributors share diverse expressions of ways in which the relationship between the ecological and social has brought new understanding to their experiences and work in the world as well as new forms of teaching, leading, healing and positive change.

It has been over fifty years since the struggles for civil rights within the US for African Americans, Latinas, Native Americans and peoples of color in general, as well as for LGBTQ communities, converged with the feminist and environmental movements. The 1960s through the early 1970s marked a time period of social unrest and demands for change, underscored by a deep unraveling of the patriarchical, racist, mechanistic, market driven paradigms we were living under. I was born in the aftermath of this time, growing up during the 1970s and 1980s, an African American, multiracial female in the first (and often last) generation that attended integrated schools. It is worth noting that the word "aftermath" holds both positive and negative connotations—it can signify either a resulting time period following a destructive event *or* new growth. Many of the framing stories of my childhood stressed the values of equal opportunity, gender and racial equity, justice, love and open doors. The post civil rights period of the 1970s and 1980s was a time of transition. There was great hope for true liberty, justice and freedom for all; yet the nation stepped into the edge of the unknown.

Tragically, the perceived massive gains for people of color, women, and for environmental protection, have, to a large extent, eroded. We are still struggling with the same issues and our nation is besieged with massive racial and social injustice, the real and threatening revocation of women's rights, as well as the continual devastation of the life systems of Earth. Currently the fervor of the activism of the 1960s and 1970s has returned with what many term as a "movement of movements," where the interlocking systems of social and ecological injustice are no longer parceled out into single issue platforms. While it is, once again, an exciting time of potential change, the promises of open doors for marginalized peoples appear dulled—those doors opened narrowly, with limited affirmative action within big business and other industry, benefiting small percentages of oppressed groups. It is disheartening to witness that, five decades since the advent of the Civil Rights Movement, peoples of color are still struggling with issues of basic civil rights and are, ironically, often positioned to teach about, unravel and push for change in response to their own oppression.

This book comes out of the intersections of the social and ecological through the varied experiences of a diverse group of women. It is birthed out of the conditions we were each born into and it moves beyond the breakdowns and criticisms of these conditions, going into the healing and emerging insights. The work here honors the uniqueness of our circumstances and gives voice and freedom to the new patterns and wisdom that come from living on these edges between ecological and social issues. In creating our chapters, we employed a subtheme of "edges of transformation."

This subtheme has many lenses. Permaculture often claims that everything interesting happens at the edges between ecosystems. Transformative learning acknowledges that our worldviews change through having experiences that confront our identities and force us to make meaning. Edges also represent crossings into liminal spaces—stepping into the mystery of nature, spirit and our psyches, not knowing what one may encounter. Edges are often hard, whether in sensory sharpness or through the psychological fear of transitioning into a different reality. Nor are edges seamless transitions—they do not embody the conventional sense of wholeness; edges are often formed when something breaks, such as a rock formation or a held sense of personal and collective identity.

As we are moving to restore our relationships with nature, including one another, in an extremely diverse globally connected planet, the knowledge we need is held by those who are crossing boundaries between fixed viewpoints, restoring relationships with place, holding multiple ways of being and reintegrating feminine wisdom. We currently have generations of peoples who straddle multiple edges—varied identities that consist of unique combinations of the indigenous and multicultural, the colonized and colonizer, the displaced and the reclaimer. We represent the joining of multiple communities, histories and identities.

As women transiting the edges between the ecological and social, we have powerful experiences that are creating new forms of healing. Our narratives cross the boundaries of place, history, trauma, worldview, restorying, compassion and healing. Our aim is to break the patterns that keep us separate from our ecological homes and one another, and moreover create power in a collective revisioning of our future.

Chapter Overviews

Within the first part, *Worldview*, the women share ideas and personal stories that speak to how our planetary worldviews have been altered by the impacts of imperialism, globalization and climate change as well as the power of emerging worldviews that take all of this in and are life-embracing. In "This is What Happens When," author and professor Mei Mei Evans queries, "...what actions we might take individually and collectively to ensure that future generations—both human and wild—will inherit a healthy, flourishing world that offers beauty, spiritual sustenance, and the continuance of both cultural and biodiversity?" Her inquiry dates back twenty-five years, to when she witnessed the irreparable damage resulting from the *Exxon Valdez* spill near to her Alaskan community. Evans brings into context the links between the oil industry, climate change and environmental injustice and how to work with the denial and psychic numbing occurring as a result of these travesties. She stresses the need to feel these issues, find empowerment through solidarity with the planet and one another and to take decentralized action with some starting steps.

In "Sustainability and the Soul," author and feminist Susan Griffin contemplates the relationship between what we see and how we tell the story of what we see, claiming that if we do not listen and embody what our interactions with nature tell us—the non-rational, unquantifiable experiences that are not valued within western culture—the destructive patterns we currently employ will continue. Griffin speaks to ways the western paradigm has silenced the natural world, including what is natural within ourselves. This silencing erases the knowledge of places and the peoples who are indigenous to them, allowing their exploitation. She dispels the reverence for western science, instead recognizing the deep wisdom of traditional ecological knowledge of indigenous peoples and their current climate justice leadership.

Within "Seeing Clearly through Cracked Lenses," author and professor Jeanine M. Canty articulates the power of being outside of any one paradigm, particularly the prevailing paradigm, in order to open up to a larger perspective—that of the Earth. This occurs when people are immersed within multiple paradigms such as those who are members of marginalized cultures (the indigenous, people of color, women, working class and poor) *and* are living within the dominant paradigm, as well as people who have experienced events that have broken their worldviews. These experiences provide an opportunity to hold a larger view that sees our collective brokenness, listens to the wisdom of the Earth and her diverse cultures, and holds the collective well-being in a way that promotes positive action and healing.

With the final essay surrounding worldview, speaker and trainer Anita L. Sanchez attends to the power of reconnecting to the ways of the ancestors and holds perspectives of emerging scientific paradigms in order to bring us back into balance with the Earth. Drawing from her multicultural background, which includes both the indigenous and the western, "Intersection of an Indigenous World View and Applied Neurophysiology" identifies shared principles within Earth-based worldviews and new areas of science that stress our interconnectedness with all of Earth's beings and how this translates to being in mutually responsible relationships with life.

The second part, *Place*, speaks to restorying our sense of place, whether in urban or rural settings, through relearning being at home in nature, as well as bringing back the place-based wisdom of one's indigenous ancestry to one's present state. It starts through addressing marginalization and healing within the urban environment with professor and community leader Ana I. Baptista's essay "Finding Hope at the Margins: a Journey of Environmental Justice." Baptista shares the story of realizing as a child that her community was marginalized and, as a result, developing a deep understanding of environmental justice—how social injustice and ecological inequity are seamless—and acting on this knowledge through community leadership. Part of the key wisdom she enacts is that "People with the lived experience of injustice are the ones that have the legitimate claim to speak about those injustices and to demand to be seen and heard." Much of her work centers on ways people within a community can transform its future.

Inhabiting the lens of cultural ecology, educator and scholar Nina S. Roberts advocates the role of women of color as environmental leaders as a means of transforming society. Her essay "Intricate Yet Nourishing: Multiracial Women, Ecology, and Social Well-being" relays how being multiracial and female instills an edge awareness of seeing oppression and challenging the status quo. Roberts interweaves seemingly unrelated areas such as the increasing multiracial population within the US, the differing relationships minority populations have with wilderness and the connections between women and the environment.

Within "Linking Ancestral Seeds and Waters to the Indigenous Places We Inhabit," indigenous scholar–activist Melissa K. Nelson and co-leader and clinical psychologist Nícola Wagenberg provide a powerful example of reconnecting youth with their indigenous connections to place. Their project *Guardians of the Waters—Tribal Canoe Revitalization Project* is "an intercultural, intergenerational, multi-tribal collaborative venture that, through tribal research, cultural practices and performances, supports the renewal of indigenous watercraft traditions of the Pacific." The story and enactment of this project is a beautiful model of decolonization and reconnection with traditional culture and ecology.

"Beauty out of the Shadows: the Indigenous Turn in a Filipina Narrative" continues the work of relanguaging and storytelling to reclaim indigenous consciousness. Professor Leny Mendoza Strobel returns to her heritage from Pampanga (a province within the Philippines) to restore her connection with place and culture, and seeks to bring this sense of being to her current home. Leaving behind academic discourse, her work is with embodied practices and reindigenization through The Center for Babaylan Studies. One of her guiding questions is: "How do we learn to dwell in someone else's land without thinking like a colonizer?"

While all of the chapters within this book offer healing pathways, the final part, *Healing*, gives us poignant models and stories of mending relationships. This part begins with educator Molly Bigknife Antonio providing another powerful example of reconnecting youth to their traditional ecological and cultural practices. "Navajo Youth: Cultivating Healthy Relationships through Traditional Reciprocity" shows how teaching youth ancestral wisdom and practices brings restoration of sacred, mutually beneficial connections, sparking healing within the larger local biocultural community. The author shares that when immersing youth into their traditions, the results include gratitude and increased altruism to humans and nature.

Artist and educator Ju-Pong Lin employs decolonial practice to model using language and ideas that lie within the borders of various identities. "A Yinyang, Ecocritical Fabulation on *Doctor Who*" centers on pattern-breaking and using language and telling our stories as a step toward healing the destruction we have done to this planet and one another, as well as to ensure our biocultural diversity. This reweaving of story through creative and off-centered form repatterns meaning and identity.

Co-founder of Bioneers and feminine leader Nina Simons models the power of allyship in crossing the boundaries of race, gender, biodiversity and justice by telling stories of how she opened her awareness and compassion around these issues. "Piercing the Shell of Privilege: How My Commitments to Environmental and Gender Justice Moved from My Head to My Heart" embodies the relationship between the personal and the political and the importance of understanding very diverse realities and deeply feeling the issues facing our planet. Her work concentrates on shifting the dynamic through collaborative, multicultural women's leadership within an Earth-centered beloved community.

Within the final essay, "Our Differentiated Unity: An Evolutionary Perspective on Healing the Wounds of Slavery and the Planet," writer and educator Belvie Rooks dives into a personal narrative of healing that responds to our collective divides as traumatized peoples. She implores the importance of creating a planetary frame of reference that includes our interconnected stories in order to heal our collective wounding. She mirrors this by sharing some of her stories as a descendant of both the enslaved and slave holding peoples of the southern US and her personal journey to hold compassion for all beings.

WORLDVIEW

Spaces In-Between, Prescott National Forest, Arizona by M. Jennifer Chandler.

Vow

Mothers
You gave what
You got; I shall not.

Honey
Hushed daughters
God privileged sons

You gave
What you got
Fathers; I shall not.

—Rachel Bagby

1

THIS IS WHAT HAPPENS WHEN

MEI MEI EVANS

We are the children of the Age of Enlightenment, and we have brought the world to the brink of ruin by acting under the delusion that humans are separate from the earth, better somehow, in control of it. We believe that humans are the only creatures of spirit in a universe otherwise made up of stones and insensate matter; that the nonhuman world was created for us alone and derives all its value from its usefulness to humanity....
—Kathleen Dean Moore[1]

We seem to think that we can substitute an irreplaceable and irretrievable beauty with something which we have created ourselves.
—Pope Francis[2]

Humanity now reaps the deadly harvest of that which the exploitation-based paradigm of western civilization has sown. Our failure to acknowledge and act in accordance with what each of us instinctively senses to be the true interconnectedness of all life has led us to the brink of an unimaginable eventuality: climate change looms as an imminent threat to earthly life as we know it.

Not only has the consumption-oriented lifestyle of developed and developing nations imperiled all human life, but it threatens equally

3

the entirety of what philosopher David Abram has called the "more-than-human" world[3] with habitat loss and mass extinctions. As Kathleen Dean Moore, self-described moral philosopher and environmental advocate, puts it:

> We believe we can destroy our habitat without also destroying ourselves… Ecological and evolutionary science tell us that this is false; that humans are part of interconnected, interdependent systems; that the thriving of the individual parts is necessary for the thriving of the whole; and that we are created, defined, and sustained by our relationships, both with each other and with the natural world.[4]

Even in the face of mounting evidence to its unsustainability, those relative few who profit from the desecration of the living world and the destruction of its diverse human communities persist in pursuing business as usual in a winner-take-all quest for supremacy. The illogic of corporate capitalism not only exhausts its own supply of resources and fouls its own nest, but it also exacts a fearsome price in human and more-than-human lives and webs of relationship.

I wish in this chapter to try to come to terms with what this juncture in global history means to each of us, to ask what actions we might take individually and collectively to ensure that future generations—both human and wild—will inherit a healthy, flourishing world that offers beauty, spiritual sustenance, and the continuance of both cultural and biodiversity. How do we act on the awareness that all beings are connected in an intricate, extensive lattice of life, now gravely imperiled? What does it mean to be a good human in these circumstances? Should I live to be old, as I hope to do, what is it that I will look back on and take solace in knowing that I did or attempted to do?

Twenty-five years ago it was my destiny to experience firsthand the environmental and social disruptions visited by the *Exxon Valdez* oil spill on the human and wildlife communities of coastal south central Alaska. I have done my best to bear witness to this tumultuous experience in my novel, *Oil and Water*, which seeks to dramatize not only the unprecedented environmental destruction of that event but something that degraded the relationships of the area's human inhabitants as well: the unholy bargain proposed by the Exxon corporation (with the federal government's and the State of Alaska's complicity) that enabled many to profit from the disaster, to become "spillionaires."[5] British Petroleum's horrific Deepwater Horizon debacle in the Gulf of Mexico in 2010, as well as Royal Dutch Shell's plundering of Nigeria, among other oil companies' questionable conduct worldwide, have done nothing to change my low opinion and mistrust of their industry. The generally unethical, rapacious, and polluting behavior of petrochemical corporations worldwide has led many of us to conclude that "the way the fossil fuel industry conducts its business is not all right with me." Happily, the divestment movement is spreading throughout the world, bringing such pressure to bear that even the philanthropic Rockefeller Brothers Fund, heir to the fortune of John D. Rockefeller's Standard Oil company, has jettisoned its fossil fuel holdings. The University of California and the nation of Norway are but the latest to commit to divestment as of this writing.

Background on Climate Change

When the Intergovernmental Panel on Climate Change (IPCC), a group of several hundred scientists from around the world assembled by the United Nations, released its most recent report in spring 2014, it forecast crop failure and ever-decreasing supplies of freshwater as well as catastrophic sea-level rise and the continued increased likelihood of violent weather events.[6] Since then, according to NASA, Earth, as of early September 2015, has experienced the warmest eight-month period since records began to be kept in 1880, surpassing even 2014's record-setting warmth.[7] Why does this matter?

James Hansen, former director of the NASA Goddard Institute for Space Studies, is widely considered to be one of the world's leading climate scientists. His book, *Storms of My Grandchildren: The Truth About the Coming Climate Catastrophe and Our Last Chance to Save Humanity*, is a call to immediate action.[8] (Hansen, a career scientist, is not exactly one to indulge in poetic hyperbole, so please take a moment to let the enormity of his book's title sink into your psyche.)

Hansen and others have concluded that the Earth can sustain no more than 350 ppm (parts per million) of carbon dioxide in the atmosphere before we are assured of global meltdown—in the form of the aforementioned cataclysmic storms (think of the hitherto unprecedented destruction wrought by the Russian and Australian heat waves of 2010 and 2013–2014 respectively, Hurricane Katrina or "Superstorm" Sandy, or 2013's Typhoon Haiyan, as well as the record-setting number and ferocity of wildfires in the western US in 2015), to say nothing of the more incremental changes to weather and climatic conditions as we have known them, including sea-level rise and ocean acidification. April 2014 marked the first month in at least 800,000 years that carbon dioxide in the atmosphere attained 400 ppm, and the level continues to climb.[9] Simply put, without immediate action to drastically reverse this trend, we increasingly inhabit a world in which the continued occurrence of climatic disruptions is no longer a question of if, but when, those disruptions will occur.

Hansen advocates that "most of the fossil fuels must be left in the ground... That is the explicit message that the science provides."[10] He writes that "the science demands a simple rule: Coal use must be prohibited unless and until the emissions can be captured and safely disposed of."[11] Dismissing the myth of "Clean Coal" entirely, Hansen states that if we hope to solve the climate crisis, "we must phase out coal emissions. Period."[12]

From Despair to Empowerment

Our individual despair, hopelessness, and sense of overwhelm in the face of seemingly irreversible climate collapse is one shared by people worldwide. We are not alone in our experience of grief. But there are strategies for confronting the sense of disempowerment we may feel and for transforming it into positive action. The work of those like deep ecologist Joanna Macy, who first designed workshops to address the notion of moving individuals and society "from despair to empowerment" in the face of environmental and technological annihilation, holds critical insights for us today.[13]

First, we must acknowledge and accept the "psychic numbing" that acts to shut down our emotional response in the face of the enormity of climate change. As one despair-to-empowerment workshop leader, Kevin McVeigh, has put it: "No feeling, no healing." According to him, we must "let in the reality of what is happening…, telling each other the truth of what we see … feeling the *pain*, …and validating it as sane and purposeful."[14] In the absence of this validation, McVeigh warns, psychic numbing results:

> [T]he *feelings* themselves may seem life-threatening … to the extent that we judge them to be too painful, frightening, or unpleasant, we may begin to turn them off completely. Believing that our feelings are the real threat, we begin to screen out systematically all data which arouse [them]… We gradually lose our ability to have any emotional reaction at all to the possibility that all life on earth could be destroyed.[15]

Once we've come to grips with the fact that psychic numbing or denial is a natural response to the fear engendered by the threats posed by climate collapse, we can develop a new perspective of reality and then reclaim our power to act. Macy, McVeigh, and others stress the importance of fostering and drawing strength and support from each other and in solidarity with the living planet. Finally, they emphasize the importance of good self-care or, as McVeigh puts it, "taking good care of ourselves and each other while we care for the world."[16]

Sandra Steingraber, longtime environmental activist and the author of *Living Downstream: An Ecologist's Personal Investigation of Cancer and the Environment*, among other books, sometimes deploys a strategy of using her subject position as a mother to examine the paradigms that lubricate the engine of corporate capitalism. In a 2013 Bioneers interview, Steingraber said that our job as parents is to make children feel safe, and that what makes children feel safe is the knowledge that grown-ups are doing things to address particular problems.[17] Regardless of whether or not we are actual parents, do we not have a moral responsibility to future generations (both the human and the "more-than-human") to safeguard the continuance of life on Earth? And doesn't it always feel better to do something than to do nothing?

Not long ago, people asked, "What is it going to take to disrupt the inertia?" But with the coming-together of 400,000 climate-change activists in New York City and the 2500 concurrent actions in 162 nations around the world on September 21st, 2014, we dare to hope that that inertia has been disrupted once and for all. The Catholic Church, President Obama, and other world leaders have finally gotten on the bus, and organizations like 350.org are helping to coordinate meaningful citizen actions in response to global warming.[18] Indeed, the groundswell of bottom-up activism bodes well for human societies that have outgrown hegemonic top-down models of governance and commerce, a phenomenon that environmentalist Paul Hawken chronicles in *Blessed Unrest: How the Largest Social Movement in History is Restoring Grace, Justice, and Beauty to the World.*

A New Economic Paradigm

Jeremy Rifkin, founder and president of the Foundation on Economic Trends, examines the impact of scientific and technological changes on the economy, the workforce, society, and the environment. He states, "Our industrial civilization is at a crossroads," noting that, among other issues, a "record one billion human beings—nearly one seventh of the human race—face hunger and starvation" and that climate change "threatens to destabilize ecosystems around the world."[19] Rifkin founded The Third Industrial Revolution Global CEO Business Roundtable to work with others in search of "a new paradigm that could usher in a post-carbon era." He foresees an increasing "democratization of energy that will bring with it a fundamental reordering of human relationships, impacting the very way we conduct business, govern society, educate our children, and engage in civic life."[20] Rifkin points to the European Union, which is "expected to draw one-third of its electricity from green sources by 2020."[21]

Canadian activist and author Naomi Klein likewise proposes that the climate crisis challenges us to discard the ideology of the "free market" that enriches an elite class at the expense of everyone and everything else. Klein, now an advisor to Pope Francis, proposes instead a restructured global economy with reconfigured political systems. Like Rifkin, she and a growing number of others argue that we have reached the end of one economic era, and that it's time to replace it with another:

> [C]limate change – if treated as a true planetary emergency... – could become a galvanizing force for humanity, leaving us all not just safer from extreme weather, but with societies that are safer and fairer in all kinds of other ways as well. The resources required to rapidly move away from fossil fuels and prepare for the coming heavy weather could pull huge swaths of humanity out of poverty... This is a vision of the future that goes beyond just surviving or enduring climate change, beyond "mitigating" and "adapting" to it in the grim language of the United Nations. It is a vision in which we collectively use the crisis to leap somewhere that seems, frankly, better than where we are right now.[22]

Womanifesto

The bad news is that we're in a real jam. The better news is that, working together, we can create a new culture of sustainability. The question remains: Will we be able to do so in time? I have decided to act as if we can, if for no other reason than it makes me feel better to do so than to give up hope.

Here are things that all of us can do: Acknowledge our own deep sense of grief. Affirm that revolutionary change is not only possible, but may well be inevitable in the face of such a massive threat to planetary life.

Slow down the pace of our days and resist workaholism and other forms of "numbing out" as antidotes to feeling scared and helpless. Practice living more mindfully in order to break old habits of consumption that put our children's lives and the lives of other living beings at risk. "Live simply so that others may simply live" remains a useful and practical adage.

Foster community. We are strongest when we stand together. Especially commit to improving the lives of girls and women worldwide because their liberation ensures the world a livable future. Confront injustice when and where we encounter it and work in the hope of a better tomorrow for all of the Earth's inhabitants.

Cultivate an ever-deepening understanding of our home-places. Insist on socially just, environmentally sustainable, spiritually meaningful lives for ourselves and for others.

We must and we can create a new culture of interconnection.

Notes

1   DeMocker, "If Your House is on Fire: Kathleen Dean Moore on the Moral Urgency of Climate Change [Interview]", 2.
2   Francis, *Laudato Si': On Care for Our Common Home*, 26.
3   Abram, *The Spell of the Sensuous: Perception and Language in a More-than-Human World*.
4   DeMocker, "If Your House is on Fire", 2.
5   Evans, *Oil and Water*.
6   IPCC WGII AR5. "Climate Change 2014: Impacts, Adaptation, and Vulnerability."
7   Holthaus, "NASA: Earth Just Experienced the Warmest Six-Month Stretch Ever Recorded."
8   Hansen, *Storms of My Grandchildren: The Truth About the Coming Climate Catastrophe and Our Last Chance to Save Humanity*.
9   IPCC WGII AR5. "Climate Change 2014: Impacts, Adaptation, and Vulnerability."
10 Hansen, *Storms of My Grandchildren*, 172.
11 Ibid., 174.
12 Ibid., 176.
13 Macy, *Despair and Personal Power in the Nuclear Age*.
14 McVeigh, "No Feeling, No Healing."
15 Ibid., 3.
16 Ibid., 3.
17 Steingraber, Sandra, "Can Towns Legally Ban Fracking?"
18 http://350.org/.
19 Rifkin, "The Third Industrial Revolution: Toward a New Economic Paradigm," 294.
20 Ibid., 295.
21 Ibid., 299.
22 Klein, *This Changes Everything: Capitalism vs. The Climate*, 7.

References

Abram, David. *The Spell of the Sensuous: Perception and Language in a More-than-Human World*. New York: Vintage Books, 1997.
DeMocker, Mary. "If Your House is on Fire: Kathleen Dean Moore on the Moral Urgency of Climate Change [Interview]." *The Sun*, 444 (2012): 2–7. Available online at http://thesunmagazine.org/issues/444/if_your_house_is_on_fire (accessed 12 March 2016).
Evans, Mei Mei. *Oil and Water*. Fairbanks, Alaska: University of Alaska Press, 2013.
Francis, *Laudato Si': On Care for Our Common Home* [Encyclical], May 24, 2015.
Hansen, James. *Storms of My Grandchildren: The Truth about the Coming Climate Catastrophe and Our Last Chance to Save Humanity*. New York: Bloomsbury, 2009.
Hawken, Paul. *Blessed Unrest: How the Largest Social Movement in History is Restoring Grace, Justice, and Beauty to the World*. New York: Penguin Books, 2008.
Holthaus, Eric. "NASA: Earth Just Experienced the Warmest Six-Month Stretch Ever Recorded." *Future Tense: The Citizen's Guide to the Future*. Available online at www.slate.

com/blogs/future_tense/2014/10/13/nasa_earth_just_experienced_the_warmest_six_month_stretch_ever.html (accessed 13 October 2014).

IPCC WGII AR5. "Climate Change 2014: Impacts, Adaptation, and Vulnerability." Intergovernmental Panel on Climate Change (IPCC), 2014. Available online at www.ipcc-wg2.gov/AR5/ (accessed 12 March 2016).

Klein, Naomi. *This Changes Everything: Capitalism vs. The Climate*. New York: Simon & Schuster, 2014.

McVeigh, Kevin. "No Feeling, No Healing [handout], 1-3." Greenfield, MA: Green River Center, 1990.

Macy, Joanna. *Despair and Personal Power in the Nuclear Age*. Philadelphia: New Society Publishers, 1983.

Rifkin, Jeremy. "The Third Industrial Revolution: Toward a New Economic Paradigm." In *Sustainability*, edited by Christian R. Weisser, 294–301. Boston: Bedford/St. Martin's, 2015.

Steingraber, Sandra. *Living Downstream: An Ecologist's Personal Investigation of Cancer and the Environment*. New York: Vintage Books, 1998.

——. "Can Towns Legally Ban Fracking?" Bioneers interview. Available online at www.bioneers.org/can-towns-legally-ban-fracking (accessed 25 November 2013).

2

SUSTAINABILITY AND THE SOUL

SUSAN GRIFFIN

> I contemplate a tree...I can assign it to a species and observe it as an instance...I can overcome its uniqueness and form so rigorously that I recognize it only as an expression of the law...I can dissolve it into a number...But it can also happen, if will and grace are joined, that as I contemplate the tree I am drawn into a relation, and the tree ceases to be an It.
>
> —Martin Buber, *I and Thou*[1]

> The bush is sitting under a tree and singing
>
> —Ojibwa song

Regarding whether we can save ourselves at this treacherous moment, both in human history and the history of the planet, the heart of the matter lies in the way we see. When we watch the white edge of a wave crashing on the shore, or gaze down an astonishingly steep slope dotted with trees and stones to the verdant valley that lies a mile below, or notice the green and yellow and blue winged humming bird as it hovers in the air over the burgundy petals of a fuchsia plant, what are we seeing?

And perhaps even more to the point, what do we *tell* ourselves that we see. Because indeed, whether we acknowledge it or not, most of us will take in more than scientifically measurable data from what we are seeing. Over and above observable data, we will be touched, if not always by a sense of awe, by the sense of a meeting with a being, a force or a phenomenon that, for better or worse, somehow completes us.

Yet in the post industrial, technologically developed culture that currently dominates the world, such experiences are either overlooked, treated as sentimental, childish, imaginary, if not bordering on insanity and above all—considering every serious decision our societies make— irrelevant. The epistemology that rules the contemporary world is lacking an essential element we need for our survival. Without an embodied and lived understanding that we are inextricably linked to every other form life takes on the planet and that we cannot survive without these infinitely various others, we will continue to make the same kind of choices that are endangering our lives and our planet right now.

The pivotal word here is *embodied*. As the philosopher Martin Buber pointed out in 1923, to know the universe as alive, sentient, intelligent, a *you* and not an *it*, is very different from what one learns from books, in school or through a series of logical deductions and experiments.[2] Understanding the principles of ecological systems with the intellect alone does not often enough lead to the passionate actions we must take if we are to save ourselves and the earth.

When I was a young woman, during his campaign for Governor of California, Ronald Reagan became famous for saying, "If you've seen one redwood, you've seen them all." Though among environmentalists, progressives and democrats he was ridiculed for this attitude, he was elected nevertheless. As I think about that moment in our collective history, I realize that these words were not that distant from the way most of us in that time were trained to think. From our youngest days, we were schooled in what has been called scientific objectivity, a perspective in which, for example, within a species one tree can stand for all the rest of a species and by implication may just as easily be replaced by another of the same species.

This schooling must have created a silent conflict in many of us. Whether we are aware of it or not, the dominant view of the natural world that we were taught contradicts and invalidates the state of mind a great many of us had as children when we considered trees and animals and even stones and streams our friends. We talked to them, heard answers, felt their presence as comforting. But gradually, in a thousand subtle ways, we were taught that such relationships are considered imaginary and to believe in such things is childish. Even if, in grammar school, we chanced to read the words of celebrated poets, such as Walt Whitman's "Smile O voluptuous cool-breath'd earth," or Emily Dickinson's "The skies can't keep their secret," we came to understand that this was "just poetry." And in case those of us who studied literature in college failed to grasp the lesson, we soon learned that these poets were guilty of what the nineteenth century critic John Ruskin had called a "Pathetic Fallacy," the mistake of endowing nature with human qualities such as intelligence, emotion or the capacity to carry meaning.

As I write this, I begin to wonder what effect this repudiation of our earliest experiences of life has had on so many of us. If it does not make you a rebel, to be set at odds with your earliest, often intensely emotional perceptions can make you less able to discern and describe what you see and feel and thus, in the end, far more obedient to authority of every kind. To belittle and ridicule the perceptions of small children once dovetailed well with various pedagogies proffered by science then, theories asserting that infants have no or little emotional life, do not feel pain in the way adults do or are "bestial" and therefore need harsh, often corporal, discipline to coax them into civilized behavior.

But the cues that lead us to abandon our earliest impressions, impressions that often run so deep they have been essential to who we are, can be far more subtle and indirect than any verbal admonition and, because they are not articulated directly, often more effective. One such sign we are given consists of the paucity of vocabulary in most modern European languages, English included, for intimate, reciprocal relationships with nature. We have little way to talk about the meaning of such experiences outside of words that are not only inadequate but vaguely pejorative, implying, as does the word "mystic," that the relationship with nature that we experienced in childhood (or indeed for some, as adults) was unreal if not hallucinatory.

One of my earliest and most indelible memories is of standing in a field near our house in the San Fernando Valley, which was not yet in those days, the late forties, entirely covered with tract houses and shopping malls. Just five years old I found myself alone, two blocks from home and slightly frightened, though too enthralled with the way the wind swept through the tall green grass that surrounded me on every side to be captured by fear. In fact, I have no memory of being rescued or of going home. That seems irrelevant to an experience through which, in a far deeper sense, I had found myself.

Though I have some memory of trying as a child to communicate what I felt on that day, I was not able to convey it to anyone until I was an adult and had encountered other systems of knowledge, such as the philosophy behind the word XAXÀ that Okanagan writer and Wisdom Keeper Jeannette Armstrong defines as the "sacred aspect of being," through the knowledge of which, she writes, we become sacred, and thus, "cannot escape knowing that all life is XAXÀ."[3]

It is no accident that a culture that tries to erase the memory and meaning of our earliest relationships with the natural world would also describe indigenous cosmologies, such as the Okanagan way of understanding existence, as "childish," "primitive" and "irrational." The idea of a hierarchy of consciousness, which places European worldview above every other cosmology, accompanied centuries of European imperialism. Whether Christianity or modern technology, from Columbus to King Leopold, to Monsanto and Exxon Mobile, the claim that the Western view is superior serves as a rationale for seizing the land and exploiting the labor of local peoples while at the same time destroying the integrity of whole regions, breaking up communities, devastating if not destroying the cultures and languages, devaluing spiritual practices, replacing meaningful work with rote tasks.

But despite this suffering, Western culture appears to be numb to the consequences of our actions, as our common discourse indulges in a kind of amnesia—an amnesia that has swallowed our own histories and our own understandings too. What words for connectedness exist in the English language before the industrial revolution? Who among our own forbearers were moved off ancestral lands filled not only with personal but collective and natural memories, along with sites in which the sacred was once present, visible, palpable? As I ask these questions I am reminded again of my own family history, the alcoholism that went at least three generations back among my Irish ancestors whose land was colonized, culture belittled. As a teenager, I paid no mind to my mother's occasional references to elves and leprechauns, chalking this up to superstition. Yet, I can see now that this fey belief had a subtext. Well aware of the anomie and isolation she felt, I came early to understand that being confined to domestic life without any participation in the wider world had wounded her. Yet as I write I also realize that not just as a setting for this injury but equal to and implicated in it was the soulless world she had been born into, in the second decade of the twentieth century, as one after another modern conveniences appeared and the contours of the natural landscape, where she grew up in Southern California, were steadily obscured by concrete blocks, freeways and smog.

Indeed, as I revealed in another volume, *Woman and Nature*, the disenchantment of nature ushered in by modern science was hardly opposed to but in fact aided and abetted the massive witch burnings that occurred from the fourteenth through the seventeenth centuries, the victims of which were usually women, who were often herbal healers practicing according to the traditions of Europe's indigenous (pagan) cultures.[4]

In the codified and authoritarian medieval world, science gave birth to many virtues, among them a new curiosity about nature, and with that the practice of observation and experiment. Yet though science is and has been liberating, it comes with a double-edged sword even now. While at the moment it gives us crucial and clear evidence of global warming, the many technological achievements wrought by Western science have also brought us global warming itself, with all its devastating effects. Perhaps now is the time to question the modern Western worldview from an indigenous perspective, through which it seems less "free of values" than ignorant of the way all life is connected.

The claim that Western science provides a superior path rests above all on the claim that the scientific method yields objective results. This attitude persists even after science itself, through relativity, has shown that objectivity is impossible. Yet above and beyond the many examples in which corporations finance scientific studies that appear to support their products, science has not been above the influence of history. As the eminent philosopher of science, Paul Feyerabend, writes in his classic work, *Against Method*:

> ...the material that a scientist actually has at his disposal, his laws, his experimental results, his mathematical techniques, his epistemological prejudices, his attitude toward the absurd consequences of theories which he accepts, is indeterminate in many ways, ambiguous, *and never fully separated from the historical background.*[5]

Indeed, modern science developed during a particular historical period, the same centuries that saw the advent of European imperialism, the colonization of Asia, Africa and the Americas and the beginning of the slave trade. Hardly free of these events, scientific theories about race, the size of skulls and brains were used to justify racism and slavery. Theories positing the inferiority of various people of color put forward by Enlightenment thinkers, from Hume to Kant to Jefferson, in the eighteenth century, brought the Enlightenment philosopher, Condorcet, to write ironically that "nature herself" was being used as "an accomplice to political inequality."[6]

Yet though overt expressions of racism have been recognized and repudiated, another more subtle form of racism continues which undermines non-Western cultures by declaring diverse local systems of knowledge to be inferior to modern science. Just as Western science contributes genuine solutions to serious problems (for instance in public health), the West's technological wizardry plays a role in advocating and even advertising the superiority of nations and conglomerates engaged in what is called "development," which more often than not is fundamentally simply a contemporary form of corporate imperialism.

California, where I was born, has a long history of taking land from indigenous peoples, whether for gold mines, industry or agribusiness. This record continues today in, for instance, Willits, California, where despite local opposition the California Department of Transportation plans to destroy a valley containing wetlands, old oak forest, the eel river where salmon run, along with ancient Pomo Indian sites, in order to build a freeway bypass.

In a backhanded, largely unconscious way, the goal of "objectivity" has allowed such violations of land, wildlife and spiritual histories to occur by invalidating the whole range of subjective feelings that are part of human emotional intelligence; thus, any empathy colonizers and developers might feel for those they are violating is dampened, if not arrested altogether.

Gender plays a crucial role in the process. No society can function long without empathy. Yet, empathy threatens the drive the West has to control the earth. So our culture solves this conflict by assigning empathy to one gender: women, while at the same time limiting women's power in the social world. In the traditional way in which our culture defines gender, women are thought to be more emotional, sensual, sensitive and as part of this equation empathetic. According to the parameters of gender, and perhaps because we are considered to be closer to nature, women do not require any training to be more emotionally intelligent or feel more empathy. Men, on the other hand, must be trained to meet the requirements of masculinity, to become more like good soldiers who do not cry in sympathy with whomever or whatever lies in the path of progress.

Men certainly are born with a capacity for a full range of emotions. Yet since, in the name of masculinity, our culture has traditionally required that they suppress much of what they feel, the empathy they feel must be repressed. Like knowledge of mortality, vulnerability, fear, tenderness, all of which they also learn to disown, the empathy felt by men who do their best to conform to the idea of masculinity will be projected on "the weaker sex," women. In this regard, the words of one of the founders of modern science, Francis Bacon, are revealing. Using the interrogation of women accused of being witches as a metaphor to describe the scientific method, Bacon said that we should put nature on the rack and torture her to reveal her secrets.[7] This is a statement rich with many connotative meanings, among them an evident rage. A rage perhaps at a part of the self which has been projected on women but which, with an almost magical power, returns again and again with a secret knowledge, a knowledge of all that the soul has lost in what is a terrible bargain for power.

One of the most important effects of empathy is that it connects us to each other and to the earth. The collective nature of existence is mirrored in the very physical structure of our brains that accrue, order and interpret perceptions by association. Indeed, our own bodies are made up of communities of cells and organs that work cooperatively to benefit the whole. As Fritjof Capra[8] and other systems thinkers have pointed out, the entire universe is made up of cooperatives, countless networks woven between atoms, molecules, bodies, ecosystems and universes.

Most indigenous cultures are based on a powerful and embodied recognition of the communal and cooperative nature of all life. (In fact, in the discourse of the eighteenth century, this quality was cited as a sign of inferiority.) An understanding of the collective nature of nature is what separates indigenous precepts and practices from what has been called "magical thinking." Though some new age programs that promote magical thinking are advertised as reflecting native cosmologies, a major difference distinguishes the latter from the former. These often over simplified and shallow approaches treat individual fate as separate from the fate of both the community and the earth. Far from reflecting any indigenous culture, the idea, for instance, that a single person can survive a tsunami caused by global warming or radiation sickness from nuclear testing simply by thinking the right thoughts, is more a shadow side of Western culture, with its solipsistic delusions of power over nature, than an example of the disciplined, communal and realistic practices developed by native peoples over millennia.

In indigenous cultures all over the world, to become a shaman, a healer or a wisdom keeper requires many years of arduous training, apprenticeship to seasoned teachers, practice and service. Indigenous cultures also have their own sciences, not recognized until recently in the West, called Traditional Ecological Knowledge or TEK, which contain understandings accrued over generations from observations, experiments, communication with plants and animals and through living in community with and respect for the earth.[9]

The achievements of TEK are many and various, including navigating the ocean for thousands of miles without the use of any compass, mapping the stars and predicting sunrises, sunsets, eclipses and other astronomical events, sustainable agricultural methods, rotation and pharmaceutical knowledge. Regarding this last, even as the West dismisses the way in which indigenous people report they have gained this knowledge, which is often by listening to plants, Western pharmaceutical corporations have attempted to steal the healing properties indigenous people have discovered in this way by patenting the results.

As well as listening to plants and animals, many indigenous societies have developed skills that the West is only beginning to recognize, such as psychic communication or using dreams to be aware of possible futures. One ground breaking Western scientist, Barbara McClintock, awarded the Nobel Prize for her work in cytogenetics, developed a unique way of visualizing maize chromosomes out of a practice inspired by her studies in Tibetan Buddhism, which led her to listen to the maize and follow "a feeling for the organism." This is an approach that, as Native American scholar Marilou Awiakta makes clear, McClintok, had she been taught more about Native American culture, would have also encountered through the teachings of the Great Corn Mother.[10]

More collaborations with cultures and peoples who have a radically different worldview are occurring now, not only in science but in the organization of movements to save the earth, for example the significant leadership of Native American and Canada's First Peoples in opposition to the Key Stone Pipeline. But today, at the brink of disaster, the collaboration we have begun must run far deeper. As Evelyn Fox Keller writes, describing McClintock's approach to knowledge, "the ultimate…task, for both artists and scientists is to 'ensoul' what one sees, to attribute to it the life one shares with it."[11] To see in this way would require an enormous shift both in the inner and the outer worlds that comprise who we are and how we live.

Change of the proportions that will be required can be unsettling, if not frightening. Yet it is also entirely possible that such a shift might not be as cataclysmic as we fear, but instead feel a great deal more like a return to a familiar, older sense of being than an alien invention. To experience the rest of existence as vibrant with meaning is not new. On the earth today there exist countless traditional cultures and even sub cultures within our post industrial societies that understand nature as replete with a plentitude of sentient, intelligent, wise, spirited, vibrant forms of being. I am thinking of the landscape of my Celtic ancestors that is inhabited by spirits, elves and faeries, the mountains held sacred by the Navajo Nation in North America, the seiti, sacred stones of the Sami people who live in the arctic, the Yoruba view of the cosmos, of the Huichol goddess Tahema, who created the firmament between her antlers, the earth spirits worshiped by the Tabwa people who live in the Congo, Kami, the water spirits of the Dogon, the animism of the Shinto tradition in Japan, a small sample to which I hasten to add peasant cultures through the Mediterranean and in the Midi in France, together with neo pagans and countless artists, poets and storytellers in the Western tradition, including W.B. Yeats, H.D., Andre Breton, Remedios Varos, Frida Kahlo, and yes, Emily Dickinson and Walt Whitman.

And, in this act of recovering our ability to see all the souls in the world around us, we will be recovering our own souls too, finding in the sound of wind or leaves falling or water rushing in a stream, in the sight of a squirrel skittering up a tree or a bevy of birds migrating across the sky, "something more—something that is not me, for which we have no language," as scholar and member of the Potawatomi Nation, Robin Wall Kimmerer, writes, "the wordless being of others in which we are never never alone."[12]

Notes

1 Buber, *I and Thou*, 57.
2 Buber, *I and Thou*, 58.
3 Cardinal and Armstrong, *The Native Creative Process: A Collaborative Discourse*, 46.
4 See Griffin, *Woman and Nature: The Roaring Inside Her*, see also Merchant, *The Death of Nature: Women, Ecology and the Scientific Revolution*.
5 Feyerabend, Paul. *Against Method*, 66.
6 Lukes and Urbinati, *Condorcet: Political Writings*, 59.
7 Griffin, *Woman and Nature: The Roaring Inside Her*.
8 Capra, *The Web of Life: A New Scientific Understanding of Living Systems*.
9 See Nelson, *Original Instructions: Indigenous Teachings for a Sustainable Future*.
10 See Awiakta, "Selu Sings for Survival;" see also Keller, *A Feeling for the Organism: The Life and Work of Barbara McClintock*.
11 Keller, *A Feeling for the Organism: The Life and Work of Barbara McClintock*, 204.
12 Kimmerer, *Braiding Sweetgrass: Indigenous Wisdom, Scientific Knowledge and the Teaching of Plants*, 1.

References

Awiakta, Marilou. "Selu Sings for Survival." In *At Home on this Earth: Two Centuries of U.S. Women's Nature Writing*, edited by Lorraine Anderson and Thomas S. Edwards, 265–269. Hanover, NH: University Press of New England, 2002.

Buber, Martin. *I and Thou*. New York: Scribners, 1970.

Capra, Fritjof. *The Web of Life: A New Scientific Understanding of Living Systems*. New York: Anchor Books/Doubleday, 1996.

Cardinal, Douglas and Jeannette Armstrong. *The Native Creative Process: A Collaborative Discourse*. Penticton, British Columbia: Theytus Books, 1991.

Feyerabend, Paul. *Against Method*. London: Verso, 1975.

Griffin, Susan. *Woman and Nature: The Roaring Inside Her*. Berkeley: Counterpoint, 2014.

Keller, Evelyn Fox. *A Feeling for the Organism: The Life and Work of Barbara McClintock*. New York: W.H. Freeman Company, 1983.

Kimmerer, Robin Wall. *Braiding Sweetgrass: Indigenous Wisdom, Scientific Knowledge and the Teaching of Plants*. Minneapolis: Milkweed Editions, 2013.

Lukes, Steven and Nadia Urbinati, editors. *Condorcet: Political Writings*. Cambridge, UK: Cambridge University Press, 2012.

Merchant, Carolyn. *The Death of Nature: Women, Ecology and the Scientific Revolution*. New York: Harper One, 1990.

Nelson, Melissa K., editor. *Original Instructions: Indigenous Teachings for a Sustainable Future*. Rochester, VT: Bear & Company, 2008.

3

SEEING CLEARLY THROUGH CRACKED LENSES

JEANINE M. CANTY

Being whole or centered is often viewed as healthy and beneficial; one is at the heart of things as opposed to residing on the outskirts, being in the minority or appearing marginalized. Yet when looking at a worldview, when one's paradigm is centered on a fixed identity, a clear resonance of right and wrong, a concrete understanding of reality, a "consensus reality," one is often unaware of all of the things one does not know and, moreover, that there are so many things that one does not see. When one experiences many challenges to one's worldview, it often cracks this fixed reality, allowing one to open up one's awareness to larger perspectives. When our lenses of seeing are cracked, we have the opportunity to expand. A broken worldview fosters a more awakened and resilient reality. Experiences with racism, social inequity, ecological oppression and other forms of personal and collective trauma provide the keys for cracking our lenses, our worldviews. They are our modern day rites of passage and can birth an opening to individual and collective insight and healing. Within this chapter, the author identifies key concepts of worldview transformation in the light of social and ecological issues as well as other forms of trauma and traces her own journey as a woman of color engaging the ecological crisis.

Presently, the planet is in a state of crisis. To a large extent, we have finally accepted that global warming is a reality and issues of climate justice are paramount. Suffering across the globe extends to both our human and more than human communities, with the direct and indirect effects of corporate globalization, whether through species loss, pollution and toxicity, wide-scale poverty, resource and religious wars, violence against women and children, racism and other forms of social injustice, mental illness, addictions and spiritual loss. We are still submerged in an era that heralded mechanistic science and the objectification of nature, including people, religious dogmatism, patriarchy, colonization, genocide, enslavement and the large-scale consumption and accumulation of surplus. On a personal and collective level, there is a psychic numbing and apathy to what is occurring around us because it is too painful to behold, as well as a continual coaxing to believe that everything is perfectly okay. In essence we are a broken society.

Ecopsychology purports that the suffering of the planet and that of people are interconnected and both are calling for healing. Moreover, it claims people living under a globalized reality, where a corporate economic system rules, are for the most part ill, and this illness resides within the framework and practice of western culture, one that has separated its identity from the rest of the natural world and, as result, views the earth as a resource for human consumption.[1] Author and psychologist Chellis Glendinning[2] parallels two states of humanity that mark the boundaries of our transition from a hunter-gatherer society to one that is disconnected from nature. The latter is the original trauma— the moment human societies broke with their earth-based traditions in order to pursue large-scale agriculture, which led to our loss of wildness and a resulting domestication. Shariff Abdullah describes the ensuing culture as *Breakers*, those who are cut off from their earth-based origins and participate in the destruction of ecosystems and peoples alike. In contrast are the *Keepers*, those communities that are still living in harmony with the natural world and practicing their original traditions.[3] Glendinning's first state, the *primal matrix*, aligns with the *Keepers*. The primal matrix describes the state of humans before they broke away from earth-based worldviews and practices and is made up of three dimensions: "a sense of belonging and security in the world, trust, faith;"

"a sense of personal integrity, centeredness, capability; the consciousness of I" and "the capacity to draw vision and meaning from non-ordinary states of consciousness."[4] These can be summarized as the abilities to feel at home within the natural world, having a unique purpose in life and experiencing the numinous. The resultant movement from the primal matrix to the original trauma is that we, and particularly those of us enculturated within western society, are broken.

In accepting our brokenness, there is yearning for wholeness. The word *healing* is related to wholeness and the myriad of forms of present age healing work seem to center on returning to a sense of wholeness that leaves us well integrated, intact, seamless—held within a community of beings that stresses our basic oneness. Yet in the light of so many stories, histories, diverse cultures, worldviews and realities, it is unreasonable to assume we will reenter a collective state of healing that is based on a common, seamless view. Instead, wholeness and healing manifests when we honor our collective wounding and allow our brokenness and resulting stories and diversities to be seen and held. Abdullah introduces a third paradigm after the *Keepers* and *Breakers*, the *Menders*—a breakthrough of people who "choose to live as conscious integral parts of a vital, sacred planet"[5] and "compassionately assist in the birth of a new way of acting in the world."[6] In embracing our brokenness, I like to visualize the *Menders* as creating a worldview that is a bricolage of our shattered selves, unified through our interconnectedness with all of life and our commitment to respect this, yet with recognition that we join together through related, yet disparate journeys of brokenness.

Brokenness: The Dark Night of the Soul, Sacred Wounds and Disorienting Dilemmas

I am always caught by a well quoted line from Leonard Cohen's song *Anthem* that utters "There is a crack in everything: that's how the light gets in."[7] The full stanza counsels:

> Ring the bells that still can ring
> Forget your perfect offering
> There is a crack, a crack in everything
> That's how the light gets in[8]

The writer seems to advise that a state of perfection will never, nor should it, be reached. It is the cracks in our lives—our mistakes, misfortunes, breakdowns and other events that mar our sense of wholeness—that are actually gifts. Plotkin relates Cohen's stanza to a practice by Navajo weavers:

> They say that perfection keeps Spirit from entering a thing. In their masterful weavings, they incorporate a deliberate irregularity, an errant line or color that looks like an unintended flaw but is actually a purposeful deviation called a "spirit line," the place where Mystery might enter.[9]

It is our cracks, our brokenness, that reorder our vision of the world, so that we may see more clearly, from a perspective that is much larger than our small sense of self. The songwriter's words invoke further meaning to me—we shall never reach states of perfection, nor shall we find the perfect model or system of explanation. Human consciousness is smaller than (what Plotkin refers to as) *Spirit* or *Mystery* and it is erroneous to try and find the full map. Instead we should choose to follow the path of encounter with challenge, learning to enter into the sacred and expand our consciousness, and act from this fuller view. This idea of being cracked, broken apart, dismembered is an ancient theme in humanity and goes by many names with current theorists such as *the dark night of the soul*,[10] our *core vulnerability* or *sacred wound*[11] and *initiation rites*.[12] From a transformative learning view, these events are disorienting dilemmas which unjar our worldviews and, if successfully navigated, transform them to access greater degrees of connectivity with all of life and the fullness of our life paths. The essence of transformative learning is when an adult permanently alters her or his worldview. Elias adds that transformative learning "is grounded in a critique of the contemporary social world, a critique of the dilemma that industrialized nations have created for the planet."[13]

A several century old concept rooted in the Catholic tradition, *the dark night of the soul* refers to one's journey back to, for a religious person, God, and for a spiritual person what might be the sacred or numinous, the force that connects all things, both visible and unseen. It is labeled dark, here meaning a painful, mysterious, solitary voyage, where one gets a temporary glimpse of the sacred which may result in "a profound abandonment depression"[14] when perceiving this separation. Bache describes the dark night of the soul as an:

> ...advanced stage of psychospiritual growth reached by only the most committed spiritual aspirants...It comes after a series of lesser trials and just before final awakening into unitive consciousness. It is the final stage of a long spiritual process of increased purification in which one's identity as a discrete self is challenged at its core and eventually surrendered.[15]

He parallels this more traditional meaning and individual path with the collective suffering currently experienced by humanity as a result of our ecological and social crisis. This presents an opportunity for our common evolutionary development met through our response, seeing our separation from all of life, letting our separative paradigms die and rejoining in collective experience with one another and the sacred: "The more in-depth healing occurs when we learn to embrace our fragmentedness from our own wholeness."[16]

Plotkin uses the terms *core vulnerability* and *sacred wound* to describe our personal marks of suffering, our sense of brokenness which leads us toward our life calling.[17] The core vulnerability is a specifically human phenomenon that is purposeful. This wounding occurs in childhood usually through a "pattern of hurtful events or a disturbing dynamic in one or more important relationships"[18] and often sets the patterns of behavior for the individual. As, and if, one matures, this wounding is addressed and develops into a unique gift, something sacred, "a key to your destiny."[19] There is a clear parallel with the dark night of the soul, but with a specific emphasis on wounding that occurs in our early years.

Similar to both the dark night of the soul and the sacred wound, Morrison sees both rites of passages and life crises as traumas which unjar consciousness. *Initiation rites* or *rites of passage* customarily transform one's ordinary life temporarily into that of "abject loss" in order to "set the stage for profound spiritual transformations."[20] Traditionally these have been facilitated ceremonially; however, trauma serves the same purpose as it manifests as a deep sense of loss and disordering of one's life meaning. Successfully navigating these initiations, whether through ceremony or life trauma, results in a maturing of one's small sense of ego identity to connect with wider frames of self, or what is called a larger Self—an identity that connects with the sacred.

West African Dagaran elder and writer Malidoma Somé also emphasizes that our life traumas are often our modern day equivalents of initiation rites, pointing out that while western peoples are often seeking rites of passages that mirror those of traditional indigenous societies, western rituals often actually lie in modern life challenges—the loss of relationships, jobs and loved ones, illnesses and other forms of crisis.

> The serious troubles we face in life are nothing other than initiatory experiences…They are a necessary ingredient in the removal of whatever stands between us and our essential self. If tribal people reach this stage through formal rites of passage, other people may do the same differently. It is as if there is a natural pull toward challenges and ordeal in the interest of gaining inner strength and living a responsible life. Hardship and ordeal therefore initiate a change from within. One emerges from them with a profound sense of having undergone a radical education.[21]

Keeping with this idea of modern day initiation rites, there is a concept within the field of transformative learning called *disorienting dilemmas* that serves a similar purpose. Transformative learning focuses on the expansion of paradigms within adults and "is grounded in a critique of the contemporary social world, a critique of the dilemma that industrialized nations have created for the planet."[22] A *disorienting dilemma* occurs when one has an experience that does not easily assimilate into one's current worldview.[23] It is a perplexing occurrence that is often prompted by some sort of trauma or loss, yet also through other events that prompt a questioning of how one makes meaning—one's worldview. A worldview or *frame of reference* is made up of two dimensions: a habit of mind and a resulting point of view. The habit of mind is how one makes meaning assumed from her or his culture and the resulting point of view is how one plays this meaning out in one's daily life.[24] One might simplify these with the habit of mind correlating with patterns of thinking and the resulting point of view as actions. When a person has a disorienting dilemma, she can choose to ignore the confliction it brings to her current worldview or to alter her worldview. If she chooses the latter, this occurs through four possible routes: "elaborating existing frames of reference," "learning new frames of reference," "transforming points of view" or "transforming habits of mind."[25]

With all of these, the transformation occurs through critically reflecting on one's initial assumptions—this is the key ingredient of worldview change. Through "elaborating existing frames of references" one might contemplate why and in what ways the disorienting dilemma confronted one's worldview, and by doing so begin to expand this to be able to integrate new information. The second possibility is to adopt a new worldview. This possibility is challenging as it is not simple to drop one's initial worldview and learn a new one—our identities come from deep rooted experiences inherited from our dominant culture and more locally situated subsets of culture. The latter two possibilities consist of changing one of the two dimensions that comprise our worldviews—through reflecting on our held assumptions and changing either our conditioned thoughts or actions.

It is important to note the danger of simply adopting a new worldview. Most people are not aware of their worldviews. Feinstein and Krippner claim each person is operating under a personal mythology, which is largely unconscious, and that "People often live their lives with very little awareness of the lens through which they are looking."[26] The notable transpersonal psychology and consciousness researcher Charles Tart claims, "The pattern of a state of consciousness deliberately maintains its integrity in a changing world,"[27] affirming that worldviews are often contained within fixed patterns. We like to think that reality is solid and fixed. Tart also introduces the terms "consensus reality"[28] and "consensus consciousness,"[29] where our worldviews come from our larger cultural conditioning which:

> [W]orks to convince us that the acquired characteristics of enculturation are actually natural, so it can be very difficult to see these

things when we are in a state of consensus consciousness. Sometimes being in some altered state...gives us an alternative view that is like an outside perspective on yourself. Then you may see the conditioned, restrictive quality of consensus consciousness.[30]

This altered state may come through many forms. The experiences of the dark night of the soul, examining a core wound and having a disorienting dilemma are all experiences that hold the potential to break and transform our worldviews.

While the classical definition of transformative learning holds critical reflection as a fairly rational process, grounded in one's everyday consciousness, Elias expands this definition to include unconscious dimensions:

[T]ransformative learning can happen through direct apprehension of an alternative framework of highly symbolic meaning, through the direct apprehension and appropriation of frameworks of meaning that emerge freshly from the unconscious. This process is described as discernment, an appreciative and receptive process that stands in sharp contrast with Mezirow's emphasis on critical reflection.[31]

Yet whether an individual has a disorienting dilemma that surfaces from everyday consciousness or a more transpersonal experience, in order for a transformation to occur the person must critically reflect on the experience.

Elias continues and outlines three conditions that are the results of the transformative learning process for the individual: (1) "a 'conscious I' capable of exercising critical reflection;" (2) an enlarged capacity for thinking that embodies holding dualities, is systematic and "perceives archetypes as partners for inner dialogue" and (3) being "a conscious creative force in the world" through an openness to perpetual learning and change. The transformative learner is continually reflecting on one's and society's assumptions without situating into a new, fixed worldview. Perhaps most importantly, the transformative learner is bringing the new levels of awareness to invoke creative change in the world.

By having multiple disorienting dilemmas, one becomes more comfortable with change through recognizing that there are larger realities within the world than those originally held. This process is known as the self-transforming self or fourth order consciousness, where one continually reforms the way one makes meaning to the extent where one moves beyond a self-centered perspective.[32] Through this type of transformation, one develops the ability to understand the perspectives of others and to even hold multiple perspectives at once.

McWhinney and Markos relate the process of the "self-transforming self" to that of ancient ritual. They contend this process occurs in Learning III (LIII), where one "challenges the interpretation of experience, relations, and truth systems, leading to broad questions such as human life, world ecology, and relations to higher powers."[33] A person who unravels the assumptions of the dominant paradigm and embarks on finding more resilient assumptions and actions, transforming to a new paradigm, often finds oneself a "wanderer" traveling a solitary path. There is often danger that this person will seek refuge in a community or group with a different paradigm, yet this new paradigm quickly becomes close minded, steeped in a new type of dogmatism. A true "self-transforming self" never becomes stagnant. McWhinney and Markos claim that "commitments to openness create a continual LIII giving birth to sages, quiet wisdom, and perhaps a sense of the Tao"[34] or to:

> [A] transcendent LIII mode, where the individual continues to question and lead others to explore beyond their habituated lives. This is an ultimate goal of transformative education: to live in perpetual self-renewal, reviewing the assumptions by which self and society are guided and given support, reflecting on and challenging their belief systems.[35]

Off Centered Worldviews: Positionality, Border Pedagogy, and the Multicultural Self

Experiencing *the dark night of a soul*, a *sacred wound, initiation rites* or a *disorienting dilemma* are clear examples of how one's worldview is broken and one is presented with the opportunity to develop a larger perspective. While all of these, to some extent, emphasize a responsibility to bring this larger perspective to the individual's actions in the world, their descriptions tend to focus on the solitary path and a unitive, universal consciousness. They are events that crack one's lenses of seeing reality, yet might be viewed as anticipated developmental episodes of the healthy life path. Moreover, they imply that the person experiencing the disorientation was previously immersed in a consensus reality, based on the accepted norms of society, and the disorienting event shifted the individual into a larger view. There are many individuals whose experiences are not centered within this consensus reality, what is identified as the common experience of society, by their backgrounds with differences of race, gender, class, sexuality, physical ability and other forms of distinction. Within our society, these are distinctions that have led to marginalization and disproportionate levels of power based on difference.

While marginalized peoples are generally at a disadvantage, in the context of worldview expansion, they often hold greater power through having experiences that cause them to question the mainstream. And moreover, with the acceptance that our current ecological and social crisis is caused, to a large extent, by the problematic western worldview, having an off centered worldview may be powerful in transforming the dominant paradigm. This seems particularly true when one holds an identity that comes from multiple intersections of race, gender, class and other distinctions that do not permit one to sit solidly in a single grouping. A person who has many experiences of identity that do not fit within the majority has, through critical reflection and action, the potential of holding an expanded worldview. Hence by being off center, one possesses power to shift the worldview to hold multiple, often conflicting lenses.

The concepts of *positionality*, *border pedagogy* and *the multicultural self* support this idea. *Positionality* is in sharp contrast to the stance of quantitative research and western tradition, which emphasizes being a distanced observer when looking at situations or assuming a position of neutrality. Instead, *positionality* accepts that we are situated in our lived experiences and that "lived experiences, particularly those of race, class, and gender, shape our worldviews."[36] This aligns with notions within transformative learning, consciousness studies and constructivism which advocate that our worldviews are constructed by our experience and as a result are and always will be partial: "we take our way of *composing* reality to be *reality*. The great embarrassment or liberation of transformation itself is the recognition that what we have been taking as reality is actually only a *construction* of reality."[37] By developing the capacities to see our constructed reality through identifying and reflecting on dimensions of our worldviews, we move away from dogmatic, binary views and develop larger perspectives.

Similar to positionality, *border pedagogy* criticizes the mainstream western paradigm as an embodiment of fixed, binary dualities. We see this within our society through classifications such as rich or poor, White or Black, male or female, Republican or Democrat—categories which sort and divide and often signify higher and lower levels of power. Moreover, border pedagogy as well as positionality critiques the western paradigm for purporting a dominant view that is singular and exclusionary, based on views of the privileged.

> Thus, historically, the privileged have often discursively subordinated less privileged groups by their flawed and often denigrating interpretations/representations and their assignment of universality and superiority to their own traits while marginalizing and ascribing inferiority to traits different from their own.[38]

To address these dogmatisms, border pedagogy encourages learners to see the spaces in between and beyond fixed identities, to work with the edges where "Borders are hovered over, crossed and criss-crossed."[39]

The *multicultural self* is the ability to identify with multiple, different human groupings. Anthony speaks to the need to learn the multicultural stories of diverse peoples as a means to shift away from the dominant western worldview that is based on whiteness.[40] He claims, "The multicultural self represents the capacity for empathy with many people and cultures, and also with our capacity for empathy with living."[41] One develops the capacity for holding multiple perspectives through experiences of engaging with diverse peoples. Bennett brings an approach that allows one to first identify one diverse perspective and ultimately move into a self-concept that integrates multiple perspectives. His training model moves from stages of denial where one has had no exposure to cultural differences to the final two stages of adaptation and integration where the self is first able to emotionally relate to one diverse world-view and finally can integrate multiple diverse worldviews into one's self-identity to such an extent that the original self-identity or world-view is transformed, the self is flexible and exposure to differences no longer results in conflict to one's worldview.[42]

People who are already situated in marginalized groups often have a "multiple consciousness" and "are better able to perceive incidents from multiple perspectives."[43] When one holds an identity that already strad-dles multiple areas of difference, one is forced to hold an expanded world-view in order to integrate these disparate notions of self because "The other is not just a boundary that we cross from time to time; the other is always within us."[44] If a person who holds a multiple consciousness or multicultural self continues to develop an open worldview as more diverse experiences are encountered, she has the potential to evolve into a self-transforming self, one who perpetually learns and applies this toward social transformation.

In outlining various experiences and identities that expands one's con-sciousness away from the dominant western paradigm and pulls one to invoke transformative change, it is important to bring in *the ecological self*. Similar to the multicultural self, the ecological self expands one's small sense of identity to holding multiple perspectives, this time with the more than human, natural world. A root cause of the ecological and social crisis is the fixation on the needs of our ego exhibited by people living within globalized realities, particularly those within western para-digms. We have developed false selves fueled by "deep-seated but unac-knowledged feelings of worthlessness and emptiness."[45] Despite having so many consumer goods, the fruit of globalization, we experience lack. Our separations from one another, from nature and from the sacred are the reasons for this sense of isolation. When we become aware of the damage we are inflicting upon the earth and start to change our world-views through both our frames of reference and resulting actions, we start to reconnect. The awakening to the ecological crisis is another form of a disorienting dilemma or the dark night of the soul. The ecological self helps to foster this process by moving from a small self or egocentric self to one that includes the perspectives of other beings within the living world.[46]

If we bring together the concepts of these various broken identities and capacities for expanding our worldviews, our sense of self, a person who holds both a multicultural and ecological self, has immense power to see and act outside of our dominant worldview that purports social and ecological oppression and instead to move toward a life affirming paradigm. It is our experiences with broken selves, paradigms and worlds that crack our lenses, our worldviews and foster a new way of seeing and acting. It is through broken lenses that we may see most clearly.

Personal Fragments

As a teacher and academic, I find it is easier to speak about the larger patterns in the world than to focus on my personal story. In light of all of the suffering on the planet, my experiences seem benign. Yet I realize that my convictions are rooted with my life experiences and I have an interesting bricolage of diversity, life events, critical reflection and practice that may be useful to others. I have encountered many cracks to my worldview. What follows are some small fragments of my personal story.

> There was a time, a state, in our childhood, when there was a vitality, a freshness, a zest, a longing for and loving of beauty that could make the earth a heaven. Light is a good metaphor for it, a metaphor that is literally true in some ways. Unfortunately, the light we once experienced gets covered over and seems lost.[47]

> By experientially exploring your core wound, you can render it sacred. Your wound holds a key to your destiny.[48]

I am sure that everyone can remember the moment they felt as their most tragic, where one's safe reality was punctured, leaving a lifelong imprint of sadness. For me, this occurred during the first grade. In the early 1970s, just a few years after the passage of the Fair Housing

Act, which among other things barred discrimination in purchasing a home, my parents moved our family from the inner city Bronx to a new suburban community outside of Princeton, New Jersey. We were the only African American family and among very few people of color. My parents had moved us there to get away from the inequitable and often unsafe conditions of New York's inner cities. They had achieved the "American Dream," buying their first home, establishing a healthy family, and living in a safe community with "good" schools. I was an infant when we moved and my earliest years there seemed normal. I was an affectionate and curious child—making friends with strangers and always eager to chat about what I found interesting in my world. Entering kindergarten was an exciting time for me—more kids to play with, new things to discover. I delighted in that first school year. But something changed for me in the first grade.

Within the first few days of that school year, a group of boys started to bully me, causing me to cry each day, and continued the entire year. The first time it happened, I doubt they intended it to be a daily game. One of them told me that I was bad because I was Black. He said that I was not a real person. I can't remember what else those boys said. I just remember how stunned I was to hear this. It was as if I was told the worst secret—of all the kids, I was a freak, unworthy, did not belong. As a very sensitive and naive seven-year-old, I burst into tears. Those boys must have been shocked by the power they had over me. All I know is that they quickly became junkies. Each day they would tease me with their bigoted, cruel remarks until I broke down and cried. At first, it did not take much to break me. One or two hurtful words could do it. Later, they started using harsher words such as the "n-word." I remember one time, they brought over the only other kid of color in my class, who was East Indian, and informed me that he was okay because he had never been a slave. As the year progressed, their tactics got worse. The taunting became longer, often taking a large portion of recess time. About mid-way through the year, they started recruiting other classmates to help. There were days when I was chased and heckled by the entire class. Going to school was so horrible, I was so dismayed, so confused. By the end of the year, I had become a different child.

When I reflect on this experience, I can put it into the context of prejudice and racism and the post-Civil Rights issues the US faced. Clearly this was not the greatest injustice of the era, lots of kids are bullied, yet for a young child this marred my sense of safety and delight in the world. I also get angry that the adults that were present did nothing. With the exception of one teacher's aide that would sometimes come to my rescue during recess, none of the adults did anything. No one talked to my classmates or contacted our parents. I did not even tell my parents until much later in life. It was the first crashing of my belief in the world. The scarring left was a sense of isolation, a fear of not fitting in, being the other and the pain this sense brought. This wound does color my worldview and while I now view not ever feeling like I truly belong to one group as a gift, there will always be underlying pain.

The following year, my parents moved my older brother and me to a very diverse community and things grew better for a while. We had another three year stint as the only African American kids in Connecticut and then moved back to the diverse community. Yet I realize that the fixed identifiers such as Black and White do not hold strongly with many of my experiences. I identify primarily as African American and hold ancestral roots from Jamaica, Barbados, the Irish, Welsh, Scottish, East Indians, the Catawba and Cherokee. Most of the stories of my lineage are lost and those I do have are partial and often mysterious and sad. I am descended from the enslaved, the colonizer and the colonized. While my parents came from poor and working class backgrounds, I grew up in an upper middle class household and hold a certain sense of privilege. And while both my parents identify as African American, they have distinct upbringings, with my mother coming from a West Indian heritage and my father's parents coming from North and South Carolina. With the coupling of the economic background and living in all White communities in much of my early years, I often find that I do not fully fit in with my cultural peers—as if I missed some important social upbringings that I would have gained if I lived in predominantly communities of color.

Interestingly, it was during those early years that I had my first encounter with a wild place. One day I wandered off with my brother and some of his friends outside of the planned, suburban community we lived in. I remember ending up by a small creek and something shifted for me—the patterns of square plots with the exact same houses with domesticated nature vanished and a new rhythm was revealed. From that time forward I was always drawn to wild places. In my mid-teens I had a peak moment when I was feeling extremely anxious about life and was sitting outside and everything simply started buzzing—the sunlight, the air, the surrounding sounds—and in that moment I first experienced peacefulness and contentment. By my mid-twenties I always lived on the edge of the forest and walking through the woods and being outside in wild places is where I feel most at home. I have had so many experiences in the natural world that have expanded my worldview and fostered relationships with living beings that I never knew were possible.

The first disorienting dilemma I recollect happened during my early teens. While in the transformative learning field disorienting dilemmas are typically experienced by adults, this was an experience that clashed with my worldview and caused me to change it. I was in my third year at summer stock, which was essentially a camp for the performing arts. This was my life passion—acting, singing, dancing and making costumes and sets. I was talented, but that summer I was frustrated because I was not getting any major parts in the productions we did. These were productions for children—*Snow White*, *Sleeping Beauty*, *Cinderella* and all of the major female parts were for White girls. Then when we did *Peter Pan*, I, the only girl of color, was cast as Tiger Lily. On top of this, the adults were doing a performance which we assisted with as the chorus. The woman playing the lead could not project her voice while singing. The director had me go up on stage with a broom, sweeping in the background and singing to add to her voice. It was at that moment that I realized that there were never going to be parts for me. Even though I was talented, I was living in a racist world, designed for people who did not look like me, and if I wanted this to change I needed to go out in the world and do something about it. That is what drew me to social justice. Prior to that, I experienced racism in a much more personal context, rather than systemically.

After finishing high school, I attended a very prestigious liberal arts school and majored in International Relations as I, idealistically, wanted to heal the world. I received a very good education and much of the overt learning was seeing the wealth and privilege of my peers. It was a somewhat segregated campus with the majority of students of color choosing to socialize with the university's community of color. I found myself again one of the only students of color in the social groups I chose and the other students of color within these groups were similar to me—growing up in situations where they were often the only person of color. Academically, I learned about so many things—particularly the framing of domination from economics, histories of colonization, cultural histories, war, politics, the dynamics of race, feminism, ecofeminism and the rise of globalization. By the time I graduated, I was disillusioned with the state of the world. Eventually I went back to school to do a teacher education program that focused on multicultural education. I was particularly interested in serving underprivileged youth and held a strong critique of the disservice received by marginalized groups.

While I learned so much through focusing on multicultural education, even its most radical iterations did not address the ecological crisis. I was disheartened with the ideal that equality meant everyone having equal access to the "American Dream" that was essentially destroying the planet. During that time I was exposed to ecopsychology which, like social justice, held a strong critique of western civilization. Suddenly my love for social justice and for the natural world merged, specifically with my exposure to the work of Carl Anthony, who, along with Belvie Rooks, became two of my dearest mentors. I finally found my passion and felt seen and understood. This spiraled into so many directions and synchronistic events and led to the completion of two more degrees, becoming a professor and developing a strong voice.

Another disorienting dilemma that stands out strongly occurred during my early thirties when I began a doctoral program in the San Francisco Bay Area. For at least six years prior, I worked at a college in a more rural to suburban region of Arizona that was extremely White with less than a handful of culturally diverse employees and very few students of color. While I, for the most part, loved this community, I

had also had some deep experiences of pain surrounding racial ignorance, tokenism and a sense of alienation as the only African American
woman. In contrast, the school I had just started was known for having
diverse students and actively seeking to increase this. During my first
intensive with the program, some of the students, who were getting
close to graduating, presented their work. I attended one session led by
an African American woman whose scholarship was on the experiences
of African American women. To be honest, I do not remember the specific content. What I do and will always remember is that she opened
with acknowledging each African American woman attending her presentation, which was most of the attendees. In fact there were probably
twelve people present, all but one an African American woman. She
acknowledged each woman by name or, if she did not know her, by "sister." She finished without acknowledging me. I froze at that moment in
disbelief, confusion and shock. There was a deep sting and sense of feeling choked, silenced and invisible. Within tens of seconds or a minute,
another woman spoke up and pointed out she forgot to acknowledge
me. The presenter apologized and I could tell she meant it, but also
that she did not realize I was African American. I burst into tears for
at least an hour—from the shielding drops that periodically roll down
the side of one's cheeks to bits of sobbing after the presentation. I was
consoled by these sisters and was grateful to be seen and comforted, but
the overall feeling was shock and sadness that I was so invisible. Most
of the women had long braids or close cropped afros and wore clothing
that seemed more cultural—flowing shirts and dresses in brighter colors, more tribal looking earrings, and many of the women had darker
skin than I. After living in a community where I stood out as the only
African American woman, I was stunned to *not* be seen as this in a
group of peers of my same culture, gender and academic status. I was
left with the sense there was no community or group that I seamlessly
fit within. I was always to be on the edge, an outsider.

I must acknowledge that the disorientations I have shared thus far
frame me as the victim—the recipient of some injustice. When I teach
disorienting dilemmas in the classroom, I often tease my students that
it is much easier to recall an incident where one was the person treated

unfairly, as opposed to the reverse or even instances where there was no perpetrator, just a causal clash in reality. Many of the cracks in my worldview have occurred through my own ignorance or through awkward, revealing situations. Yet I must admit it is the disorienting dilemmas that come with a touch of heartbreak that come most readily to mind. When we can pull apart and see our conditionings, learn to see those of others and start to work with those edges, a new level of compassion and understanding can arise.

New Vision: Seeing Clearly through Cracked Lenses

> No one person has the horizons of meaning adequate to fully interpret any social situation, but this is not necessarily a bad thing; rather than being an argument for an exclusive representation of the other, it is an argument for the most inclusive possible representation of any group. The greater the number of interpretations, the fuller our understanding of others' experiences will become. No doubt, many of these representations will conflict with one another.[49]

> [N]o single unifying force in today's complex civilization is powerful enough to preserve cohesion amid the multiple of contrasting mythologies people are exposed to now.[50]

Our world is diverse, complex, fragmented and experiencing extremely high levels of suffering. Our ecological and social crisis, which I believe is also a spiritual crisis, indicates a deep need for us to connect with one another, the living world and a sense of the sacred— the numinous. Much of our societies, particularly those nested within western, globalized realities, are holding and enacting worldviews which are destructive. We need to shift our paradigms so our lenses not only see the damage we are causing, but they also include the widest frames of life. So much of the control and order that has been created through western tradition has been to establish a singular worldview in order to exert authority and silence dissenting paradigms. While having a common story certainly creates order and common vision, if it is not based on the truth of our diverse experiences, it is not authentic. By embracing the power of our broken identities, the cracks in our worldviews, as a means of enlarging our perspectives, we have the power of unifying in common experience through difference.

Notes

1 Davis and Canty, "Ecopsychology and Transpersonal Psychology;" Fischer, *Radical Ecopsychology: Psychology in the Service of Life*; Roszak, *The Voice of the Earth*.
2 Glendinning, *My Name is Chellis & I'm in Recovery from Western Civilization*.
3 Abdullah, *Creating a World that Works for All*.
4 Glendinning, *My Name is Chellis and I'm in Recovery from Western Civilization*, 20–21.
5 Abdullah, *Creating a World that Works for All*, 4.
6 Ibid., 87.
7 Clarke, "The Crack in Everything," 63; Plotkin, *Wild Mind: A Field Guide to the Human Psyche*, 177.
8 Cohen, "Anthem."
9 Plotkin, *Wild Mind: A Field Guide to the Human Psyche*, 177–178.
10 Wilber, "The Spectrum of Psychopathology;" Bache, "The Eco-crisis and Species Ego-death: Speculations on the Future."
11 Plotkin, *Wild Mind: A Field Guide to the Human Psyche*; Plotkin, *Nature and Human Soul: Cultivating Wholeness and Community in a Fragmented World*.
12 Morrison, "Trauma and Transformative Passage."
13 Elias, "It's Time to Change Our Minds."
14 Wilber, "The Spectrum of Psychopathology."
15 Bache, "The Eco-crisis and Species Ego-death: Speculations on the Future," 91–92.
16 Plotkin, *Wild Mind: A Field Guide to the Human Psyche*, 27.
17 ——, *Wild Mind: A Field Guide to the Human Psyche*; Plotkin, *Nature and Human Soul: Cultivating Wholeness and Community in a Fragmented World*.
18 Plotkin, *Nature and Human Soul: Cultivating Wholeness and Community in a Fragmented World*, 262.
19 Ibid., 262.
20 Morrison, "Trauma and Transformative Passage," 40.
21 Somé, *The Healing Wisdom of Africa: Finding Life Purpose through Nature, Ritual, and Community*, 278.
22 Elias, "It's Time to Change Our Minds."
23 Mezirow, *Learning as Transformation: Critical Perspectives on a Theory in Progress*.
24 ——, "Learning to Think Like an Adult: Core Concepts of Transformative Theory."
25 Ibid., 19.
26 Feinstein and Krippner, *Personal Mythology: The Psychology of Your Evolving Self*, 1.
27 Tart, *Waking Up: Overcoming the Obstacles to Human Potential*, 5.
28 ——, *States of Consciousness*.
29 ——, *Waking Up: Overcoming the Obstacles to Human Potential*.
30 Ibid., 16.
31 Elias, "It's Time to Change Our Minds."
32 Debold, "Epistemology, Fourth Order Consciousness, and the Subject-Object Relationship: Or How the Self Evolves with Robert Kegan."
33 McWhinney and Markos, "Transformative Education: Across the Threshold," 19.
34 Ibid., 29.

35   Ibid., 30.
36   Alkon and Agyeman, *Cultivating Food Justice: Race, Class, and Sustainability*, 3.
37   Debold, "Epistemology, Fourth Order Consciousness, and the Subject-object Relationship," 146.
38   Briscoe, "A Question of Representation in Educational Discourse: Multiplicities and Intersections of Identities and Positionalities," 27.
39   Cook, "'Nothing Can Ever Be the Case of "Us" and "Them" Again': Exploring the Politics of Difference through Border Pedagogy and Student Journal Writing," 15.
40   Anthony, "Ecopsychology and the Deconstruction of Whiteness."
41   Canty et al., "Roundtable: Race, Environment and Sustainability (Part One)," 240.
42   Bennett, "Towards Ethnorelativism: A Developmental Model of Intercultural Sensitivity."
43   Briscoe, "A Question of Representation in Educational Discourse: Multiplicities and Intersections of Identities and Positionalities," 25.
44   Ibid., 30.
45   Kanner and Gomes, "The All Consuming Self," 79.
46   Naess, "Self-realization: An Ecological Approach to Being in the World."
47   Tart, *Waking Up: Overcoming the Obstacles to Human Potential*, xi–xii.
48   Plotkin, *Nature and Human Soul: Cultivating Wholeness and Community in a Fragmented World*, 262.
49   Briscoe, "A Question of Representation in Educational Discourse: Multiplicities and Intersections of Identities and Positionalities," 35.
50   Feinstein and Krippner, *Personal Mythology: The Psychology of Your Evolving Self*, 7.

References

Abdullah, Shariff. *Creating a World that Works for All*. San Francisco: Berrett-Koehler Publishers, 1999.

Alkon, Alison H. and Julian Agyeman, editors. *Cultivating Food Justice: Race, Class, and Sustainability*. Cambridge, MA: The MIT Press, 2011.

Anthony, Carl (as interviewed by Theodore Roszak). "Ecopsychology and the Deconstruction of Whiteness." In *Ecopsychology: Restoring the Earth Healing the Mind*, edited by Theodore Roszak, Mary E. Gomes, and Allen D. Kanner, 263–278. San Francisco: Sierra Books, 1995.

Bache, Christopher M. "The Eco-crisis and Species Ego-death: Speculations on the Future." *The Journal of Transpersonal Psychology*, 32, 1 (2000): 89–94.

Bennett, Milton J. "Towards Ethnorelativism: A Developmental Model of Intercultural Sensitivity." In *Education for the Intercultural Experience*, edited by R. Michael Paige, 21–71. Yarmouth, ME: Intercultural Press, 1993.

Briscoe, Felecia M. "A Question of Representation in Educational Discourse: Multiplicities and Intersections of Identities and Positionalities." *Educational Studies*, 38, 1 (2005): 23–41.

Canty, Jeanine M., Randall Amster, Carl Anthony, Suzanne Benally, Drew Dellinger and Belvie Rooks. "Roundtable: Race, Environment and Sustainability (Part One)." *Sustainability: The Journal of Record*, 4, 5 (2011): 238–241.

Clarke, Isabel. "The Crack in Everything." In *GreenSpirit: Path to a New Consciousness*, edited by Marian Van Eyk McCain, 63–75. Washington: O Books, 2010.

Cohen, Leonard. "Anthem." In *The Future*. New York: Columbia, 1992.

Cook, Ian. "'Nothing Can Ever Be the Case of "Us" and "Them" Again': Exploring the Politics of Difference through Border Pedagogy and Student Journal Writing." *Journal of Geography in Higher Education*, 24, 1 (2000): 13–27.

Davis, John V. and Jeanine M. Canty. "Ecopsychology and Transpersonal Psychology." In *The Wiley-Blackwell Handbook of Transpersonal Psychology*, edited by Harris L. Friedman and Glenn Hartelius, 597–611. West Sussex, UK: Wiley-Blackwell, 2013.

Debold, Elizabeth. "Epistemology, Fourth Order Consciousness, and the Subject-object Relationship: Or How the Self Evolves with Robert Kegan [Interview with Robert Kegan]." *What is Enlightenment: Redefining Spirituality for an Evolving World*, 22 (2002): 143–154.

Elias, Dean. "It's Time to Change Our Minds." *Revision*, 20, 1 (1997): 2–7.

Feinstein, David and Stanley Krippner. *Personal Mythology: The Psychology of Your Evolving Self.* Los Angeles: Jeremy P. Tarcher, Inc., 1988.

Fisher, Andy. *Radical Ecopsychology: Psychology in the Service of Life.* Albany: SUNY Press, 2002.

Glendinning, Chellis. *My Name is Chellis & I'm in Recovery from Western Civilization.* Boston: Shambhala Publications, 1994.

Kanner, Allen D. and Mary E. Gomes. "The All Consuming Self." In *Ecopsychology: Restoring the Earth Healing the Mind*, edited by Theodore Roszak, Mary E. Gomes, and Allen D. Kanner, 77–91. San Francisco: Sierra Books, 1995.

McWhinney, Will and Laura Markos. "Transformative Education: Across the Threshold." *Journal of Transformative Education*, 1, 1 (2003): 16–37.

Mezirow, Jack, editor. *Learning as Transformation: Critical Perspectives on a Theory in Progress.* San Francisco: Jossey-Bass, 2000a.

——. "Learning to Think Like an Adult: Core Concepts of Transformative Theory." In *Learning as Transformation: Critical Perspectives on a Theory in Progress*, edited by Jack Mezirow, 3–33. San Francisco: Jossey-Bass, 2000b.

Morrison, Reed A. "Trauma and Transformative Passage." *International Journal of Transpersonal Studies*, 31, 1 (2012): 38–46.

Naess, Arne. "Self-realization: An Ecological Approach to Being in the World." In *Deep Ecology for the 21st Century: Readings on the Philosophy and Practice of the New Environmentalism*, edited by George Sessions, 225–239. Boston: Shambhala Publications, Inc., 1995.

Plotkin, Bill. *Nature and Human Soul: Cultivating Wholeness and Community in a Fragmented World.* Novato, CA: New World Library, 2007.

——. *Wild Mind: A Field Guide to the Human Psyche.* Novato, CA: New World Library, 2013.

Roszak, Theodore. *The Voice of the Earth: An Exploration of Ecopsychology.* New York: Simon & Schuster, 1992.

Somé, Malidoma P. *The Healing Wisdom of Africa: Finding Life Purpose through Nature, Ritual, and Community.* New York: Penguin Putnam Inc., 1998.

Tart, Charles T. *States of Consciousness.* New York, NY: E.P. Dutton & Co., Inc., 1975.

——. *Waking Up: Overcoming the Obstacles to Human Potential.* Boston: New Science Library, an Imprint of Shambhala Publications, Inc., 1986.

Wilber, Ken. "The Spectrum of Psychopathology." In *Transformations of Consciousness*, edited by Ken Wilber, Jack Engler and Daniel P. Brown, 107–126. Boston: New Science Library/Shambhala, 1986.

4

INTERSECTION OF AN INDIGENOUS WORLDVIEW AND APPLIED NEUROPHYSIOLOGY

ANITA L. SANCHEZ

When I gazed into the face of the Achuar leader/warrior/family man I saw such clear eyes. It was as if I were looking into a mass of brilliant stars in the unpolluted sky, deep in the Ecuadoran rainforest. His eyes reflected all that the Achuar had showed me of how they live as part of the forest, the animals, the water, the birds, dreams, and spirits. The children are confident, as they live in harmony with their surroundings. Able to articulate with words and body movement the care in which they hold each other and the natural world, for they understand that everything is interconnected, everything is sacred. The words of my own elders and leaders who taught me of the sacred circle in which the people, the earth/natural world, and spirit are all connected—that at the core, we are all of the same root. My knees buckled and tears of gratitude flowed down my face—it struck me that I was seeing in the Achuar leader's eyes what my ancestors may have looked like before. Before they were overcome by the insatiable hunger of others for more land, more resources, more control *over the world*, rather than seeking to live *with the world*.[1]

This indigenous worldview of interconnectedness has largely been lost in modern society, to our detriment at many levels, degrading our environmental, physical, and spiritual health. However, science, especially neurophysiology (and ecobiology), is now discovering and demonstrating the utter interconnectedness of people with each other and with the environment around and within them. Daily, we are finding proof that our individual and societal health depends on the balance in our physical bodies and social systems that is generated by and supported through a life-giving connection to others and our surroundings. The philosophical and practical lessons of the indigenous worldview provide excellent guides to applying our learnings from science for greater balance and mutually supportive relationships with the earth and all life. We are discovering that the merger of these two ways of knowing has the potential to transform our interactions and open the door to a long-term, sustainable human presence on the planet.

Drawing on these powerful recent findings in the sciences, learnings and spiritual knowledge from my teachers and elders, and my own experience as a student of human and organizational development, I am convinced that this moment in time is extraordinary for its potential to combine our powerful indigenous wisdom tradition, and this new western science worldview, for an enormous expansion of our species' capacity to survive and thrive, creating a world in balance.

An Indigenous Worldview—All My Relations

If you grow up as a Native American in ceremony and everyday practice, you will hear this concept—thousands of times—we are all connected. This is what is encompassed in the nearly universally used phase, "All my relations." "My relations," my family, includes everything in the world around me: life, the earth, and the spirit that is woven throughout everything and everyone. The indigenous worldview is that the spirit, the people (human beings), and the earth—all nature and the cosmos— are interconnected. All are my relations, for each is part of an intimately interconnected whole. When I do something that hurts the people, it also hurts the earth and the spirit. When I do something that is caring for the river, then I care for the people, the earth, and the spirit. Even

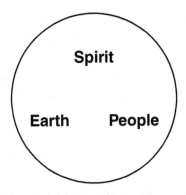

Figure 4.1   An Indigenous Worldview: We Are All Connected, One.

though I was brought up in multiple heritages, I understood that this mindset, this worldview, was how I was to practice my everyday life—to be in connection with the sacred, with all.

When I say then that all is connected, all my relations, I am reminding myself that the sacred is not separated from everyday life; it is impossible to disconnect any aspect of my life, for they are all part of the sacred. As I studied the sciences of organizations, human behavior, and the physical world, I came to understand that this indigenous worldview is also a methodological tool for obtaining knowledge. Just as I grew up learning to observe the natural world by identifying the relationships between various things, in the same way, I observe organizations and systems that people have created, looking for the relationships between the elements in them. In this worldview, everything and everyone in the natural world has relationships with every other thing and the total set of relationships makes up the natural world as we experience it. Vine Deloria, Jr, speaks of this Indian principle of interpretation and observation as simplicity itself. "We are all relatives...This concept is simply the relativity concept as applied to a universe which people experience as alive and not as dead or inert."[2] So, too, my grandmother taught me that the stones were the ears of the earth. The sacred energy of the stone has much to teach us and we are to care for them just as we care for all the other beings in the universe. We have a human–human relationship. We have a human–plant relationship. We have a human–animal relationship.

We also have a direct relationship with Spirit, Grandmother and Grandfather, God, Allah, Universe energy. The spiritual dimension of reality is always an experience in the world. Spirit, earth and people are all connected. All is part of the sacred. When one holds this truth, then one must respect that the natural world is filled with intelligence and knowledge. Just as I saw that the Achuar begin each day listening to one another, sharing their dreams and then determining what is to unfold that day, I too learned that dreams and spiritual experience are a method of gathering data.

In western science, some would say that you must discard anything that has a remote relationship with the subjective experiences of human beings and other forms of life. Yet, many of the greatest thought leaders in western science have relied deeply on intuition, dreams, and visions. As Vine Deloria, Jr, teaches:

> Western science tries to take this phenomenon as evidence of an individual genius of the scientist, whereas we, indigenous thinkers, sense that these data are derived from external sources or drawn from a reservoir of subjective information available to all individuals who are open to the connection. For indigenous people living in a world where everything is interconnected, much cannot be explained within the limits of mathematical models.[3]

It is clear to me from my teachers, elders, and scientists, that reliance solely on numbers excludes critical information that provides understanding of the depth and complexity of natural phenomena.

To be fair, not all science has distanced itself from a holistic worldview. There are models such as complexity theory, succession theory, and geophysiological approaches to learning and knowledge that embrace a holistic worldview. While providing diversity leadership training, one holistic model identified to me by Lee Klinger, a scientist at the National Center for Atmospheric Research, is Lovelock's Gaia theory, which views the activities of the living organism as the primary influence for planetary conditions favorable for life.[4] Our growing understanding of cosmology, the science of the origins and development of the universe, similarly underscores that we are all made up of the atoms of the first stars, while ecobiology demonstrates that we humans are actually an enormously complex, interrelated set of organisms living in symbiotic harmony.

Nor does the approach of western science have to necessarily reduce phenomena to mathematical equations, and disparate parts. Nuclear physicist, Claude Poncelet, says most clearly:

> My direct experience of what I have called the spiritual dimension of reality has always been an experience of the world. While I could not explain this experience using standard scientific knowledge, and while my spiritual experience did not fit ordinary-reality scientific models, I could not deny or reject it or call it merely imagination without violating what is for me the basic approach of science: *science does not reject the experience of reality,* whether or not such experience fits scientific models... The validity and acceptance of any model depends upon its agreement and consistency with our direct experience of the physical world. The final word is what the world tells us about itself, not what we think the world is like.[5]

This provides a near-perfect match to most tribal traditions that I have observed in the Americas. No data is discarded as unimportant and irrelevant: individual experiences, accumulated wisdom of the community gathered by previous generations, dreams, visions, prophecies, and information received from plants, animals, birds, and sky, are all data to be categorized, evaluated and understood as a unified body of knowledge. By poignant contrast, we now see the tendency for traditional knowledge to be "validated" only once a match between indigenous wisdom and data/theory from western science is discovered. As we begin to embrace this interconnectedness, perhaps we can accept or expand our thinking to say that the traditional model of western science is not the sole criterion for all truth, credibility, and accuracy.

The traditional indigenous worldview reminds us of the symbiotic relationship of all things and the importance of balance in the universe. Within this worldview, one is guided to live as a whole human being who is connected to her/himself, both mind and heart, as well as caring for the connection to other beings. When we adopt such a perspective, it directs not only the science we do but also directs our daily life. Our ability to recognize our connection within the larger web of life helps us to understand how other individuals, groups, and systems impact us and how we influence them. We can then more easily discern meaning in our lives, care for each other and all beings, and facilitate more effective collective change efforts to resolve the many crises before us.

Let's return, for a moment, to the Achuar man who inspired the opening paragraph of this chapter. The Achuar are a people living deep in the Amazon rainforests of Ecuador and Peru. They provide a powerful example of how traditional wisdom is coming to influence not only our scientific understanding of the world around us, but also our sense of our own role in life on the planet. The Achuar have lived for millennia in the forest, until recently isolated from outsiders, and completely integrated into their environment. Their senses are acutely tuned to the natural world around them, and their perception of connection to the earth, their community, and all living things is central to their understanding of the world. However, two decades ago, impelled by their collective, prophetic dreams of coming destruction, the Achuar reached out to people in the modern world to help them understand the nature and cause of the threat they perceived, the threat to their very existence from oil exploration, mining, timber harvesting, and more. In the process of making that connection to the modern world, they generated an understanding, in us, of the true nature and implications of our culture's insatiable hunger for things and resources and control that disconnects us from harmony with the natural world around us.

The lessons learned from the Achuar led to the creation of the Pachamama Alliance, a global organization dedicated to empowering indigenous people of the Amazon rainforest to preserve their lands and culture and "using insights gained from that work, to educate and inspire individuals everywhere to bring forth a thriving, just and sustainable world."[6] The vision of the Pachamama Alliance is of "a world that works for everyone: an environmentally sustainable, spiritually fulfilling, socially just human presence on this planet—a New Dream for humanity."[7] This intersection of an intact indigenous worldview and the modern world generates a new understanding of what it will take to transform our society for the coming millennia—an understanding that everything we face is inextricably interconnected. Today, the Pachamama Alliance helps people in 87 countries around the world understand that we cannot be individually at our best unless everyone around us is thriving, that environmental health and socially just and fair human systems, and our individual and collective spiritual fulfillment, are all utterly interwoven. We can only achieve one goal by achieving them all. In this way, the Achuar–Pachamama Alliance partnership is an exemplar of the highest best synergy of these worlds and allows an inspired creativity to come forth.

Now, let's consider a scientific discipline that provides one of the most robust demonstrations of interconnection—applied neurophysiology.

Basics of Applied Neurophysiology—Mind–Brain–Body Connection

The latest brain–body research highlights the impact of purposefully being in connection with our inner physiological and psychological states and the relationship of those states to the people and environment around us. Using a basic understanding of brain–body mechanics, we can delve into the causes, impacts, and interactions of stress and resilience. We can see the principles of an indigenous worldview demonstrated in this relatively new science, and identify the potential for expanded synergies in mindful application of native wisdom combined with neurophysiological self-awareness.

The Brain

One of the most amazing things about the brain is that we all have one by birth, and yet most of us have not been taught how to most effectively operate it. There was no instruction manual with this complex organ, so for the most part our training has been cultural.

The brain comprises 3 percent of our body mass and yet consumes 20 percent of our available energy. Our brain is always running, seven days a week, twenty-four hours daily. It generates enough electricity to light up a light bulb. The brain processes about 400 billion bits of information per second, yet we are consciously aware of only about 2,000 bits of that data at any one time.[8] The brain's functions change when we are under stress, whether momentary, acute, or chronic. These changes are linked to physiological changes that occur in our body at the same time. The good news is that we are learning essential facts about this environment–brain–body interaction and, with knowledge and skill practice, we can positively influence our mental and physical health and well being and, in fact, the well being of those around us.

Our drive to survive is centered in the functions linked to the brainstem, which manages a large portion of our bodies' operations. The brainstem and cerebellum regulate most of the autonomic and automatic functions, keeping our hearts beating, our lungs breathing, controlling our digestion and balance, and keeping all of our organs functioning. This is analogous to control central and is the first part of the brain to develop. This part of the brain is directly connected to all of our senses and continuously processes incoming data for signs of threat to our well being.

Our drive to connect with others is at the center of our brains. Sometimes referred to as the emotional brain, it is the home of our socio-emotional life and much of our ability to relate to other beings. We live a large part of our lives in this part of the brain—responding to various scenarios, real or imaginary, befriending and caring for family and coworkers, and connecting to a larger sense of community. This emotional part of the midbrain, or limbic system, can also trigger physiological responses that interfere with our connection to healthy community, leaving us struggling to connect with family and friends. Emotional energy draws upon a very large amount of our overall daily brain energy expenditure.

Our drive to understand, to create, to assign logic and meaning—big picture thinking—is represented in the upper brain, the neocortex. This is what most people visualize when they hear the word "brain." It is the largest part of our brain mass, yet it gets the least priority in terms of energy allocation (glucose blood sugar) when we perceive threats and risks to our survival. In essence, any sense of threat drives us into our lower brain and triggers powerful stimulation of the body. Thus, when we are under stress, the neocortex—the rational, reflective, planning, creative, imaginative belief system center—drops to third place in energy rationing, limiting our ability to reflect, look forward, and make calculated decisions based on present information. The neocortex is also the part of the brain that gets overloaded by too much of everything, good and bad, coming at us in a world that requires us to consciously think—activities, plans, schedules, budgets, decisions, and more.

What are the implications of this brain functioning vis-à-vis the indigenous worldview?

Sense of Safety or Sense of Threat? It Matters

When we are immersed in the belief of interconnectedness with the people and the world around us, we are more likely to have a sense of safety and community. That feeling of safety moderates, or down-regulates, the lower brain and midbrain response to signals in the environment, allowing the neocortex more opportunity to analyze and plan for positive outcomes. We are more likely to create collaborative relationships, care for each other, and build shared understanding of what is and what we can co-create. When this happens, we are flooded with the hormone oxytocin, often called the "happy hormone." When we feel a positive, caring connection to other humans (and nature) our body is filled with this hormone and our reflection, understanding, rational abilities, and creative abilities are heightened.

By contrast, when we feel any threat to our survival, real or imagined, we have a fight, flight, or associated freeze reaction, which sets off a complex series of physiological responses in our brain and body. When we engage the fight–flight–freeze responses, two systems are activated in the midbrain: the sympathetic nervous system and the adrenal-cortical system. In part, through the release of the stress hormone cortisol, these systems insure that we are able to react almost instantly for survival, producing the action that is required. For this reason, energy is shunted from our upper brain to insure that we are able to fight the threat, run from it, or freeze (the freeze state can prepare us for death or possible recovery by initially conserving energy). The fight–flight–freeze response and associated release of stress hormones is an emergency act. During this response, the available energy is not directed to thinking, speaking, reflecting, creative solutions, or collaboration. The demand is to act or freeze, now, because one's very survival is at risk.

The stress release hormone cortisol is not bad, in fact cortisol is essential to life—assisting in regulation of blood sugar utilization, increasing energy, and masking fatigue and pain. It is a potent ingredient in both ongoing body function and threat response. The problem with cortisol occurs when human beings are triggering a fight, flight, or freeze response to events that are not actually life-threatening. Our daily lives are too often filled with distress signals from a myriad of events such as traffic jams, financial pressures, problems with bosses, fears of losing our job or position, difficulties with children, television news, in-box overload, and much, much more. Scientific research indicates that the average American is having a fight–flight response up to 50–60 times per day.[9] Our brains, body, and neurophysiological system are not built to sustain this constant state of threat response.

The cortisol, which was only meant to come online when in survival situations, is now flowing into our bodies on a nearly continuous basis. An overabundance of cortisol flooding directly contributes to many illnesses—hypertension, sleep disruption, diabetes, heart diseases, and other ailments too many to describe here. Fatigue, overwhelm, isolation, and chronic illness are costs of living in a world we experience as disconnected, uncaring, and alienating, a world we imagine as dangerous, rather than safe and suffused with support from "all my relations."

The Heart

When walking in nature, a park, a rainforest, a desert, it is easy for me to begin to relax and fall into the rhythm of life around me. And yet, it seems to take more conscious attention to listen to my own heart. As our hearts beat, the rhythm of life and one's feelings are reflected. Our elders share the story of how our heart rhythms and emotions impact others around us and now science, too, shares this story of our impact on others.

> Be careful of what you are feeling, what you say, and even what you think, for once your feeling and words are out in the wind they can never return.[10]

The Institute of HeartMath has spent many years researching the rhythms and frequencies of the heart. They explain that the beat-to-beat rhythm of your heart varies in direct relation to your brain and nervous system. This is known as heart rate variability or HRV. You may have heard from popular culture that an average heart rate is 70, but the reality is that your heart rate is constantly changing: accelerating and decelerating. When we inhale, our heart beats faster; when we exhale, it slows down. The average over a one-minute period might be 70, but the pattern of beats during that minute will directly reflect the continuous changes in our neurophysiology, including threat response and perceptions of safety and connection. The difference in the rate of heartbeats in the span of each full breath, "heart rate variability," is easily measured and displayed as a series of spiky curves (when we are stressed) or wide, smooth curves (when we are relaxed and feeling connected to others or nature).[11] This would be an interesting footnote to our physiology were it not for one well-documented effect of HRV—it has a simultaneous effect on the others around us. The simultaneous effect is called "entrainment," which means that people within six, eight, or ten feet of each other tend to have their HRV correspond to the HRV of the other. This means that our physiological threat response, or lack thereof, reflected in our HRV curves, responds to that of nearby people, whose HRV curves come to more closely mirror ours, and vice versa. Thus, due to the equivalent of emotional contagion, we may feel calmer around a calm person, or tense in the presence of an agitated person. We are, in fact, connected.

All My Relations and Modern Science's View of Life's Interconnectedness

> We are related, we are all one. The Indian acknowledges this and so discovers the most liberating aspect of Native science: life renews, and all things which support life are renewable.[12]

> Carbon is the foundation of life. It exists in every living organism, in every cell. While some is stilled, preserved in fossils over long stretches of time, most is continually recycled... Humans are mostly water, and, after that, mostly carbon – carbon that has been passed down through the ages, from the flesh of a fish, the ear of an elephant, the leaves of a plant. Somewhere in each of us is a cell whose carbon elements may have nourished the planet's nascent life.[13]

We are indeed completely connected. As we learn about the intricacies of our neurophysiology, we begin to see functional strategies and skills for influencing and managing our perceptions of threat, our stress responses, and our feelings of safety and connectedness. These include conscious breathing techniques, developing and maintaining positive mental images of relationships, nature, and desirable outcomes, and strategies for turning off threat responses through rapid conceptual reframing of situations that could initiate one. Each of these approaches has parallels in venerable spiritual or philosophical traditions. At the same time, they also rely implicitly, or often explicitly, on a model of the world in harmony that is grounded in an understanding of the connection between all things, all life. In fact, the most effective neurophysiology/stress management strategies draw directly on teachings in disciplines such as meditation, qigong, yoga, prayer, contemplation, and nature awareness.[14] All are suffused with the spirit of "all my relations," leading to the insight that we are, with the impetus of recent scientific discoveries, returning to the wisdom of our indigenous forebears and contemporaries. Honoring and applying that wisdom, it turns out, is an excellent strategy for skillfully using our new scientific knowledge to improve our physical, mental, and spiritual health.

We've examined some potent interweaving of indigenous and modern scientific worldviews on the philosophical and individual level. Happily, we are also beginning to find our way toward enacting this worldview of interconnectedness in our organizations. Let us now look at an example in the world of business.

Interconnectedness in Organizations: An Exemplar

Many of us spend half or more of our waking hours in organizations. We invest enormous effort and energy in these collections of people and functions. It is far too seldom that we experience the sense of community, relatedness, and higher purpose that we might wish for if we stepped back and really considered what would fully support our creativity, joy, and sense of fulfillment at work. The latest Gallup employee engagement surveys tell us that only 30 percent of US employees are actively engaged and inspired at work. The other 70 percent are either merely present (50 percent) or actively unhappy (20 percent) in their work.[15] With this as a backdrop, consider a company whose engagement profile is off the charts, in a positive way, one that truly embraces interconnectedness as a moral and a business imperative, creating extraordinary results.

The voice of Bob Chapman, CEO of Barry-Wehmiller Companies, echoes up from the bottom of the auditorium where he greeted a new cadre of 50 Communication Skills Training professors. He says, "Your purpose as a professor, a leader, can be to build great people. That is what we value at Barry-Wehmiller; we build great people who do extraordinary things."[16] With a smile and twinkle in his eyes, he continues:

> I get up each morning happy to go to work and to shine the light on every person. Like my family at home, each one of our B-W employees is a gift and they, individually and together, make this a place where every employee says that they want their sons, daughters, friends to work here, too.[17]

The Barry-Wehmiller Company (B-W), over 100 years old, is a capital goods manufacturing and engineering consulting business headquartered in St. Louis, Missouri. They employ 11,000 people around the world and, in 2014, had annual sales of $2.4 billion.[18]

In these regards they are not exceptional, but in their philosophy and commitment to creating and maintaining an organization that is, first and foremost, about fostering and rewarding interconnectedness, they may be unparalleled in their value and appreciation of every person regardless of rank and tenure. In their words:

> We're Building A Better World. We're more than just a successful capital equipment and engineering solutions firm. We're an organization fiercely committed to improving the lives of our team members across the globe. By providing meaningful work in an environment of care and compassion, we send them home fulfilled by their time with us, rather than drained by it. We understand what every human being on the planet desires: to know that who they are and what they do matter. As a business, we have a unique opportunity to let them know that they do.[19]

B-W demonstrates this in every aspect of their organization. They have acquired several dozen companies across the US and around the globe. Every one of those companies was kept in the same city, no one was laid off, and they all received the same or better pay. Those employees were brought in as full members of the B-W family, valued for who they are and what they could contribute to the success of their coworkers and the company.

In 2008, when the recession hit B-W company, they saw a 30 percent drop in customer demand for their services. Bob and the other leaders stood by their commitment to their interconnectedness.

> We will all take unpaid leave each month, from CEO to the newest entry to the organization, across the entire global company… that way the pain is carried by all of us and not totally burdensome on a few of us.[20]

Six months later, sales picked back up, everyone moved back up to full time, and sizeable bonuses were awarded to every employee at the end of the year.

This mindset of "WE" is: we each are valued, we each are interconnected, we each are leaders with gifts and an inner light that we are here to acknowledge in each other. In all parts of the organization, weekly group gatherings begin with what they call "high touch meetings," giving effective appreciation. Effective appreciation is totally authentic, describing the feelings, actions, and impact that someone's behavior, presence, and contributions have brought to your or a colleague's personal and work life. Their Communication Skills Training class supports this idea by requiring all leaders to attend before they can participate in any other educational training. Why?—"Because listening to your people is the most important thing that you can do, giving each employee the grace and space to be heard and acknowledged for their unique gifts."[21] This training has been so successful that employees report powerful improvements in their family relationships—so much so, that the course is offered free in several communities to family members and the public who want to learn the skills of actively building connection to others that they see B-W employees are gaining. Finally, an impressive financial postscript to this story of intentional interconnectedness: B-W has returned 18 to 24 percent profits on their sales every year since 1994, through thick and thin, recessions and expansions.[22]

Conclusion

> Native America views humans and their surroundings as interconnected within a sacred circle. It holds the essences of being and becoming.[23]

"All my relations," the emblematic benediction of indigenous worldview, stands to inform and even lead us into a new sense of relationship with each other and with the entire natural world around us. It is exciting to be alive at a time when we can be a part of the growing number of communities in the western world who are not breaking life into separate compartments in an attempt to understand the secrets of the universe. Modern sciences, in particular applied neurophysiology and modern organizational experience, are discovering the wisdom of this indigenous perspective, generating a new renaissance in our understanding of how we can live enormously full, healthy, and productive lives as members of the human and natural community. I encourage us all to explore how these threads are woven into our lives, our organizations, our communities, and to expand our worldview and discover many more aspects of the interconnectedness with "All our relations" and ourselves.

Notes

1 Sanchez, *The Four Gifts: How Native Wisdom Transformed My Life*, 70.
2 Deloria, "Relativity, Relatedness and Reality," 34.
3 Deloria, "Ethnoscience and Indian Realities," 16.
4 Windham, "Bridging Two Worlds," 39 and through personal conversation during a diversity leadership training.
5 Poncelet, *The Shaman Within: A Physicist's Guide to the Deeper Dimensions of Your Life, the Universe, and Everything*, xxii–xxiii.
6 Tucker, "Pachamama Alliance's Journeys Leader Manual," 4.
7 Ibid., 1.
8 Dispenza, *Evolve Your Brain: The Science of Changing Your Mind*, 11.

9 Rankin, *Mind Over Medicine: Scientific Proof that You Can Heal Yourself,* 143.
10 Grandmother Ruth (Navajo) through personal conversation during healings in Boulder in 1992.
11 HeartMath, *emWave2 Quick Start Guide,* 3.
12 Dr. Pam Colorado (Oneida), quoted in Hill, *Words of Power: Voices from Indian America,* 33.
13 Cramer, "Science Notebook: Scientific Observations," 1.
14 Scaer, *The Trauma Spectrum: Hidden Wounds and Human Resiliency,* 157–158.
15 Gallup, "State of the American Workplace: Employee Engagement Insights for U.S. Business Leaders," 47.
16 Bob Chapman, CEO of Barry-Wehmiller Corporation, personal notes from his oral presentation at professor training for Communications Skills Training class, University of Washington, St. Louis, March 7, 2013.
17 Ibid.
18 Barry-Wehmiller Companies, "Snapshot of the Organization."
19 Barry-Wehmiller, "Overview."
20 Remarks by Bob Chapman to a private gathering. See also Chapman, "How a Family Shared a Burden."
21 Barry-Wehmiller University, *Our Community Listens Communication Skills Class Notebook,* Module 4, 3.
22 Blakeman, "Barry-Wehmiller – Another Great Participation Age Company," 1.
23 Lakota Elder, quoted in Wilson, *The Little Wisdom Library: Native American Wisdom,* 13.

References

Barry-Wehmiller, "Overview." Available online at www.linkedin.com/company/barry--wehmiller-companies-inc (accessed 30 March 2016).

Barry-Wehmiller Companies, "Snapshot of the Organization," 2016. Available online at www1.barry-wehmiller.com/our-business/snapshot-of-the-organization (accessed 30 March 2016).

Barry-Wehmiller University. *Our Community Listens Communication Skills Class Notebook.* 2013.

Blakeman, Chuck. "Barry-Wehmiller – Another Great Participation Age Company." 2014. Available online at www.chuckblakeman.com/2014/07/texts/barry-wehmiller-another-great-participation-age-company (accessed 14 March 2016).

Chapman, Bob. "How a Family Shared a Burden." *Truly Human Leadership* [blog], April 24, 2013. Available online at www.trulyhumanleadership.com/?p=645 (accessed 30 March 2016).

Cramer, Deborah. "Science Notebook: Scientific Observations." *Science News,* 174, 11 (2008): 4.

Deloria, Vine, Jr. "Ethnoscience and Indian Realities." *Winds of Change,* 7, 3 (1992): 12–18.

Deloria, Vine, Jr. "Relativity, Relatedness and Reality." *Winds of Change,* 7, 4 (1992): 34–40.

Dispenza, Joe. *Evolve Your Brain: The Science of Changing Your Mind.* Deerfield Beach, FL: Health Communications, Inc., 2007.

Gallup. "State of the American Workplace: Employee Engagement Insights for U.S. Business Leaders." Gallup, Inc., 2013. Available online at www.gallup.com/strategicconsulting/163007/state-american-workplace.aspx (accessed 14 March 2016).

HeartMath. *emWave2 Quick Start Guide.* Boulder Creek, CA: Institute of HeartMath, 2011.

Hill, Norbert, Jr. (Oneida), editor. *Words of Power: Voices from Indian America.* Golden, CO: Fulcrum Publishing, 1994.

Poncelet, Claude. *The Shaman Within: A Physicist's Guide to the Deeper Dimensions of Your Life, the Universe, and Everything.* Boulder, CO: Sounds True, 2014.

Rankin, Lissa. *Mind Over Medicine: Scientific Proof that You Can Heal Yourself.* Carlsbad, CA: Hay House, Inc., 2013.

Sanchez, Anita L. *The Four Gifts: How Native Wisdom Transformed My Life* [manuscript]. Boulder, CO: Sanchez Tennis & Associates, LLC, 2014.

Scaer, Robert. *The Trauma Spectrum: Hidden Wounds and Human Resiliency.* New York: W.W. Norton & Company, 2005.

Tucker, David. *Pachamama Alliance's Journeys Leader Manual.* San Francisco: Pachamama Alliance, 2014.

Wilson, Terry P. *The Little Wisdom Library: Native American Wisdom.* San Francisco: Chronicle Books, 1994.

Windham, Thomas. "Bridging Two Worlds: Native American Students Bring Traditional Knowledge to the Study of Atmospheric Sciences." *Winds of Change,* 12, 1 (1997): 38–42.

PLACE

Self-Impressions, California by M. Jennifer Chandler

No one
Caresses
My feet like the Earth
                    —Rachel Bagby

5

FINDING HOPE AT THE MARGINS

A JOURNEY OF ENVIRONMENTAL JUSTICE
ANA I. BAPTISTA

Growing up, the City of Newark, New Jersey was most notable as the punchline of bad jokes about urban blight and decay, but to me it was home. This city shaped my understanding of the environment, community, social justice, and ultimately what I would dedicate my life to pursuing: environmental justice. I came to discover the full depth of meaning of this term, "environmental justice," as my personal experiences of struggle combined with my professional knowledge of the way physical spaces are formed by ecology, social, economic, and political practices. Growing up, I knew intuitively what environmental *injustice* was—what it looked and smelled like, what it felt like to feel resentment and despair about the physical conditions around you. Later I came to understand the multiple dimensions of environmental *justice* in the form of recognition, distribution, and structural justice. The spaces where environmental degradation and marginalized communities of color and low-income people come to coincide are fertile spaces for gaining insight into the ecological and social processes that are often hidden from society. These invisible places are the products of an unequal, throwaway society that lives a comfortable existence at the expense of sacrifice zones, referred to as environmental justice communities. To achieve environmental justice means to have access not just to a clean and healthy environment, but to have the ability to help shape the conditions of your environment and be shaped by it in positive, empowering ways. My journey of finding voice through the environmental struggles of my community is a starting point for understanding how we might come to see and contribute to this ideal of environmental justice.

The Ironbound

On the easternmost edge of the City of Newark, surrounded by rail lines, the Passaic River, and the New Jersey Turnpike, lies a neighborhood called the "Ironbound." Growing up in a place called *Ironbound* gives one an acute sense of boundaries. This is a place whose very name references the rail lines that surrounded an industrialized landscape and gave rise to a vibrant community of poor and working class people of color and immigrants. The area was borne out of a vast marsh ecosystem that is part of an area of northern New Jersey known as the meadowlands. Although this delicate ecosystem once thrived as part of a complex estuary, it was historically seen as treacherous land, filled in with garbage dumps and tamed to accommodate the industry that grew up around the rivers. Growing up, the steel girded borders and the toxic Passaic River were boundaries to be respected and feared. Millions of people today fly over and drive through our city but few give it much thought. All the underbelly infrastructure of the metropolitan area—trash incinerators, sewage plants, seaports, airports, chemical plants, power plants, and prisons—are relegated to these marginal lands. If you look closely, you can see these sacrifice zones or fenceline communities all across the country. They coexist alongside concentrated pockets of poor communities of color, long segregated by decades of industrial pollution, unfair housing practices, and economic divestment. These are places Carolyn Merchant describes as spaces of "otherness."[1] Cities in particular were socially constructed in contrast to the images of the American Eden that western colonizers sought to preserve as pristine wilderness. Merchant reminds us that:

> The 'Others' were the colonized indigenous people, immigrants, and people of color who were outside the controlled, managed garden ... what lay beyond the periphery were wastelands and

deserts, the places of outcasts, of waste, of people of color, and of immigrants – in short, those colonized 'Others' not admitted into the enclosed space of the reinvented garden.[2]

But how did the creation of places like the Ironbound happen and why? This question haunted me as a child. Why do we accept that certain people and places are disposable, and pushed to the margins by our society?

Finding My Voice on a Toxic Tour

It wasn't all smokestacks and struggle in the Ironbound. I loved my neighborhood. As much as it frustrated and angered me to see how degraded our environment was, it was a place where families and neighbors took care of each other and mounted fierce resistance to the steady stream of dumping in the community. The first time I realized my neighborhood was not quite like New Jersey's leafy suburban experience came when I spent a summer at an environmental enrichment program in the Pine Barrens of New Jersey. As part of the environmental curriculum, they included a field trip to Newark to learn about environmental pollution. This bus of sheltered suburban children and instructors filled an itinerary with stops through the Ironbound like a stroll through a house of horrors. Stops included glimpses at the world's largest superfund site contaminated with deadly Agent Orange, the state's largest garbage incinerator, and many more examples of environmental destruction, which they had never before seen. I was at a crossroads. Before this bus rolled past my house, I had to decide whether I would share with them that this place they were touring was my home or whether I would remain silent as they took in my neighborhood like visitors to a zoo. My hesitation stemmed from a deep fear that they would equate the physical conditions of my environment as an assessment of my own value as a person. Ultimately I decided to speak up. I spoke up mostly out of anger and wounded pride. How dare these people judge my community? So I stood up on the bus and, before they exited the Turnpike, I began to share with them the stories of my community's efforts to fight new incinerator proposals, to get the superfund sites cleaned up, to create more parks, and to stop the dumping in our city. It was my first impromptu toxic tour. It would be the first of many that would help me find my voice and also help me to discover the full meaning of environmental justice.

In Giovanna Di Chiro's essay "Nature as Community" we come to understand that the feeling of alienation from nature and the process of framing and recounting the experiences of living in an environmentally degraded environment can also be a pathway toward transformation.

> Often the only functional relationship with nature for many city-dwelling people or those living near toxic waste sites becomes the core of their political strategy. In other words, their knowledge of the destruction of nature and natural systems in their local communities may function to mobilize them to act on these negative experiences.[3]

The act of narrating a tour of the most toxic places in my community was a powerful way to link people living a comfortable distance from the ecological and material destruction in my community to their lived experiences. It helped give meaning and make real what was a painful lived experience of environmental injustice. It was also a way to reclaim a different kind of relationship to nature than the one we were learning about in the Pine Barrens of New Jersey.

The act of "speaking for ourselves" is also a central tenet of the environmental justice movement. People with the lived experience of injustice are the ones that have the legitimate claim to speak about those injustices and to demand to be seen and heard. This notion is tied to the concept of environmental justice as a form of recognition. David Schlosberg reminds us that environmental justice is not solely attainable via a just distribution of material resources, but is also linked to identity and recognition.

> The bottom line here is that environmental justice activists often see themselves as outside the cultural mainstream. As such, their identities are devalued. The movement, then, turns to recognition as a key component of the justice of environmental justice.[4]

Justice in this case goes beyond the recognition and empowerment of individuals and extends to the whole community. In this sense, speaking up on the bus that day I was not only reclaiming my own voice in relation to a place, I was demanding that the group recognize the integrity and dignity of the community as a whole. The toxic tour was a reminder of our interconnectedness and the importance of authentic voice and recognition in countering environmental injustice.

The Concentration of Environmental Burdens

Out of sight, out of mind. This is the reality for environmental justice communities. You flush your toilet, you throw out the trash, you turn on the lights, you purchase those new sneakers you wanted. All of these simple, daily acts reverberate in the communities that are at the points of extraction, production, transport, and waste dumping. These acts are made possible by the existence of places and people that are mostly out of sight of our everyday lives. They do not exist in our popular imaginations. We have no idea where the garbage goes or where the sneakers come from and so the illusion of cheap, efficient, fast consumption is a reality we take for granted. What if we were forced to live next door to the incinerators where our garbage goes or where the power is produced? Would we still think it is easy and efficient, would we view the concomitant environmental impacts as normal byproducts of the marketplace?

In the Ironbound and places like it throughout the globe, environmental destruction is allowed or "permitted" to occur either unfettered by the needs of industry or meted out based on passive regulatory limits set by the state, chemical by chemical, stack by stack. Robert Bullard, the stalwart of environmental justice, reminds us that:

> Communities are not all created equal. In the United States, for example, some communities are routinely poisoned while the government looks the other way. Environmental regulations have not uniformly benefited all segments of society. People of color (African American, Latinos, Asians, Pacific Islanders, and Native Americans) are disproportionately harmed by industrial toxins on their jobs and in their neighborhoods ... Why do some communities get dumped on while others escape?[5]

This was THE question that confounded me as a young person trying to make sense of the environmental injustices in Newark. The question goes beyond questioning the logic of the industry doing the dumping, but extends to the role of the government that endorses or ignores the disproportionate impacts of that dumping. On that first toxic tour of Newark, the indignant questions from my fellow students included statements like, "Surely the government will intervene to address these problems," said with the air of outrage and assurance afforded to those lucky enough to have grown up in places protected from these injustices. But at the ripe old age of sixteen, I was already very cynical about the role of government to do anything but support industries and ignore community concerns. I didn't know about Dr Bullard yet, but his words rang all too true in my world. I had witnessed time after time in my own community the way environmental agencies, elected officials, and even scientific "experts" sided with polluting industries to make the case to locate yet another polluting facility in our midst.

The notion that environmental burdens are disproportionately located in communities of color and low-income communities is at the heart of the environmental justice movement. Luke Cole and Sheila Foster suggest that the structure of government decision-making on environmental issues is complicit in the unequal burdens placed on these communities where "Permitting laws and policies both mediate and legitimize the dependence of private decision makers on structural inequalities in choosing facility sites."[6] The State's narrow conceptualization of environmental problems as facility siting and emissions controls decisions after the pollution is generated makes consideration of environmental justice seem outside the purview of traditional environmental regulation and decision-making processes. Absent the consideration of the cumulative, disproportionate nature of environmental pollution burdens and the differential health and environmental impacts of these burdens, environmental decision-making is rendered useless, or worse, complicit in the degradation of already vulnerable communities.

The emergence of the environmental justice movement has been a powerful response to the entrenched problems of disproportionate environmental burdens. Communities like the Ironbound have mounted forceful opposition to environmental burdens through community organizing, direct action, litigation, and the building of coalitions across issues not traditionally considered "environmental." But the chronic fight over unwanted land uses puts already struggling communities with limited resources on the defensive. These battles are an exhausting and often disheartening process that can wear down the will to fight. David Harvey challenges the environmental justice movement to look beyond localized battles or "particularist militancies" to find a universal politics of social justice that can create lasting responses to environmental injustice.[7] Environmental justice organizations throughout the country have in fact sought relief from the endless battles in their backyards by linking up their grassroots efforts to systematic responses to inequality while still maintaining their authentic voice embedded in community.

In the Ironbound, I found one such environmental justice organization focused on social justice called the Ironbound Community Corporation (ICC), which was the organization that often called those late-night meetings and incinerator protests I attended as a child with my family. They helped organize residents to mount opposition to very powerful economic and political interests pushing more pollution on our neighborhoods. The leaders from ICC were neighbors that lived down the street and knocked on our doors to tell us about what was happening and encouraged us to participate, even though my parents didn't speak English and we had no money or political clout. The people in this organization were my mentors, and when I later joined them as a graduate student I became part of a long tradition of community based planning and activism grounded in social justice. Instead of focusing solely on the never-ending litany of polluters, we also dedicated our energy to organizing residents and together developing a vision for the future. This future included a community with more green spaces, a clean river, parks, and the creation of jobs with the potential to break the cycle of poverty and pollution. These planning and organizing exercises laid the foundation for campaigns to create new parks, clean the river, and conduct our own monitoring and clean ups. In this way, environmental justice was not just about fighting for less of the burdens but fighting for the right to shape our own destiny. Together we created an alternative vision of economic and environmental justice while maintaining a radical critique of the underlying systems that give rise to material inequalities.

The Racialization of Space—Structural Racism and Urban Development

The central question that Dr Bullard posed, "why do some communities get dumped on," has driven my professional exploration of environmental racism through the lens of urban planning and public policy. Today when I give "Toxic Tours," I ask people to consider that the City of Newark is home to one of the largest seaports in the country, in the middle of one of the largest consumer markets, among the wealthiest metropolitan regions in the world, yet Newark suffers under the weight of chronic, intergenerational poverty, one of the highest residentially, racially segregated places with some of the most toxic pollution concentrations in the nation. These extreme contradictions cry out for attention and reflection. I couldn't comprehend the notion that these material realities of inequality were simple byproducts of a rational economic system. I was often confronted with statements like "well if it's so bad you should just move" or "there's nothing wrong with this, it's just that Newark has cheap land close to the highways so that's where the industries naturally want to locate." Simple—the unfettered market leads environmental pollution and urban blight to our doorstep and if we can't stomach it, then we have the right to relocate. Something about this supposedly rational market logic seemed irrational and unfair and anyone who has grown up poor or a person of color knows that the "just move" strategy is a lie. You can't "vote with your feet" if you don't get a vote and you're wearing lead shoes. The currency of upward mobility in American society has been closed off to people of color for generations through institutional racism in a variety of ways.

The processes by which the City of Newark became a segregated city with chronic concentrations of poverty, pollution, and disinvestment were not coincidences of the marketplace. The story of Newark is the story of many inner cities throughout the country where the confluence of deindustrialization, White flight, and racist housing, urban policy, and environmental programs created ghettos alongside wealthy outer ring suburbs. I'm always shocked how few of my planning students have any knowledge of the history of explicitly racist government programs related to housing in particular. Everyone knows the images of segregated restaurants and buses from the civil rights era, but few of them have any notion of how deeply this racial project extended into our systems of banking, real estate, transportation, and urban development. These policies shaped the physical reality, the form and function of cities like Newark, and the growing suburbs for generations. Practices like redlining and discriminatory mortgage lending structured the choices of where people could go to school, live, or work. Many of the public housing complexes in the Ironbound and throughout Newark were segregated by race and were built in those areas of the city considered the least desirable places to live, marginal pieces of swampland at the edges of communities like the Ironbound. Even after being legally outlawed, the practices of steering people and subtle discrimination continue to pervade the marketplace. john a. powell reminds us that "The racialized use of space is a deliberative yet ever changing set of practices that isolates and subordinates marginalized populations."[8]

Newark cannot exist as a space of concentrated poverty and people of color without the existence of predominantly White, wealthier communities that surround it. These dichotomies embedded in our geography serve as a constant reminder of the legacy of institutional racism that continues to permeate the life choices and physical forms of cities that are often brushed aside as seemingly pure market decisions. I remember reading Laura Pulido's article, "Rethinking Environmental Racism," for the first time as a graduate student in urban planning.[9] It was the articulation of what I experienced my whole life growing up in Newark but could never quite unlock. No amount of rational planning could've explained what Pulido so beautifully summed up about the relationship of space, racism, and urban development.

> A brief example may demonstrate how white privilege allows us to historicize environmental racism: A polluter locates near a black neighborhood because the land is relatively inexpensive and adjacent to an industrial zone. This is not a malicious, racially

motivated, discriminatory act. Instead, many would argue that is economically rational. Yet it is racist in that it is made possible by the existence of a racial hierarchy, reproduces racial inequality, and undermines the wellbeing of that community. Moreover, the value of black land cannot be understood outside of the relative value of white land, which is a historical product. White land is more valuable by virtue of its whiteness, and thus it is not as economically feasible for the polluter. Nor is it likely that the black community's proximity to the industrial zone is a chance occurrence. Given the Federal government's role in creating suburbia, white's opposition to integration, and the fact that black communities have been restricted to areas whites deemed undesirable, can current patterns of environmental racism be understood outside a racist urban history?"[10]

Here was an explanation of structural racism that opened up a new way of thinking about the environmental injustices in Newark but also helped link the local struggles of my city to a larger narrative of urban development. It made tackling the issues of environmental injustice even more daunting, because it was not simply a matter of redistributing the environmental burdens in society, or doing better physical planning of cities, or even protecting the environment for all people. Structural forms of racism, like White privilege, meant that environmental justice could only be achieved through a thoughtful project to systematically undo generations of intentional and unintentional racist decisions. john a. powell reminds us that the project of countering and dismantling structural racism and racialized spaces is firmly rooted in collective action and expansive notions of belonging in society:

> This history of metropolitan dynamics in the United States is one of multiple structures inscribing racial hierarchies into the fabric of our geography. Countering this history will require not only collective action and a bold commitment to the ideals of democracy and justice but also a new way of seeing.[11]

My journey working for environmental justice means that it is necessarily a collective journey, of continually finding ways to draw people into knowing, understanding, and acting in ways that counter institutional racism and the spacialization of race.

Spaces of Transformation and Hope

Albert Hirschman said of people who grow up in blighted communities, that they have three choices—loyalty, exit, or voice.[12] According to Cynthia Duncun, "By 'voice' Hirschman means staying, working for change, and advocating for the kind of public and private investment that widens opportunities."[13] In my journey toward environmental justice I have chosen the path of *Voice*. I found my voice by first trying to make sense of the ways in which my own community was ravaged by racism, inequality, industrialization, capitalism, and consumption. The toxic tours I host these days are not just a retelling of tales of horrors of environmental destruction, but a call to action for those people within the community and outside of it. For those residents that live in Newark and communities like it throughout the globe, we have to continually work to inspire action not apathy, empowerment not disillusionment, and authentic voice. But even more importantly, the work of the environmental justice movement must incorporate a sense of connectedness and responsibility that extends to those living comfortably outside the sacrifice zones. In the places at the margins—where society has hidden its dirty little secrets about the real impacts of economic growth, White privilege, and environmental destruction—there is an opportunity for real transformative change. Environmental justice communities must become a priority not just for those living in these areas, but for all those who claim to care for the earth, for social justice, and for human dignity. john a. powell reminds us that in trying to build new, more inclusive metropolitan regions requires our hearts and minds. "To succeed in creating better regions, more participatory democratic processes, and equal access to opportunity, we must make this work a project of the imagination and a project of the spirit."[14]

Environmental justice requires us to link together both the physical spaces that form our communities as well as the civic, political, and economic forces that can create more just places. The work of environmental justice includes grassroots organizing, coalition building, political and social movement solidarity—these are the building blocks for a transformative and radical approach to environmental justice. Most importantly, we must do the hard work of making these invisible spaces visible to all, felt by all, and tackled by all if we are to have any hope at redemption and social justice.

Notes

1 Merchant, "Shades of Darkness: Race and Environmental History."
2 Ibid., 389.
3 Di Chiro, "Nature as Community: The Convergence of Environment and Social Justice," 313.
4 Schlosberg, "The Justice of Environmental Justice: Reconciling Equity, Recognition, and Participation in a Political Movement," 89.
5 Bullard, "Anatomy of Environmental Racism and the Environmental Justice Movement," 15.
6 Cole and Foster, *From the Ground Up: Environmental Racism and the Rise of the Environmental Justice Movement*, 74.
7 Harvey, *Justice, Nature and the Geography of Difference.*
8 powell, "Reinterpreting Metropolitan Space as a Strategy for Social Justice," 25.
9 Pulido, "Rethinking Environmental Racism: White Privilege and Urban Development in Southern California."
10 Ibid., 16.
11 powell, "Reinterpreting Metropolitan Space as a Strategy for Social Justice," 32.
12 Hirschman, "'Exit, Voice, and Loyalty': Further Reflections and a Survey of Recent Contributions."
13 Duncan, "From Bootstrap Community Development to Regional Equity," 10.
14 powell, "Reinterpreting Metropolitan Space as a Strategy for Social Justice," 32.

References

Bullard, Robert D. "Anatomy of Environmental Racism and the Environmental Justice Movement." In *Confronting Environmental Racism: Voices from the Grassroots*, edited by Robert D. Bullard, 15–39. Boston: South End Press, 1993.

Cole, Luke W. and Sheila R. Foster. *From the Ground Up: Environmental Racism and the Rise of the Environmental Justice Movement*. New York: New York University Press, 2000.

Di Chiro, Giovanna. "Nature as Community: The Convergence of Environment and Social Justice." In *Uncommon Ground: Rethinking the Human Place in Nature*, edited by William Cronon, 298–320. New York: W.W. Norton Company, Inc., 1996.

Duncan, Cynthia A. "From Bootstrap Community Development to Regional Equity." In *Breakthrough Communities: Sustainability and Justice in the Next American Metropolis*, edited by M. Paloma Pavel, 9–14. Cambridge: The MIT Press, 2009.

Harvey, David. *Justice, Nature and the Geography of Difference*. Malden, MA: Blackwell Publishers, Inc., 1996.

Hirschman, Albert O. "'Exit, Voice, and Loyalty': Further Reflections and a Survey of Recent Contributions." *Social Science Information*, 13, 1 (1974): 7–26.

Merchant, Carolyn. "Shades of Darkness: Race and Environmental History." *Environmental History*, 8, 3 (2003): 380–394.

powell, john a. "Reinterpreting Metropolitan Space as a Strategy for Social Justice." In *Breakthrough Communities: Sustainability and Justice in the Next American Metropolis*, edited by M. Paloma Pavel, 23–32. Cambridge: The MIT Press, 2009.

Pulido, Laura. "Rethinking Environmental Racism: White Privilege and Urban Development in Southern California." *Annals of the Association of American Geographers*, 90, 1 (2000): 12–40.

Schlosberg, David. "The Justice of Environmental Justice: Reconciling Equity, Recognition, and Participation in a Political Movement." In *Moral and Political Reasoning in Environmental Practice*, edited by Andrew Wright and Avner D. Shalit, 77–106. Cambridge: Massachusetts Institute of Technology, 2003.

6

INTRICATE YET NOURISHING

MULTIRACIAL WOMEN, ECOLOGY, AND SOCIAL WELL-BEING
NINA S. ROBERTS

The increasingly diverse US population is contributing to a growing complexity of understanding multiracial and multiethnic identity. This includes reshaping conventional wisdom concerning environmental awareness and opportunities for spiritual rejuvenation resulting from visiting parks and enjoying recreation outdoors. In particular, this chapter will elucidate connections between nature, parks, and women across multiethnic boundaries in ways that can also develop economically and socially vibrant communities. I will integrate sample demographic and social trends relating to ethnic shifts among women across US society, broadly. These trends will be woven through my stories of how cultural ecology has impacted my social evolution, spiritual growth, and unleashed my transformation as a leader and scholar. In brief, cultural ecology characterizes ways in which culture change is prompted, or induced, by how we adapt to the natural environment around us. As noted in Bowser, Roberts, Simmons, and Perales, "Personal stories from women of color can help guide future leaders in developing community support, mentoring, and inclusiveness in environmental leadership."[1]

While focusing on the positive and affirming is vital, social pressure to assimilate into dominant cultural ways of being is still somewhat intense; this is conveyed in key points made about my own multiracial experience in my chapter of the landmark book *Speaking Up and Speaking Out*.[2] Consequently, it can be either too easy not to "rock the boat" when we know we should, or risk being criticized if we step out of the norm. How do we break the cycle and challenge the system? How do we respect difference, challenge oppression and the status quo, and still be heard? These concepts will also be expanded upon in this chapter as this important topic of social and cultural ecology, integral to my personal and professional life, surfaces deeply with the passage of time. As Maria Root states so well: "Multiracial people blur the boundaries between races...and [our] existence challenges the rigidity of racial lines...Oppression always fragments people, as energy and attention are diverted from the experience of wholeness."[3] When we refuse to fragment ourselves or others, we become less fearful and learn to approach differences with respect; it is this respect that gives us courage and ultimately heals the soul.

On the Edge

Being both multiracial and female is much like standing at the edge of a cliff. You can see what's beyond your feet—the rocks jutting out in odd places, the river rushing below, and details only you could be privy to from your position are evident; most other people cannot see the view from your vantage point although they'll say "I know how you feel." One could say this is the case with many things in life. Only those who find themselves in the pan know what the ingredients truly are. Still, living in a multicultural and multiracial world is not only about "knowing;" it's also about taking the fragmented world around you and piecing it all together, striving to make sense of it within your specific experience. Myself being of East Indian, West Indian, and White origins, I was called many names growing up, including "half-breed, mixed up, oreo, and confused."[4] As multiracial women, we stand on the edge of the boundary looking out, exploring in, and always prepared to be the recipient of name calling, misunderstanding, and even intrigue and jealousy. Maeda Allman suggests that, indeed, "race, gender, and sexuality exist as a sort of unstable triad; shifts in one create disturbances in the other two."[5] Nowhere do the concepts of balance and awareness become more potent and relevant than in discussions about race and gender.

It is always important to have the ability to transcend cultural boundaries in perception, to see and appreciate the grass on the other side—something a person with mixed blood can usually understand. This is the main benefit a settled multicultural environment can give us. A renowned scholar, and someone I'd love to meet, Maria Root discusses how the concept of a multiracial world might help to pull apart a negative construction of race.[6] The world is not such an easy place, though, so more often than not we run the risk of having to justify ourselves, or those connected to us, in a bid to explain why and how our differences exist. A multiracial woman has many glass ceilings to break through, for color, gender, and sexuality become more complex discussions in this context and within the realm of identity formation. The awareness of gender and body here take on a whole new meaning. Jaggar and Bordo have collected a selection of author works focusing on feminist ways of knowing, and these are from the philosophical, sociological, and psychological points of view, among other areas.[7] One essay, by Ruth Berman, discusses western science as a "fundamentally oppressive" discipline.[8] She calls for the transformation of science in order to remove bias against women, but this could only be achieved in a more egalitarian society. Basically, it is proposed that western intellectual tradition is undergoing a period of crisis.[9] Traditional intellectual and political ideals have fizzled out, and this has led to social unrest and economic change. Never has it proved more important for the true feminist to go back to her roots and get more in touch with the environment she occupies.

King posits that the true feminist today cannot ignore the world's state of ecological crisis, not simply for obvious reasons, but also because this crisis "is related to systems of hatred of all that is natural and female by the white, male western formulators of philosophy, technology, and death inventions."[10] The author believes that "the goals of feminism, ecology, and movements against racism and for the survival of indigenous peoples are internally related; they must be understood and pursued together in a worldwide, genuinely prolife, movement."[11]

Meanwhile, Zimmerman[12] speculated that environmentalists have been criticized by deep ecologists for not being effective in attempting to cut down human exploitation of the environment. This brings forth the concept that being an ecologist at heart required a much more pronounced commitment than being pro-environment. Yet, ecofeminists claim to be more radical and committed than deep ecologists (and, by inference, reform environmentalists) in combating the patriarchal culture and perception that dominates nature in the western world. By setting aside these long-standing, male-incorporated concepts (including hierarchialism, dualism, androcentrism, and atomism), people and their environment can finally live on in harmony with each other.

In light of the foregoing, this chapter will discuss the pressure to accept and become one with dominant cultural ways and, because of this, the necessity to break away and challenge the status quo. The key phrase is "accepting differences" while struggling for the ability to be heard in an increasingly multicultural world. The voices of humanity are many, no longer limited to a dominant few; however, the chorus often consists of muddled voices where the individual tones and cadences are difficult to make out. By manipulating the sounds, it is possible and desirable to make the individual stand out within the whole, creating a compelling, harmonious melody. Social and cultural ecology presents the need for a less fragmented world within the multicultural and multiracial contexts. We can be whole, while still being different, and in this sense of wholeness and mutual respect we can make the world a better place through fearless and impactful strategies. Hence, the central theme exposed in these pages reveals layers of the spirit often untapped. A look at demographic and social trends follows.

Keeping Up or Getting Left Behind

To analyze social and behavior patterns and identify reasons for both challenges and progress being made in the ecological and environmental fields, and diversity issues, concurrently, it is important to first offer a cursory overview of basic demographics of the US; sharing information regarding the overall picture of sample social trends offers a valuable framework.

As of the last Census, 2010, the US was at 308 million people and climbing steadily; as of June 2014, the total nationwide resident population of over 318 million made us the third most populous country in the world (behind China and India). Two important demographic and social aspects to consider are the facts that women are living longer than men and, broadly, people's health has moved swiftly to the forefront of public discourse. Individual efforts to live a healthy lifestyle have lacked in success and sustainability.[13]

Lee et al.,[14] for example, discussed how women of color are vulnerable to the harmful effects of poor dietary habits and physical inactivity. Subsequently, *Health Is Power* (HIP) was set up as a trial to study the efficacy of group cohesion intervention aimed at increasing physical activity and improving the eating habits of African American and Hispanic women in Houston and Austin, Texas.

Lee and others ultimately stress the importance of identifying factors needed to "adopt and maintain physical behavior changes"[15] for health purposes. They add especially that "[w]omen serve as important behavioral gatekeepers, as they continue to be the primary family caretakers, and hold multiple roles in the family, workplace and community."[16]

Additionally, the Pew Research Center[17] goes beyond gender and discusses the decline of marriage and rise of new family forms over the last half century. Their report sheds light on new family dynamics, taking into account shifting attitudes and behaviors differing by class, age, and race, as well as social, educational, cultural, and environmental factors. The findings of their study were complemented with a thorough analysis of demographic and economic data provided by the US Census Bureau. The final report presented some interesting and, in some cases, not so surprising findings.

One of these findings supported the trend that, while marriage is the status of choice among people with a higher education, it is decidedly not as prevalent among people on lower socioeconomic and education levels (e.g., reflected in a 16 percent gap in marriage rates between college graduates, 64 percent, and those possessing a high school diploma or less, 48 percent). Despite the desire for marriage, economic security plays a huge role in the decision to marry, and is often indeed a condition for marriage. This can be added to the fact the current generation of young people in many cases opt not to marry (a decline in marriages of 20 percent from 1960 to 2008) and are decidedly more open to cohabitation, compared to their counterparts from the 1960s. Still, despite the decline in marriage rates and the prevailing perception that marriage is "not the only path to family formation,"[18] the family unit stays strong and remains one of the most important elements in life. Cohabitation rates have nearly doubled since 1990. In addition, the modern generation tends to view new types of families, such as single parenthood, interracial marriage, and same sex marriage, in at least a neutral if not a positive light. Still, there is much headway to be made. Although there has been a 48 percent increase since 1977, only 62 percent of survey respondents in the Pew study endorsed a marriage where both spouses work outside the home while taking care of the children and sharing household chores. Therefore, the traditional male breadwinner and figurehead continues to be a driving force and a man is required to be able to support his family—while only a third of survey respondents made this statement about a woman.

On the multiracial front, 25 percent of survey respondents claimed that interracial marriages are "good for society"[19] while 60 percent were neutral and 14 percent expressed their displeasure at such a trend. The report states that the decline in marriage rates has been most noticeable among Blacks. By 2008, only 32 percent of Black adults were married, compared to 61 percent in 1960. According to this report, it transpires that Blacks are more likely to live as single parents than have a family living arrangement of a household with two spouses raising kids. The number of Blacks in single parent households in 2008 ranked at 19 percent, driven by births of children to Black women outside of wedlock (72 percent), compared to a lower rate among Hispanic women (53 percent), and an even lower one among Whites (29 percent). Hence, by 2008, approximately half of all minor Black children lived in a single parent household. Meanwhile, the report highlights that Blacks tend to be exceedingly critical of this trend and contend that children should be raised by two parents. This is not the case among Hispanics and Whites.

Perhaps as a result of this, only 64 percent of Blacks claim to be satisfied with their family life.

The Rise of Interracial Marriages

In another study, the Pew Research Center[20] investigated the rise of intermarriage rates from demographic and economic perspectives. Comparisons of interracial couples with other couples who marry within their race were also conducted. Newlywed couples were grouped by race and ethnicity of the individual spouses, and then compared in terms of the following factors: education, income, spouse's age, place or region of residence, and other factors. Key findings brought to light the increasing popularity of intermarriage (15 percent of all new marriages in 2010, compared to 6.7 percent in 1980), broken down in 2010 as follows: Whites (9 percent), Blacks (17 percent), Hispanics (26 percent), and Asians (28 percent) married outside of their race. This said, the report found gender patterns varied considerably in this respect among mainly Blacks and Asians, with Asian females carrying the torch at 36 percent entering an interracial marriage. This was followed by 24 percent of Black males, 17 percent of Asian males, and 9 percent of Black females. Interracial marriages among Whites and Hispanics did not register wide variations in gender patterns. White/Asian newlyweds also registered earning a considerably higher median salary (over $70k annually), as well as a higher educational status (over half possess a college degree), than any other interracial couple.

In addition, it is interesting to note that, among Hispanics and Blacks, those in interracial marriages with Whites tended to have a higher education than those who married within their own race or ethnicity. As far as regional differences go, the highest prevalence of interracial marriages in the US occurred in, or toward, the West. In addition, 35 percent of Americans claim that someone closely related to them is in an interracial marriage. The majority of people surveyed (63 percent) claim to have acceptance of interracial marriage, in comparison to the mid-1980s, when public opinion on the subject was significantly more divided, with 28 percent claiming interracial marriages were unacceptable, and only 33 percent stating it would be acceptable for them and everyone.

What all of these numbers loudly imply is how rapidly the face of America is changing. The children born of these families are altering the color wheel, spreading "half-breed fever", as I call it, wherever they go. A biracial male made it as far as the US presidency, the highest office imaginable, and whatever your political creed or affiliation, you will recognize this as a phenomenon that could only happen now, at this time, paving the way for others to reach for the stars. Currently, 7 million people in the US identify themselves as multiracial or biracial—not an insignificant number by any measure. Indeed, it seems to be some kind of trend to ride the wave of this open generation, judging by this scenario. It is a shifting world, one that pleads further exploration.

Environmental Awareness, Stewardship, and Conservation: Changes and Challenges

So, what to do in changing times? One goal could be to relearn the world, rediscover it, and taste its new flavors, much like one would a foreign, never-tried-before, gourmet dish of ingredients brought together in a complex way. This new world needs many champions to help drive awareness toward its protection and upkeep—and to engage in the ongoing discussion about Earth management. Women have a flexible but undeniable role to fill when it comes to averting the Earth's crisis. Joanna Macy is one such woman, and she has traveled from one continent to the next, imparting knowledge and awareness through writing and teaching to mentor and inspire activists all around the world.

In an article meant to serve as a compendium of interviews granted to Macy,[21] this remarkable woman talks about her experiences, causes, and meanderings. One of her important projects, Nuclear Guardianship, strived for the closing down of all nuclear reactors and proper handling of the radioactive remains. One of her most striking statements must be her view that the current economy and growth of an industrial society focused on technology and market forces cause our experience of time to be limited and narrow. As we live fast-paced, occasionally blurred lives, our experiences become fleeting and fragmented at best. She states:

> We often blame ourselves for having poor time-management skills, but the source of the problem is in the nature of the industrial-growth society. To be more precise, it is in its technology and its market forces. Searching for efficiency, we develop technologies to increase the speed of every operation and machine, and start measuring time in ever more minuscule fragments—nanoseconds and fractions of nanoseconds. [...] Corporations seek to show not only a greater profit every quarter but also a rising rate of growth. This makes for exceedingly short-term thinking. There is little or no room for reflection or weighing consequences.[22]

Furthermore, there is the intense feeling that things are spiraling out of control. Thoughts are hurried through our brains, and often remain unfinished when new distractions fast arise. And, this is where the problem starts with respect to conservation, because with our brains processing things so fast, and time becoming a scarce commodity, we rarely stop to wonder about the consequences our present actions may have on the future. Hence, we thoughtlessly waste our resources, and siphon everything we can from the Earth—its forests, coal, oil, fisheries, and all other natural resources. We then destroy that which we cannot use or consume. The mentality that we must build, protect, and strive for future generations has pretty much fizzled out, replaced by worship at the altar of instant gratification. Macy's reasoning for this is not that humans are bad, but that they are trapped "in a mind-destroying acceleration of time."[23] To live a better life, we must break this cycle, develop a more open and intuitive perspective of time, and create harmony between us and our natural environment.

Emergence of Environmental Justice

In order to achieve such balance, however, we must consider the issue of equal access to the environment and/or activities in or around nature. The emergence of the environmental justice movement had its seeds sown in the 1980s. This radical, multiracial, socially aware movement started making waves by bringing attention to participation barriers through grassroots efforts.[24] Of relevance here is the discussion regarding socioeconomic barriers that restrict access. Floyd,[25] for instance, mentions the historical barriers, such as lack of expendable income or transportation born of education and employment constraints. This barrier creates the marginalization of a certain demographic to which access is often denied for affordability reasons. Floyd lists different hypotheses and factors that explain participation in recreational activities among minority groups, including cultural factors (sub-cultural hypothesis) and assimilation issues, the functioning of which requires sensitive educational practices and higher staff diversity.

At the core of this hypothesis we find that different cultures view nature differently. As a result, discrimination rears its ugly head in both interpersonal interactions and institutional practices. Hence, there is a need for environmental agencies to devise culturally relevant programs while providing services and protection across the board to sometimes eclectic visitors and participants in environmental-based activities.

The Color of Climate

Does climate have a color? If one looks at the way cultural and racial minorities are underrepresented in the ecological and environmental sciences majors and departments at universities, then from this context, yes, climate does have a color, as well as a gender—and it is decidedly not female or most shades of brown, according to policy makers and organization leaders. These minorities therefore do not have a voice in negotiations. In more specific terms:

> [C]limate and color are defined as dualities for minority women— where these women may have a double burden, being underrepresented in the sciences as a whole and extremely rare in the environmental fields. In this context, color signifies "green" environmentalism as well as the many shades of brown, reflective of women of different racial, cultural, and ethnic backgrounds.[26]

Women of color have long been at the forefront of the struggle to bring attention to challenges that continue to devastate minority communities and their environment. As noted many years ago by Taylor, issues such as exposure to toxins, health and safety issues in the workplace, lead poisoning and asbestos issues, sub-standard housing, pollution, environmental contamination,[27] and more, affect minority neighborhoods in ways that the environmental justice movement continues to change decade after decade. While this is not fresh news, what needs to be brought back into the core is that with the nation's demographic shifts come more women of color who are well educated, politically minded, and breaking new ground.

Such conditions are necessary for these women to become stewards of the environment. To achieve this, one must first connect with others to advance the cause and change stunted perspectives, shaping new ideas into opportunities for progress. In order to set about a journey of discovery, however, one must remain cognizant of, and open to, the notion of "otherness"—be it in issues of gender, race, sexuality, or something else—which should invoke an empowering and not crippling conscious exploration of an environment full of colors and character. As race in relationships is an ever present, albeit sometimes silent and unmentioned construct, the act of building meaningful networks would involve seeking connections and establishing boundaries "with" and not "through" or "over" others.[28]

Connections between Nature, Parks, and Women of Color

Along these lines, Unger[29] discusses women, sexuality, and environmental justice in US history. The author goes deep into the discussion of various organizations' interest in the human genome and genetics research, specifically within the purview of environmental health policy. At the core, therefore, broken down to the bare bones, we find the link between humans and their environment—and how the health of one is inextricably connected to the health of the other.

Ecofeminism is a contemporary philosophical term utilized by Besthorn and McMillen[30] to suggest an expanded, revised ecological model, mainly from the social work practice perspective, but this model can be applied in the wider, practical ecological context. The way a person interacts with their environment requires an integrated approach within a world that is viewed in holistic and ecological terms.[31] Despite some controversies surrounding ecofeminism, one must admit it has made a significant contribution to understanding humanity and the creation of a relevant connection to planetary ecosystems. Ecofeminism has its own language in relation to nature and the individual, and the way one connects with the other. Therefore, it has much to do not only with respect to nature itself, but with personal and community empowerment as well, including being commensurate with social justice initiatives and anti-discrimination and oppression efforts. The only way to move forward is by seeing humanity and nature as two halves of a whole—indeed, as Besthorn and McMillen suggest, "in large measure social, political, economic and environmental issues are interrelated and fundamentally associated with humanity's philosophical understanding of its relationship with nature and the practices that stem from it."[32] Most importantly, "an expanded ecological model [...] must address those powerful systemic oppressions that maintain human alienation."[33]

Taylor has written about the topic of race, class, gender, and the environment for many years. In her paper "Women of Color, Environmental Justice, and Ecofeminism," she reminds us that while ecofeminists have organized themselves with broad definitions of the "environment," they have never paid much attention to how the issues they explore have disproportionately impacted people of color.[34] While times have changed, this seems to still hold true in the twenty-first century. "Compared with feminism and ecofeminism, movements in which the gender dimension dwarfs the other dimensions of the struggle, the environmental justice movement wages a struggle which is more balanced, with race, gender, and class forming the basic elements."[35] As Taylor continues, "women-of-color environmental justice activism is not just feminism or ecofeminism; it is broader and more complex than either of these movements."[36] Important to note is that many women of color in the environmental justice movement really see themselves as social justice activists because they prefer not to use any of the labels we encounter, such as "environmental," "feminist," or even "ecofeminist," to describe or define themselves.[37]

I like to use multiple subject positions and emphasize the binary axis of White and non-White should no longer be used to regard the social construction of race and how this operates within racism. As noted by Sturgeon,[38] such dualistic thinking does not encourage discussions of the way in which racism in the US affects various women of color differently. If we comprehend the historical perspective of ways racism has operated yet focus on the consequences of racism today, this would put White ecofeminists in a position to form greater coalitions with the movement of environmental racism, which grounds its analysis in both of these elements. Hence, in conclusion, "issues of environmental degradation and concerns for a re-animated human/nature consciousness cannot be separated from those systemic forces that function to maintain all forms of injustice, whether toward nature or other human beings."[39] However, perhaps the most significant contention is that barriers to a serene human–environment relationship come in the form of factors that in turn promote human oppression, such as racism, gender inequality or sexism, patriarchal systems, and economic exploitation. Ecofeminist writers have, if anything, presented the claim that everything is interconnected in this world, and from this premise, action can take place to stake a deeper commitment to social and environmental justice. In such an ideal world, gone shall be the model of dominance, oppression, and aggression, in favor of compassionate, sensitive systems that plant the seeds of awareness and connectedness across communities. This brings me to a necessary discussion: the need for culturally competent leadership in the environmental sector.

Leadership and Cultural Competency, Where the Two Shall Meet

Taylor[40] writes about women of color, environmental justice, and ecofeminism, and brings this debate full circle under themes of women and culture, spirituality, and social well-being. The most vital of Taylor's contributions in this work might possibly be the spotlight she provides on the insights that women (and indeed, people) of color have brought to the environmental debate—such as the light shed from stories of inequities and environmental racism condoned by traditional environmental activists and often ignored by the radical ones. All of this happened historically because nobody took note of seeing the issues affecting people of color as simply environmental issues. One problem compounded another, and community struggles became rampant, impeding the harmonious coming together of people and nature in highly diverse urban and rural areas. Yet, as previously indicated, Taylor puts forward that:

> [W]omen of color have been at the forefront of the struggle to bring attention to the issues that are devastating minority communities—issues such as hazardous waste disposal; exposure to toxins; occupational health and safety; lead poisoning, cancers, and other health issues; housing; pollution; and environmental contamination.[41]

And what is the reason for this? Women of color have had to assume this role because "their communities, some of the most degraded environments in this country, are the repositories of the waste products of capitalist production and excessive consumption."[42]

But, discourse of ethnicity in relation to environmental justice is not the simplest of topics to tackle. Race is not a straightforward issue and I have maintained in my prior writings how misunderstandings and lack of knowledge in regards to mixed-race people—our existence and contribution to the world—oftentimes pose a threat to the conventional wisdom. My eclectic and uncommon heritage has aided me in understanding issues of diversity from a unique and dynamic perspective. Human relationships are complex enough, and when you throw other elements into the mix, such as socioeconomic status, gender, and race differences, things get a little more complicated. For these reasons, I have studied the multicultural phenomenon for over two decades. In my chapter in *Speaking Up and Speaking Out*,[43] one of my main goals was to explain how diversity—in terms of mixed-race participants in environmental programs and park and recreational activities—is actually changing the face of the parks and environmental education industry.

Furthermore, in my work in "The Color of Climate Change," I stressed the crucial nature of engaging "into the psychological paradigms of diversity management, and to identify the link between the commitment of leaders and diversity outcomes."[44] This is because, despite the fact scholars have drawn attention to the topic of diversity within the workforce (e.g., Taylor 2007[45]), equality has not yet been achieved on a practical level, that is, via legislation and programs aimed to eliminate discrimination and advance the interests of women in the workforce.

Yet, before we begin to tackle diversity with respect to race and gender, it helps to first have an understanding of marginalization. Tucker (1990) defined marginalization as a daily process "by means of which certain people and ideas are privileged over others ... ignored, trivialized, rendered invisible and unheard, perceived as inconsequential, de-authorized, 'other' or threatening, while others are valorized."[46] The goal is to therefore create a world where marginalization is a thing of the past. Under an environmental justice umbrella, environmental racism should be eradicated, as the Environmental Protection Agency (EPA) sustains many efforts.[47] In her work, Gnyawali[48] discusses how environmental injustice is, indeed, a feminism issue. For instance, in developing countries that do not even have proper waste disposal or a health care system, or experience environmental degradation, to have population-control legislation in place and rein in the wasteful use of the world's resources would have an impact on the lives of women. The health and well-being of women is crucial if we want societies to progress. Environmental hazards and toxic waste dumping, for example, can have severe negative effects on women's reproductive and general health; therefore, we cannot ignore the direct link between women's health and the health of the environment that surrounds them.

So how do we give women a stronger voice so they get to decide what kind of place they need to live in? The best kind of power is a shared decision-making power inclusive of building solid relationships across cultures. Social well-being for women is assured when they are afforded options for environmental leadership as participants and stakeholders in the environmental justice system their state provides.

Environmental Leadership: Women, Culture, Spirituality, and Social Well-being

To teach people awareness and respect for the environment and culture, one must become a leader and steward of nature. In an interview with Llewellyn Vaughan-Lee, the concept of "Spiritual Ecology" is presented and "loss of soul" discussed as prompted by the global ecological crisis.[49] According to Vaughan-Lee, ecological problems cannot be tackled simply by looking at their outward manifestation, but by looking inward, at hidden worlds that the naked eye cannot see. This connection with inner worlds is a practice that indigenous cultures are not strangers to, while modern, western society seems to have lost its way over time, losing the vital link to the soul realm and becoming slaves to a culture of materialism. The more we move away from the inner world, creating for ourselves needs that we do not really have, the more we are stuck in the outer one, thus losing the very meaning of life and balance along the way—what Vaughan-Lee refers to as "loss of soul." To regain knowledge of and connection with our spiritual center, we need to nourish our inner selves with positive energy, insight, and awareness of our spiritual nature within the human realm we inhabit. Here, the spiritual and the physical come together in a sort of communion, nourished by our words and concepts. Our sense of life and leadership feeds our soul and, in turn, celebrates the beauty of the nature that surrounds us. Yet to effect this change, we must draw upon our inner power and engage an evolution of consciousness to devise a paradigm shift and counter the influences that keep us stuck within a selfish, greedy cycle of want and need. If we end up living in a world with no connection to nature—no link with the sacred—then, what is the purpose of life?

Throughout my career and personal journey, for instance, my purpose has shifted to mentoring young minds and being a positive influence. My goal in mentoring is to facilitate the learning of my protégés and coach them to move away from their materialistic self, avert commercialism, and develop a more sustained connection with nature and outdoor spaces. Creating a sense of place with special environments enables us to explore the cultural ecology as well as share experiences and stories helping us to connect that place to our soul and to transmit feelings of place from generation to generation.

From Place to Space in Politics and Science

During the 55th United Nations Commission on the Status of Women, one of the main topics discussed was the impact of a shifting climate on vulnerable populations, as well as the need for a stronger female presence and voice in the science fields. "How can we address a global problem, using only half of the global intellectual capacity?"—Former US Secretary of State Hilary Rodham Clinton's words.[50] Still, it remains a fact that White women continue to dominate the fields of biological and social sciences. Furthermore, despite the increase in female science students, the number of female faculty members or women in positions of power has not changed so readily with time.

Such a state of affairs—whether it continues as it is or makes a three hundred sixty degree shift—is therefore a matter of politics, and the cultural awareness and perspective of those who make the ultimate decisions about race and gender. It is of course vital to elect people with a sensitivity to issues of diversity, which should lead to an improvement in the way organizations operate with respect to equal opportunity hiring and workforce design.

As we become a more diverse nation, starting from where I am as a cultural medley of identities, the age-old point of view of urban heritage and status quo no longer hold much water. The end goal is for diversity to become so accepted, so commonplace, that we barely need to mention it any more, but rather begin to embrace it as a vital part of our everyday lives. This notion does not support colorblindness, but rather focuses on a conscious effort to integrate diversity, the environment, and women as leaders in policy decisions. While White privilege still exists and inequity is alive and well, women of color have a special relationship with the land and the natural environment, and our spirit needs to tell the story.

Conclusions and Final Thoughts

Glass and Wallace say it best—"it can be so easy to speak of race and to forget about racism, to speak glibly of harmful social realities without taking responsibility for transforming injustice."[51] The world can only change through fresh perspectives imparted through education and new approaches within the realm of environmental stewardship. If White ecofeminists stopped being so ideological in their separation of nature from culture, they would not become tribal people, for example;

rather, they would be challenged to creatively deal with the politics of their daily lives.[52] They would have to start envisioning nature as including the urban and constructed landscapes in which so many of us live. Ecofeminists need to share in developing strategies that can provide a basis for more effective coalitions, and more effective advocacy for political change, not just between White ecofeminists and everyone else, but across a multiplicity of differences that merely divide women within our own gender and across various races.

Moreover, students of social, racial, and environmental studies are, if nothing else, a promise to the future. With open eyes and extended hands, they can step into worlds heretofore unknown, to see what goes on over their fence, which others, such as misguided caregivers, had erected too high and too thick for them to see through. Glass and Wallace continue, "If and only when the shared family histories of […] students who have been forcibly socialized to experience separate racial statuses are recognized, appreciated and nurtured can false, rigid, and unequal boundaries be transgressed and transformed."[53] We all have crucial roles to play.

Awareness is vital, and providing women of color with access and opportunity changes lives across cultures. As such, awareness can be taught, molded, and expanded through education. As much as I dislike that word—"molded"—it does bring everything down to the gist, the tiniest atom of understanding from which all knowledge and acceptance stems and grows. Mixed-race scholarship has something to contribute to contradictory and constraining race and gender narratives.[54] This educational vision can be expanded into the professional world. When you think about the work you've done in the past, what you're doing now, or want to do in the future, we're all in different places with our skills and abilities as well as our fears and limitations. Actions and impacts can be documented, whereas attitudes and intentions are debatable. We may not know what's in the hearts and minds of specific people, policymakers, or power holders—and it's not worth the energy to make guesses or assumptions. But we can and should hold them accountable for their actions, commitments, and decisions, since those have a bearing on outcomes. The rewards are greater when we seek to develop trust and learn to be an ally to others, versus those who are sitting back and observing, because without action we can watch our natural environments disappear.

Notes

1   Bowser et al., "The Color of Climate: Ecology, Environment, Climate Change, and Women of Color—Exploring Environmental Leadership from the Perspective of Women of Color in Science," 61.
2   Roberts, "What are You, Anyway? From Tea at High Noon to Curry and Masala Dosa: How Identity and Experience Interact to Challenge the System."
3   Root, *The Multiracial Experience: Racial Borders as the New Frontier*, 14.
4   Roberts, "What are You, Anyway? From Tea at High Noon to Curry and Masala Dosa: How Identity and Experience Interact to Challenge the System," 32.
5   Maeda Allman, "(Un)Natural Boundaries, Mixed Race, Gender, and Sexuality," 279.
6   Root, *The Multiracial Experience: Racial Borders as the New Frontier*.
7   Jaggar and Bordo, *Gender/Body/Knowledge: Feminist Reconstructions of Being and Knowing*.
8   Ibid., 8.
9   Ibid., 9.
10 King, "Healing the Wounds: Feminism, Ecology, and Nature/Culture Dualism," 115.
11 Ibid., 116.
12 Zimmerman, "Feminism, Deep Ecology, and Environmental Ethics."
13 US Census Bureau. "United States Census 2010: It's in our hands."
14 Lee et al., "Health is Power: An Ecological, Theory-based Health Intervention for Women of Color."
15 Ibid., 922.
16 Ibid.
17 Taylor, "The Decline of Marriage and Rise of New Families."
18 Ibid., ii.
19 Ibid., 9.
20 Wang, "The Rise of Intermarriage Rates, Characteristics Vary by Race and Gender."
21 Gates et al., "Woman on the Edge of Time: Interview with Joanna Macy."
22 Ibid.
23 Ibid.
24 Taylor, "Women of Color, Environmental Justice, and Ecofeminism."
25 Floyd, "Defining Best Practices in Boating, Fishing, and Stewardship Education: Challenges and Opportunities for Reaching Diverse Audiences."
26 Bowser et al., "The Color of Climate: Ecology, Environment, Climate Change, and Women of color—Exploring Environmental Leadership from the Perspective of Women of Color in Science," 60.
27 Taylor, "Women of Color, Environmental Justice, and Ecofeminism," 39.
28 Maeda Allman, "(Un)Natural Boundaries, Mixed Race, Gender, and Sexuality," 290.
29 Unger, Nancy C. "Women, Sexuality, and Environmental Justice in American History."
30 Besthorn and McMillen, "The Oppression of Women and Nature: Ecofeminism as a Framework for an Expanded Ecological Social Work."
31 Robbins et al., *Contemporary Human Behavior Theory: A Critical Perspective for Social Work*.
32 Besthorn and McMillen, "The Oppression of Women and Nature: Ecofeminism as a Framework for an Expanded Ecological Social Work," 227.
33 Ibid., 228.

34 Taylor, "Women of Color, Environmental Justice, and Ecofeminism."
35 Ibid., 65.
36 Ibid., 65.
37 Ibid.
38 Sturgeon, "The Nature of Race: Discourses in Racial Difference in Ecofeminism."
39 Bile, "The Rhetorics of Critical Ecofeminism: Conceptual Connection and Reasoned Response," 27.
40 Taylor, "Women of Color, Environmental Justice, and Ecofeminism."
41 Ibid., 39.
42 Ibid., 39.
43 Roberts, "What are You, Anyway? From Tea at High Noon to Curry and Masala Dosa: How Identity and Experience Interact to Challenge the System."
44 Bowser et al., "The Color of Climate: Ecology, Environment, Climate Change, and Women of Color—Exploring Environmental Leadership from the Perspective of Women of Color in Science," 64.
45 Taylor, "Diversity and Equity in Environmental Organizations: The Salience of These Factors to Students."
46 Tucker, "Director's Foreword."
47 Gnyawali, "Environmental Justice and Ecofeminism."
48 Ibid.
49 Ecobuddhism. "On Spiritual Ecology: Interview with Llewellyn Vaughan-Lee."
50 Alber, Gotelind. "Statement on the Behalf of Gender and Climate Change (GenderCC) to the United Nations Framework Convention on Climate Change."
51 Glass and Wallace, "Challenging Race and Racism: A Framework for Educators," 343.
52 Sturgeon, "The Nature of Race: Discourses in Racial Difference in Ecofeminism."
53 Glass and Wallace, "Challenging Race and Racism: A Framework for Educators," 345.
54 Streeter, "Ambiguous Bodies, Locating Black/White Women in Cultural Representations."

References

Alber, Gotelind. "Statement on the Behalf of Gender and Climate Change (GenderCC) to the United Nations Framework Convention on Climate Change" [press release]. Cancun, Mexico, 2010. Available online at www.gendercc.net/metanavigation/press.html (accessed 10 October 2014).

Besthorn, Fred H. and Diane Pearson McMillen. "The Oppression of Women and Nature: Ecofeminism as a Framework for an Expanded Ecological Social Work." *Families in Society*, 83, 3 (2002): 221–232.

Bile, Jeffrey. "The Rhetorics of Critical Ecofeminism: Conceptual Connection and Reasoned Response." In *Ecofeminism and Rhetoric: Critical Perspectives on Sex, Technology, and Discourse*, edited by Douglas A. Vakoch, 1–38. New York: Berghahn, 2011.

Bowser, Gillian, Nina Roberts, Denise Simmons, and Kathy Perales. "The Color of Climate: Ecology, Environment, Climate Change, and Women of Color—Exploring Environmental Leadership from the Perspective of Women of Color in Science." In *Environmental Leadership: A Reference Handbook*, edited by Deborah Rigling Gallagher, 60–67. Thousand Oaks, CA: Sage Publications, 2012.

Ecobuddhism. "On Spiritual Ecology: Interview with Llewellyn Vaughan-Lee." 2012. Available online at http://spiritualecology.org/article/spiritual-ecology (accessed 25 July 2014).

Floyd, Myron F. "Defining Best Practices in Boating, Fishing, and Stewardship Education: Challenges and Opportunities for Reaching Diverse Audiences." In *Defining Best Practices in Boating, Fishing and Stewardship Education*, edited by Anthony J. Fedler, 87–97. Alexandria, VA: Recreational Boating and Fishing Foundation, 2001.

Gates, Barbara, Susan Moon and Wes Nisker. "Woman on the Edge of Time: Interview with Joanna Macy." 2011. Available online at http://spiritualecology.org/article/woman-edge-time (accessed 18 September 2014).

Glass, Ronald D. and Kendra R. Wallace. "Challenging Race and Racism: A Framework for Educators." In *The Multiracial Experience, Racial Borders as the New Frontier*, edited by Maria P.P. Root, 341–358. Thousand Oaks: Sage Publications, 1996.

Gnyawali, Urmila. "Environmental Justice and Ecofeminism." In *Environmental Justice and Women* [blog]. 2013. Available online at http://environmentaljusticeandwomen.blogspot.com/2013/04/environmental-justice-environmental.html (accessed 7 September 2014).

Jaggar, Alison M. and Susan R. Bordo, editors. *Gender/Body/Knowledge: Feminist Reconstructions of Being and Knowing*. Rutgers, NJ: Rutgers University Press, 1989.

King, Ynestra. "Healing the Wounds: Feminism, Ecology, and Nature/Culture Dualism." In *Gender/Body/Knowledge: Feminist Reconstructions of Being and Knowing*, edited by Alison M. Jaggar and Susan R. Bordo, 115–141. Rutgers, NJ: Rutgers University Press, 1989.

Lee, Rebecca E., Ashley V. Medina, Scherezade K. Mama, Jacqueline Y. Reese-Smith, Daniel P. O'Connor, Marcella Brosnan, Catherine Cubbin, Tracy McMillan, and Paul A. Estabrooks. "Health is Power: An Ecological, Theory-based Health Intervention for Women of Color." *Contemporary Clinical Trials*, 32, 6 (2011): 916–923.

Maeda Allman, Karen. "(Un)Natural Boundaries, Mixed Race, Gender, and Sexuality." In *The Multiracial Experience, Racial Borders as the New Frontier*, edited by Maria P.P. Root, 277–290. Thousand Oaks: Sage Publications, 1996.

Robbins, Susan P., Pranab Chatterjee, and Edward R. Canda. *Contemporary Human Behavior Theory: A Critical Perspective for Social Work*. Boston: Allyn and Bacon, 1998.

Roberts, Nina S. "What are You, Anyway? From Tea at High Noon to Curry and Masala Dosa: How Identity and Experience Interact to Challenge the System." In *Speaking Up and Speaking Out: Working for Social and Environmental Justice through Parks, Recreation, and Leisure*, edited by Daniel Dustin and Karen Paisley, 32–40. Urbana, IL: Sagamore, 2010.

Root, Maria P.P., editor. *The Multiracial Experience: Racial Borders as the New Frontier*. Thousand Oaks, CA: Sage Publications, 1996.

Streeter, Caroline. A. "Ambiguous Bodies, Locating Black/White Women in Cultural Representations." In *The Multiracial Experience, Racial Borders as the New Frontier*, edited by Maria P.P. Root, 305–320. Thousand Oaks, CA: SAGE Publications, 1996.

Sturgeon, Noël. "The Nature of Race: Discourses in Racial Difference in Ecofeminism." In *Ecofeminism: Women, Culture, Nature*, edited by Karen J. Warren, 260–278. Bloomington, IN: Indiana University Press, 1997.

Taylor, Dorceta E. "Women of Color, Environmental Justice, and Ecofeminism." In *Ecofeminism: Women, Culture, Nature*, edited by Karen J. Warren, 38–81. Bloomington, IN: Indiana University Press, 1997.

Taylor, Dorceta E. "Diversity and Equity in Environmental Organizations: The Salience of These Factors to Students." *The Journal of Environmental Education*, 39, 1 (2007): 19–43.

Taylor, Paul, editor. "The Decline of Marriage and Rise of New Families." PEW Research Center, Social and Demographic Trends Project, 2010.

Tucker, Marcia. "Director's Foreword." In *Out There: Marginalization and Contemporary Cultures*, edited by Russell Ferguson, Martha Gever, Trinh T. Minh-ha, and Cornell West, 7–8. New York: MIT Press, 1990.

Unger, Nancy C. "Women, Sexuality, and Environmental Justice in American History." In *New Perspectives on Environmental Justice*, edited by Rachel Stein, 45–62. New Brunswick, NJ: Rutgers University Press, 2004.

US Census Bureau. "United States Census 2010: It's in our hands." 2010. Available online at www.census.gov/2010census (accessed 18 March 2016).

Wang, Wendy. "The Rise of Intermarriage Rates, Characteristics Vary by Race and Gender." Washington, DC: Pew Research Center, 2012.

Zimmerman, Michael E. "Feminism, Deep Ecology, and Environmental Ethics." *Environmental Ethics*, 9, 1 (1987): 21–44.

7

LINKING ANCESTRAL SEEDS AND WATERS TO THE INDIGENOUS PLACES WE INHABIT

MELISSA K. NELSON AND NÍCOLA WAGENBERG

When the ocean comes to you as a lover,
marry at once,
quickly, for God's sake!

Don't Postpone it!
Existence has no better gift.[1]

What Waters Do You Come From?

My name is Nícola Wagenberg; I grew up in Bogotá, Colombia. My grandparents immigrated to Colombia from Eastern Europe around WWII. They were Jewish. I am not sure what waters my ancestors would identify with. Perhaps if I look way back, at least some of them would have come from Palestine—could be The Red Sea. Growing up in Colombia, even though I lived high up in the mountains, we traveled to the Atlantic and Pacific Oceans, in particular the Caribbean. I love the ocean. I feel very connected to the warm waters, the waves, the sound and breeze. I have been hearing the call of the ocean. I feel it deep in my gut. A love and passion that when I follow it, feels like I am doing what is right. The spirit of the ocean has guided me to participate in *Guardians of the Waters* through The Cultural Conservancy. I am here to tell you about this story, a response to the call.

My name is Melissa Nelson; In the Ojibwe language, my name is *MakoonziGaba-wiik*. I grew up on the South Fork of the Eel River in Mendocino County, on the "Lost Coast" of northern California. I am a river lover and forest dweller. My parents are from Willow Lake and Fish Lake in the Turtle Mountains of North Dakota. My parents and grandparents are lake people but they are also river people, as they grew up and lived by the Souris River. Before them, my maternal great-grandparents lived and worked on the Red River. Interestingly, the Souris and Red Rivers both flow north into Canada across the arbitrary political border at the 49th parallel. My ancestral waters and seeds come from the Deep North, potentially, through my maternal Cree side and my paternal Norwegian side, all the way to the Arctic Circle. Another set of grandparents came from Minnesota area at the headwaters of the *Mishi-ziibi* ("great river" in the Ojibwe language) also known as the Mississippi River. I am a river lover and forest dweller and my love of water stems from my swimming, fishing, playing, and exploring in the Eel River and other coastal streams of the North Coast for the first 18 years of my life. I also spent a lot of time at the confluence where these fresh streams meet the ocean. I love the mighty Pacific, but where I grew up the ocean is too wild and dangerous to go into beyond the knees. These experiences gave me a profound relationship with both fresh and salt waters. I have dedicated much of my life's work to honoring the spirit of water and forests and restoring humans' intimate relationship with the more-than-human world, starting with myself. I enjoy working and playing on the edges and ecotones of land and water, forest and sea, human and more-than-human, urban and rural, science and poetry, and the visible and invisible. I am fortunate to do experiential education and indigenous, cultural work through The Cultural Conservancy.

Both of us work at The Cultural Conservancy (TCC). TCC is a Native-led indigenous rights non-profit organization based in San Francisco. For the past 30 years we have worked with Native communities locally, nationally, and internationally on cultural revitalization, land and water protection, indigenous rights, education, and community health. We have diverse programs that include growing and promoting Native foodways, producing and teaching Native media, providing small grants to international indigenous rights groups, protecting and revitalizing Native songs, stories, and languages, and, for the past five years, working with Native artists and Pacific communities on an exciting project, *Guardians of the Waters.*

TCC's *Guardians of the Waters—Tribal Canoe Revitalization Project* is an inter-cultural, inter-generational, multi-tribal collaborative venture that, through tribal research and cultural practices and performances, supports the renewal of indigenous watercraft traditions of the Pacific, beginning with Native California. We respectfully use this phrase, "Guardians of the Waters," which was generously shared with us by our brother and sister, Wikuki Kingi and Tania Wolfgramm, from the Maori tradition of *Aotearoa* (New Zealand). In their traditional knowledge, lifeways, and practices, there is a long tradition of honoring humans' role as guardians, *Tiaki*, with a fundamental responsibility to an ethic of guardianship, *Kaitiakitanga*, which is relational and reciprocal.[2] As peoples of the Pacific, for both the Maori and Hawaiian extended community and the coastal California communities (where we live and work), we take this ethic of guardianship seriously and are joining and expanding a movement to bring back and strengthen Native watercraft traditions and our original responsibility and primary role as water guardians; most indigenous traditions around the world have such concepts in their cosmologies and original instructions.

Out of this larger Native water revitalization program grew the *Native Youth Guardians of the Waters Program* (GOTW), which provides Native and indigenous young adults access to Native watercraft traditions, cultural healing, multi-media explorations, and creative modalities of self-expression. Through listening, group discussion and processing, immersion in nature, and interaction with Native artists and knowledge holders, participants explore the connections between cultural healing and ecological health, personal and collective identities, and traditional and new arts. In 2013, a group of Native and indigenous young women participated in the first GOTW. What follows is an account of this unique experiential and transformative educational experience, including the activities, learnings, and transformative aspects.

We are a cultural psychologist and a cultural ecologist and we see this work as traversing the edges of several larger movements and practices related to decolonization (decolonizing methodologies,[3] addressing historical trauma and internalized oppression[4]) and eco-cultural revitalization (cultural health and healing, renewing indigenous ways of knowing and learning) as well as ecopsychology's and ecoliteracy's emphasis on igniting *biophilia*, humans' innate love for the natural world.

As author Melissa Nelson shares in "River of Memory, Lakes of Survival: Indigenous Water Traditions and the Anishinaabeg Nation:"

> Harvard biologist and author E.O. Wilson has noted in his books *Biophilia* and *The Biophilia Hypothesis*, that humans have an intrinsic attraction and connection to other life forms, or what he calls biodiversity (Wilson 1986; Wilson & Kellert 1995). Likewise, since our bodies and the Earth itself are both approximately seventy percent water, I suggest that humans have a deeply ingrained "aqua-philia"—a visceral, sensuous, creative attraction to water. It is a relationship that feeds our souls and imaginations.[5]

As Guardians of the Waters we surrender to our *aquaphilia*, and out of this passion and obligation we work to protect our waters by honoring the ancestral waters we come from and follow the rivers of memory to our current habitats. Through ancestral explorations and contemporary place-making, we understand and support the argument that an informed and personal connection to place is essential for human wholeness and well-being and ultimately for social justice and ecological sustainability. Theories of indigenous resurgence and methods of decolonization and revitalization inform our approach as we experiment with transdisciplinary and holistic strategies for individual and cultural transformation.[6]

For our GOTW pilot program, five urban, inter-cultural young women, between ages 17 and 22, were selected among the youth that answered the call to "Become Guardians of the Waters." They came from different parts of the San Francisco Bay Area. Their names and ethnic backgrounds are: Napaquetzalli Martinez (Yaqui/Apache/Purépecha/ Xicana), Monserrat Rueda-Hernandez (Mexican-American), Natalie Isabel Contreras (Michoacan/Purepecha/Tarascan/Durango/Tarahu-mara/Jalisco/Nahuatl), Kiva McGahan (Salvadorean/Apache/Calo/ Mayan/German/Irish), and Stacie Aori (Kenyan/Kikuyu/Luhya). The main facilitators were Nícola Wagenberg (Colombian/Jewish), who also served as project director, youth mentor Valerie Ordoñez (Salvadorean/ Mexican) and Mateo Hinojosa (Bolivian-American), who was the media director. Throughout the program, participants interacted and learned from many diverse Native scholars, artists, and cultural bearers.

There were many ways that the Native artists and scholars interacted with the participants. They gave talks, gave demonstrations, and held talking circles. They taught specific skills supporting a process of embodied learning. Most importantly, they communicated and passed on traditional knowledge that otherwise the participants would not have been exposed to or able to learn. Because of this, the young women demonstrated a deep commitment to the learning process. It was a demanding yet very fulfilling experience at the intellectual, physical, emotional, and spiritual level. Through a focus on indigenous knowledge, learning, and identity exploration, the young women were exposed to a type of indigenous education that they otherwise would not have been able to experience. It became evident that the participants were hungry for this kind of engaged, holistic immersion.

The group met for a total of 20 sessions. The sessions were four hours long, including one camping weekend. At the beginning of the sessions, we had creative check-ins giving a chance for participants to share how they were doing personally, and anything related to the project: dreams, reflections, challenges, and concerns. At the end of each session we had a closing circle to reflect on the day, share what they were taking with them, and provide feedback. These are some of the activities the program offered: art-making, journaling, photography, dream sharing, and expressive arts activities on personal, family, and collective struggles and personal and community resilience. These activities helped create a safe space to share and learn. Participants were able to share from a deep emotional place and provide support to each other. In regards to this experience Stacie, a participant, reflects: "I have become closer to a group of people in ways I haven't before. I have learned more about myself when we had to think about who we are and where we come from."

The program offered an opportunity to learn from artists that are holding, continuing, researching, and embodying ancestral traditions. One of them was artist and "decolonizationist" L. Frank Manriquez (Tongva/Ajachmem), who gave a presentation and demonstration on Southern California Native canoe traditions. L. Frank has been key in leading the efforts of California Native watercraft revitalization with TCC, engaging the inter-generational and inter-tribal community in doing research and building a Ti'aat, a southern California style red-wood sewn plank canoe, only the second one of its kind to be built in 250 years. For L. Frank, Native watercraft revitalization includes connecting with the stars, language, waters, and others in community. Its purpose is also to bring awareness and to protest the colonization and destruction of indigenous sacred sites and waters. L. Frank talked to the youth about her people's lands: "The most sacred spot, the center of the universe and the navy uses it to bomb for target practice, for years." Natalie, one of the participants, talks about how L. Frank carries ancestral memory and sees her as a treasure, "not something to be held and kept, but something to care for and listen, that kind of treasure."

The group went on various field trips to experience different bodies of water outside of the city. For many of the young women it was their first time visiting the ocean, being by a waterfall, and swimming in a pond. One of these very special sites was Indian Canyon, the only federally recognized Ohlone territory. Ohlone Cultural Bearer Ann Marie Sayers and artist Kanyon Sayers-Roods (Ohlone/Chumash) taught about indigenous water and land struggles and victories and led the group in a water ceremony by the historic waterfall that, poignantly, at the time had no water. The group was very affected that the waterfall was dry when it usually has water. Natalie comments that even though she felt cheated, "it was also good because it shows that we're messing up." She expands: "This place that usually has water doesn't have even a drop and what does that mean to us?" During the ceremony the group prayed to bring the health back to the land and to the waters, and to ourselves. We asked the ancestors to please listen to the prayers. Kanyon shared that in the Mutsun Ohlone language water is *rama*, which not only means water, but also the flow of the water, the essence of the power of water. She says: "you are not just one word, you are everything." This conveys the interconnectedness with nature: we are not separate from nature, we are water. "For all Indigenous Peoples of the world, water is the source of material, cultural and spiritual life."[7]

As part of learning about indigenous canoe traditions and doing hands on work, participants learned to carve their own wooden paddles. Ethan Castro (Wailaki/Pomo) and Maori Master Carver and canoe-maker Wikuki Kingi taught the young women wood carving skills using traditional and modern tools. For many of them it was their first time carving or using a power tool. Natalie observed: "I'm so small and I held a power drill like nothing. I remember when I finished my hands were trembling." Wikuki also taught about Maori watercraft traditions, including water spirits, stories, and voyages. The young women learned the Maori war canoe paddling chants and dance movements. Napa, one of the participants, expressed how empowering it was for her to be learning with a group of women from someone expert at their craft. She observed that it gave them an opportunity as urban indigenous women to reclaim the traditions and skills; to take them into their own hands so they can learn and pass them on. As we engaged in these creative activities that included traditional arts, the group had time to reflect through journaling, sharing their dreams, and dialoguing with each other. Natalie expressed deep insight at the fact that:

> The survival of indigenous water traditions and the epistemology that supports its fundamental understandings has required several forms of resistance against dominant society's attempts to force Indigenous culture and identity to assimilate...since then, knowledge about indigenous worldviews, values, and culture has survived through aesthetic forms of expression such as art, poetry, craft making, and dance.

Another important activity that included learning from Native artists and knowledge holders as well as learning from plants and doing hands on work was through being with tule (*Schoenplectus acutus*), a special California Native plant that lives in freshwater. The group learned the many traditional uses of tule, including harvesting it, eating it, and making tule dolls, mats, and building a collective tule boat. We had the great pleasure and opportunity to learn from the "tule lady," Diana Almendariz (Maidu/Wintun), and renowned California Indian basket weaver and teacher Kathy Wallace (Yurok/Karuk/Hupa). The making of the collective tule boat was a community event in partnership with the local Miwok and Pomo tribes that took place at Occidental Arts and Ecology Center (OAEC). For most of the participants, it was their first time canoeing a tule boat they built from tule they harvested. Kiva, one of the participants, shares that it was at that moment, while harvesting tule by a beautiful lake, her feet immersed in the mud, that she realized what she was missing: "I didn't allow myself to enjoy nature as much as I thought I had, the relationship between the land and the waters was really eye opening in that moment for me." Natalie describes how being in such close contact with tule reed was when she began to see and feel the recuperation of an indigenous self-identity. She explains:

> I felt myself being transported in space and time by several sets of thousands of years, to some watery place in the valley of central Mexico... I visualized the importance of this act of remembering in myself, and re-membering myself.

While the group experienced firsthand what it is like to be with water and connect with water in a very different way than they had before, participants began to think and relate to water in a new way, from an indigenous perspective. In her presentation on Native water consciousness, co-author Melissa Nelson (Turtle Mountain Chippewa) shared with the group:

> We are out of balance and our life fully depends on treating water differently. We need a paradigm shift in the way we think about

water, it's urgent and our life depends on it. Indigenous water consciousness is really about identifying with water on a very visceral level.

Participants were asked to think about the waters they come from and to see water as an ancestor. Monse, a participant, shares about her process of shifting paradigms and expanding her western mindset:

> I remember thinking at one point when we were learning about our connection to waters, Monse, you need to stop being so literal (water is just water) but then I caught myself: *this is literal...* I understood the *literal fact* that the waters are my relatives, my ancestors... I had a big shift of mindset when it came to rebuilding a relationship with water and understanding it from a different perspective.

Some of the young women did not have the answer as to the waters their ancestors come from. We created a space within the circle to share and mourn the not knowing, the disconnection to the past due to colonization, genocide, immigration, and displacement. Monse, whose parents emigrated from Mexico, talks about how shame comes up for her from not knowing her lineage, who her people are, and where her ancestors come from. She describes:

> If you look at me I probably have indigenous blood in me, but I have no way of knowing that, it's been so disconnected, torn apart, so there is shame and frustration, it is internalized but you do not talk about it... we are trying to reconnect all these pieces that have been torn away from us.

In regards to not knowing the answers, Valerie talks about how she learns from her senses as well as from asking the questions. She believes that being able to ask the questions, even though she might not have the answers, is an important place to start. She feels that in western educational institutions there is not even a place where she can ask the unanswered questions. She is thankful to be able to have a shared space to ask the questions and as she does this, she renews her relationship to the past.

Natalie talks about how participating in this kind of project is a way to reconnect with ancestral memory and to strengthen her indigenous identity. She observes: "this project is important to me because of its relevance to the unfolding of ancestral memory inherent to us all, but much less developed as a result of a traumatic history of colonialism." As a youth of color, she struggles with her identity, especially in the US educational institutions, where she feels displaced. She reflects: "This project is important because it counters all those negative experiences by encouraging the value of being in touch with my indigenous cultural identity, and its active practice in the recuperation of forgotten traditions, now remembered." For her, the writing exercises were the most helpful in triggering memories: "they led me to remember old memories of a certain longing to be one with the ocean, feeling the immensity and wonder about water, even at a young age." This is one of the poems Natalie wrote during a writing exercise in which they were asked to start their poem with "I am":

I am
I am who I am
The daughter of man, of woman
The child who learned and began
to sway with the water at sand.
This memory of days spent at sea,
while in the womb I followed my mama's feet.
To listen to the way it would speak,
the waves crashing on rocky ocean peaks.
The streams ashore they would wash
and snake their way through tule marsh.
To carve the path in which daughter marched
from a fragile seed to a girl with a warrior's heart.

If water is an ancestor, then connecting with water is a way to reconnect with the ancestors, as life giving and ever-present. Napa remarks that she felt the ancestors and ancestral knowledge of every single participant were very present in all of the meetings. At the beginning of the program, each participant brought water they identified with and poured it in a container, mixing it with everyone's water. This collective water was present in all of the meetings. Connecting with water as ever-present and life giving can facilitate a process of healing the disconnection and historical trauma, especially if we learn from indigenous paradigms about how to connect with water as our mother. In reflecting about the most powerful learning that she received from the project, Kiva observes: "You treat it [water] as an ancestor rather than as an element that you are supposed to conserve, you think of it as a mother that is giving you your life."

The mothering presence brings mirroring and holding which allowed the young women to feel the shame, guilt, anger, and sadness that comes up as a result of the disconnection and historical trauma. The young women in the program talked about how the program allowed for a space to feel some of the feelings of shame and frustration, which are very uncomfortable and can be very painful and scary to feel. In her dissertation, co-author Nícola Wagenberg describes how where there is trauma, in order to enter into affective states such as grief, anger, fear, and shame, it is necessary to connect and bring forward the "mothering other" as well as those aspects of the feminine that allow entry into authentic states.[8] Engagement with affective states can be an alternative to staying frozen as a result of trauma. As Mohawk scholar Taiaiake Alfred has written, "stepping into our fear is crucial, because leaving the comfort zone of accepted truth is vital to creating the emotional and mental state that allows one to really learn."[9] Reclamation of the feminine is one way to cultivate openness and surrender to the depths of experience and feeling while trusting that one can come up after dwelling there. Through such surrender and trust, transformation and stepping into authentic power become possible.

For many of the young women this was the first time that they were with a group of mostly women, with the exception of Mateo who played a key role as a male ally to the women. Being with a group of women, and in particular *indigenous* women, was very significant for all. Many of them talked about how this helped create a safe space to learn and share. For some of them it facilitated a process of learning to trust other women. The presence of water as the mother, and the support that they gave each other as indigenous women, created a holding space that allowed for healing and transformation of the feminine as well as indigenous self.

Women are seeking healing and they are also the healers of their own and others' trauma. They have powers they can bring forward that are needed to recover from historical trauma and internalized oppression. It is important to recognize that they are the leaders in this process and must trust themselves and each other with what emerges. It is inspiring to see how these modern, urban indigenous women reconnected to the long tradition of women as water guardians and therefore guardians of their *own* waters, those of their bodies, minds, hearts, and spirits, which connect them, and all of us, to the sources of life. The body of the Earth and the bodies of women are deeply tied as we both carry seeds, waters, gifts, trauma, and the ability to flow, be resilient, and heal ourselves.

This group of young women answered the call to become Guardians of the Waters. Perhaps they responded to the call of their ancestors to join indigenous women, who for centuries have played and continue to play the role of water keepers for their communities. Perhaps they responded to the call of future generations yearning for clean water to dwell in. When asked what attracted them to the program, the young women said that the words "Guardians of the Waters" sounded familiar, that they sounded right; they felt this was where they needed to be.

They knew it was going to be an initiation process and they were ready for it. They were excited to reclaim their water traditions and, in Kiva's words, "go on a journey with other Native youth and find ourselves." Natalie beautifully describes how for her becoming a Guardian of the Waters is a revolutionary act of defiance "against every force that in the past had delayed the process of the recovering of water traditions of connectivity and interdependence." As she was doing the work, she was recuperating a piece of herself that had been taken away for generations, "like unwrapping a present of gold aura, memories from a close and distant past."

At the end of the program Monse describes how she found her calling, to care for all living things. Napa calls indigenous youth to reclaim and remember:

> [I]n a time when too many youth are distracted from our living ancestors: the earth, the air, the water, the fire; it is now the work of young indigenous leaders to reclaim and remember our ancestral teachings and sacred connections, this way we will build a sustainable future for all of our relations.

Reclaiming and remembering the ancestral teachings was one of the most powerful learnings from the program. As the women struggled to reclaim these traditions it is important to acknowledge that they were doing it in their own way. They were discovering their own relationship with these teachings, and as Valerie notes, they were able to "acknowledge that traditions are in constant flux." There is no right way to reconnect or to remember or to carry on the traditions. We have to create our own relationship with these teachings and with our ancestors, one that makes sense to us, and is going to help us the most. For Kiva it was very powerful to be able to go through this program and find her voice. She shares how her mother has passed down the traditions to her, but by going through this program she got to reclaim the culture for herself and in her own way. She expands: "I always felt like I had to prove who I am to myself, so that [discovering for herself] was really spiritually awakening and emotional." In this way, as Kiva points out, we find ourselves, we determine who we are, and we create our own traditions. There is no perfect or pure way. The ancestors were not perfect or pure. We acknowledge that this might be controversial and taboo to say but it is the truth.

The culmination of the program was the creation of a six-minute video, "Guardians of the Waters," which beautifully and powerfully follows the young women's journey and shares the crucial and urgent teachings they received.[10] Learning media literacy and Native media production was a key component of the program. The Cultural Conservancy acknowledges that new media is a powerful educational, artistic, and political tool. It is a way to animate our voices in modern contexts and reclaim our long tradition as storytellers. We believe that it is imperative that Native communities have access to these new communication technologies so that they are the ones telling their own stories. The young women learned audio and video recording, and collectively created the video. Mateo, The Cultural Conservancy's media director, explains that the video "connects the world of our youth with the world of our ancestors and those who will come."

The journey and learnings from this program can be summarized as follows:

Ocean Calls: the youth feel called to participate and become Guardians of the Waters, and they bravely sign up for a demanding yet unique indigenous educational experience.

Ice Hurts: as they explore their indigenous identity and connect with Native waters and lands, the young women feel the trauma and painful disconnection from ancestors, from the elements, from self. They see the devastating results of colonization and capitalism upon their communities, lands, and waters. They feel the grief, shame, and anger.

Lakes are Ancestors: ancestors show up as allies, and call upon the young women to join them to help heal and transform. The young women connect with their own as well as their ancestors' courage, resilience, and medicine.

Rivers Connect and Heal: through sharing with Native teachers and with each other, the youth re-member and re-connect. As Napa eloquently shares in the video: "by reclaiming indigenous health, indigenous perspectives, Native media, Native arts and skills, and the watercraft traditions, not only are we transforming ourselves but we are also transforming our communities because we are able to share that knowledge now."

Rain is Cycle of Life: the young women feel inspired to share, become leaders in their communities, advocate, and work for a better future. They share their work and video with many communities, such as Bioneers, schools, colleges, and universities, Native film festivals, and through online channels and social media.

We are incredibly grateful to this group of young women for their participation and contributions. We learned from them as much as they learned from us. Young people today are hungry and feel the urgency to search for and find their own ways to reconnect, create, and fight for a healthy relationship with each other, their ancestors, nature, and themselves. This program was a life changing experience because of the initiative, leadership, vulnerability, hard work, and brilliance that these young women came with and exhibited throughout. And for that we are deeply honored and grateful. As it transformed them, it also transformed us. It helps us feel hopeful. Next, we want to share our personal stories and journey as they relate to this program, including our work around eco-cultural revitalization and personal transformation.

Nícola's Story: Inter-cultural Sharing and Healing

I grew up in a very small post-holocaust Jewish community in Colombia, where I lived the first 20 years of my life. As a third generation descendant of survivors of the Jewish holocaust, I have done a lot of research and process around what it means to be a third generation descendant, how the trauma has been passed down to me through the generations, and whether I could and how I could heal and transform it. Through my doctoral research I learned that, as a third generation descendant, I feel guilt and shame around healing and transforming the trauma—because it could mean that I am betraying and leaving my ancestors behind. After all, the main message that I heard growing up was that I needed to remember, that I could not forget what had happened. In part because of fear that it could happen again, but in a big part, and what is not talked about, because of the belief that to heal and move on means we are leaving behind those that suffered and sacrificed their lives for us.

One of the main learnings that I come away with from this work is that there is not a pure way or a right way to be and to connect with our ancestors and traditions. Although it feels taboo to say it, I believe that recognizing this is essential for our liberation. We have the power to decide, to experiment, to create and co-create, and connect in the way that is the most helpful to us. In my work to heal inter-generational trauma I called my ancestors, and some of them showed up to support me in my journey. I was afraid that my ancestors were angry at me because I was choosing a different path than the traditional one I was supposed to take. I felt guilty. Nonetheless, I have been pleasantly surprised and immensely appreciative to be able to connect with ancestors that want the best for me and support me in wanting to heal, transform, and follow my own path in a fully empowered and distinct way. I realize that as we do this work we also provide healing to them. Together we co-create and transform.

As part of the inter-generational trauma that was passed down, the other messages that I received have been that I need to be pure, that I should not mix with others, that I should stick to my tribe, that I needed to fear the other, that I was superior, that I was inferior, that the suffering of our people made us special, and that as a woman my job was to stay and marry in the tribe. However, I believe that in order to heal I need to connect and build bridges with "the other." My healing deeply depends on that.

As part of this youth project, we held a workshop where we presented and dialogued on historical trauma. Melissa talked about it from the Native perspective and I shared from my Jewish perspective. It was very illuminating and exciting for all of us to see that there are similarities between our experiences. Of course there are also a lot of differences, and our present situations are very different, but we shared similar questions around what we want to honor and reclaim as well as what we want to transform and release. Through this process of reclaiming and releasing we create space for authentic power so that we can proactively and creatively do what we need to do to take care of ourselves, our communities, and our planet.

I realize that our ancestors, and in particular the Native ancestors and the current older generations, have had to keep their culture very close to them—if at all possible—because of the genocide, the appropriation, stealing, and destruction that has happened. This program and our work is built around giving indigenous youth the opportunity to interact with these older generations who have fought so hard to reconnect and revitalize indigenous knowledge and life ways, as well as mourn and have compassion for those who gave them up altogether to try to survive and be accepted. I have also observed that the younger generations appear to be at a point in time where they are freer and safer to build bridges among tribes and cultures, and assert a modern indigeneity. While we need to continue to respect our own cultures and the cultures of others, inter-cultural sharing, integration, and collaboration is possible and essential for our evolution.

Inter-cultural sharing is key in helping us connect with all of the ancestors, including our own, and in this way heal cultural trauma. While writing this article, I had a beautiful and pertinent dream. I was in front of a table, like an altar, with many special objects. I was there with a co-worker from TCC, smudging the space. We were lighting a candle in the shape of a buffalo. It felt like we were praying for both the buffalo and for her. Next to it there was a silver wine cup. It looked like the one I grew up with that we used to pray in Hebrew for the sweet wine, and the sweet waters. At that moment I connected deeply with my ancestors and tradition. I felt it in my heart. It was a healing moment as I felt a deep and beautiful connection with them, the sweet waters, and with myself, without fear, guilt, or shame, but instead with immense joy, beauty, and appreciation. We all want to heal, including the ancestors, the buffalo, and the sweet waters.

I am deeply grateful for the doors that the Native and indigenous community has opened for me, to be able to feel my own indigeneity. For me it has been a process of decolonizing my mind, body, and psyche, in particular being able to question and transform the colonial, patriarchal, hierarchical, and oppressive paradigm and system in which I grew up. To me that has meant connecting deeply with the feminine, with nature, with the spirits in nature, to feel my deep love and commitment to the ocean and the waters, and to have the permission and courage to feel both the pain and the joy. As an immigrant to California, I am deeply thankful to the California Native community for teaching me about the local plants and waters, and sharing your cultural practices. Thank you for your friendship. These intimate, reciprocal, and respectful relationships have helped me to deepen my sense of belonging, connection, and responsibility to place, and to all beings past, present, and future.

Melissa's Story: From Birch Trees to Redwoods—All on Turtle's Back

I grew up as a mixed-blood, second-generation relocatee 2,000 miles from my parents' homeland. From the epicenter of North America in the Turtle Mountains to the wild, Northwest Coast of California, my parents deliberately left the Indian/White polarized territory of North Dakota for the more progressive culture of northern California in the early 60s. My mom was first coerced into moving to Oakland, California in 1954 as part of the first wave of the federal Indian relocation program. Unlike many others, she managed to eke out a living working at the Alameda Hospital and immediately liked the diverse, multicultural, open attitude of the San Francisco Bay Area.

I grew up in a tiny town in Mendocino County knowing of my Native heritage yet not living within an Anishinaabeg or Cree context. My mom often shared extraordinary stories of her childhood and our relatives' rich heritage and she shared some language and foods, but basically we lived as modern Americans. I felt disconnected from my Native roots but deeply connected to the local botanical roots of the redwood, bay laurel, Douglas fir, coastal live oak, madrone, and manzanita of my riverine home, the ancestral lands of the Pomo, Yuki, and Wailaki peoples. Even though I knew that my ancestral trees were birch not redwood, and even though I knew the Eel River was not *my* ancestral river, I knew it was *someone's* ancestral river. This stimulated a deep curiosity and commitment to learn about the local Native peoples on whose land I was living. I knew deep in my bones that there was some link between honoring my own ancestral seeds and waters and respecting the First Peoples of the indigenous place I inhabited.

While my physical body was fed by the clean air, water, and food of that redwood forest river landscape, my heart and spirit had inherited mixed-blood shame and the pain and trauma my mother carried from reservation life, Catholic boarding school, and relocation. Being Métis or Michif, my mom was never quite "Indian enough" or "white enough" and was shunned and discriminated against for her Indianness for her whole life until she came to California. Silence, forgetting, and "passing" were keys to getting by. As Anishinaabeg sister and scholar/writer Leanne Simpson has written, "my ancestors resisted and survived what must have seemed like an apocalyptic reality of occupation and subjugation in a context where they had few choices."[11] Few choices indeed for my mom too, and things did not get much better as that internalized trauma and oppression, without being directly addressed, becomes a soul wound that requires daily self-medication.[12] In the shadow of alcoholism, domestic chaos, and rural malaise, the river and the forest became my community, my solace, my learning place, and my sacred refuge.

The more I yearned to learn about my own Native heritage, the more I yearned to learn about the First Peoples of the land and waters that held me together. It has been these two yearnings that have set me on my life's learning journey. As cultural anthropologist Les Field has written about in reference to the Muwekma Ohlone, "absence and loss are as much a real part of heritage for the Muwekma Ohlone [or any other colonized people] as presence and continuity, and only by understanding the former can the latter manifest."[13] Thus, my interest in service to my own Native heritage and to other colonized peoples and places. Integral to this is a commitment to exploring multiple ways to repair, mend, and revitalize ourselves and our places after disruption and loss. This legacy of pain due to genocide and oppression, and especially the internalized racism instilled in boarding schools, has led to generations of what the Aborigines of Australia call the "stolen generations," and in Canada some First Nations call the "lost generations." Chickasaw law expert James Sakej Henderson refers to these generations, those of my mother, as members of the "Split-Head Society."[14]

As I've written in "Mending the Split-Head Society with Trickster Consciousness,"[15] the process of decolonization and revitalization requires a fierce and compassionate commitment to self-understanding, to community, and to "all our relations." In this essay I demonstrate how learning indigenous cultural arts and Native languages are two direct ways to disrupt the Cartesian dualism of Eurocentric conditioning, embody the wholeness of cultural heritage from the inside out, and open up new pathways for re-creation and indigenous imagination. After experimenting with these ways for decades, I was thrilled to see how the use of these indigenous methods in our Native Youth Guardians of the Waters Program was positively received and utilized by these courageous young indigenous women. They embraced, expanded, and transformed their experiences in novel and multidimensional ways. As we shared earlier, there is an openness and experimental nature to the

youth we were privileged to work with, who are interrogating colonialism and affirming and re-creating new forms of indigeneity. These
women Guardians of the Waters are today's new warriors. As Taiaiake
Alfred has written:

> The new warriors are committed in the first instance to self-trans-
> formation and self-defense against the insidious forms of control
> that the state and capitalism use to shape lives according to their
> needs—to fear, to obey, to consume. When lies rule, warriors reveal
> new truths for the people to believe.[16]

I am extremely fortunate to be able to do this work through The Cultural Conservancy with these "new warriors," with Native mentors and
knowledge holders, and with colleagues and friends who come to these
issues from their own cultural experience and ancestral waters, demonstrating that the family of humanity shares so many core themes and
aspirations. We are able to envision, remember, restore, and experiment
on the edges of transformation with urban and rural communities and
places and be a part of a contemporary resurgence toward eco-cultural
health and liberation.

In my Anishinaabeg oral tradition, we have the Seven Fires Proph-
ecy, which tells of the colonial invasion and the ensuing disruption and
loss of indigenous lifeways.[17] It foresees the creation of the Split-Head
Society in the fifth and sixth Fires and the damage to our Earth and
extended kin of more-than-human relatives. It speaks to our time, the
time of the Seventh Fire, when many of us would look back into our
ancestral seeds and waters and pick up the fragments of song, the shards
of memory, the threads of story, and the fragments of sacred places to
re-member and put ourselves back together again. We are in this time
and many of us, in my generation, are engaged in this revitalization
work. What is also exciting to see is the emergence of the Eighth Fire,
today's indigenous youth from both urban and rural settings, who are
hungry for these connections and opportunities to decolonize and renew
themselves after generations of trauma and forgetting. Re-tracing our
ancestral seeds and waters (for me, the Birch Tree and the Red River of

the North) not only connects us to our own personal songlines but to the seeds and waters where we grew up and live (for me, the redwood tree and the Eel River).

Embodying holistic connections to ancestral places requires us to learn about and understand the historical legacies and contemporary struggles of the First Peoples who call these places their ancestral territory. The local Pomo, Wailaki, Yuki, and Ohlone and Coast Miwok peoples of Northern Coastal California, have taught me how to respect their lands and waters in ways that have given me greater understanding of my own heritage. Likewise, my growing understanding of my Anishinaabeg traditions enables me to be a better resident and ally to the local peoples and places. It is a type of inter-tribal, inter-cultural, and inter-species reciprocal learning and sharing process that strengthens all and facilitates a sacred kinship. And these connections remind me we are *all* on Turtle's back (Turtle Island) in North America and *all* on our Earth Mother on this planet, so that root will always inextricably bind us, especially if we listen to the call to be a guardian of our waters and our places.

Notes

1   Rumi, "The Seed Market," 153.
2   See Wolfgramm, et al., *The Dynamics of Traditional Ecological Knowledge in Changing Realities of Home: A Maori Economy Perspective* and Roberts et al., "Kaitiakitanga: Maori Perspectives on Conservation."
3   Smith, *Decolonizing Methodologies*; Waziyatawin and Yellow Bird, *For Indigenous Minds Only.*
4   Freire, *Pedagogy of the Oppressed*; Brave Heart, "Wakiksuyapi: Carrying the Historical Trauma of the Lakota;" Duran, *Healing the Soul Wound: Counseling with American Indians and Other Native Peoples*; Duran and Duran, *Native American Postcolonial Psychology*; Walters et al., "Dis-placement and Dis-ease: Land, Place, and Health Among American Indians and Alaska Natives."
5   Nelson, "River of Memory, Lakes of Survival: Indigenous Water Traditions and the Anishinaabeg Nation."
6   Simpson, *Dancing on Our Turtle's Back: Stories of Nishnaabeg Re-Creation, Resurgence and a New Emergence.*
7   Tlatokan Atlahuak Declaration, March 2006, 4th World Water Forum.
8   Wagenberg, *Holocaust Kickboxer: Descent and Transformation of Intergenerational Trauma,* 95.
9   Alfred, *Wasase, Indigenous Pathways of Action and Freedom,* 33.
10 Watch the "Guardians of the Waters" video at: http://vimeo.com/77668178.

11   Simpson, *Dancing on Our Turtle's Back: Stories of Nishnaabeg Re-Creation, Resurgence and a New Emergence*, 15.
12   See Duran, *Healing the Soul Wound*.
13   Field, *Abalone Tales: Collaborative Explorations of Sovereignty and Identity in Native California*, 44.
14   Nelson, "Mending the Split-Head Society with Trickster Consciousness."
15   Ibid.
16   Alfred, *Wasase, Indigenous Pathways of Action and Freedom*, 44.
17   See Benton-Banai, *The Mishomis Book*; Simpson, *Lighting the Eighth Fire: The Liberation, Resurgence, and Protection of Indigenous Nations*; and Kimmerer, *Braiding Sweetgrass: Indigenous Wisdom, Scientific Knowledge, and the Teachings of Plants*.

References

Alfred, Taiaiake. *Wasase, Indigenous Pathways of Action and Freedom*. Toronto: University of Toronto Press, 2005.

Benton-Banai, Eddie. *The Mishomis Book*. Minneapolis: University of Minnesota Press, 2011.

Brave Heart, Maria Yellow Horse. "Wakiksuyapi: Carrying the Historical Trauma of the Lakota." In *Tulane Studies in Social Welfare*, 21–22 (2000): 245–266. Available online at www.pasadena.edu/files/syllabi/stvillanueva_39362.pdf (accessed 30 March 2016).

Duran, Eduardo. *Healing the Soul Wound: Counseling with American Indians and Other Native Peoples*. New York: Teachers College Press, 2006.

Duran, Eduardo and Bonnie Duran. *Native American Postcolonial Psychology*. Albany: State University of New York, 1995.

Field, Les. *Abalone Tales: Collaborative Explorations of Sovereignty and Identity in Native California*. Durham: Duke University Press, 2008.

Freire, Paulo. *Pedagogy of the Oppressed*. New York: Herder and Herder, 1970.

Kimmerer, Robin Wall. *Braiding Sweetgrass: Indigenous Wisdom, Scientific Knowledge, and the Teachings of Plants*. Minneapolis: Milkweed Editions, 2013.

Nelson, Melissa. "Mending the Split-Head Society with Trickster Consciousness." In *Original Instructions: Indigenous Teachings for a Sustainable Future*, edited by Melissa K. Nelson, 288–298. Rochester, VT: Bear & Company, 2008.

Nelson, Melissa. "River of Memory, Lakes of Survival: Indigenous Water Traditions and the Anishinaabeg Nation." In *Deep Blue: Critical Reflections on Nature Religion and Water*, edited by Sylvie Shaw and Andrew Francis, 67–86. London: Equinox Publishing, 2011.

Roberts, Mere, Waerete Norman, Nganeko Minhinnick, Del Wihongi, and Carmen Kirkwood. "Kaitiakitanga: Maori Perspectives on Conservation." *Pacific Conservation Biology*, 2, 1 (1995): 7–20.

Rumi, Jalal-al Din. "The Seed Market." In *The Essential Rumi: New Expanded Edition*, translated by Coleman Barks, 153. New York: HarperOne, 2004.

Simpson, Leanne. *Lighting the Eighth Fire: The Liberation, Resurgence, and Protection of Indigenous Nations*. Winnipeg: Arbeiter Ring Press, 2005.

Simpson, Leanne. *Dancing on Our Turtle's Back: Stories of Nishnaabeg Re-Creation, Resurgence and a New Emergence*. Winnipeg: Arbeiter Ring Press, 2011.

Smith, Linda Tuhiwai. *Decolonizing Methodologies: Research and Indigenous Peoples*. New York: Palgrave, 1999.

Tlatokan Atlahuak Declaration, March 2006, 4th World Water Forum. Available online at http://tribalinknews.blogspot.com/2006/09/tlatokan-atlahuak-declaration-4th.html (accessed 30 March 2016).

Wagenberg, Nícola. *Holocaust Kickboxer: Descent and Transformation of Intergenerational Trauma*. Dissertation. Meridian University, 2012.

Walters, Karina L., Ramona Beltran, David Huh, and Teresa Evans-Campbell. "Dis-placement and Dis-ease: Land, Place, and Health Among American Indians and Alaska Natives." In *Communities, Neighborhoods, and Health: Expanding the Boundaries of Place (Social Disparities in Health and Health Care)*, edited by Linda M. Burton, Susan P. Kemp, ManChui Leung, Stephen A. Matthews, and David T. Takeuchi, 163–199. Seattle: University of Washington, 2011.

Waziyatawin and Michael Yellow Bird, editors. *For Indigenous Minds Only: A Decolonization Handbook*. Santa Fe: SAR Press, 2012.

Wolfgramm, Rachel, Chellie Spiller, C. Houkamau, and M. Henare. *The Dynamics of Traditional Ecological Knowledge in Changing Realities of Home: A Maori Economy Perspective*. Unpublished Manuscript.

8

BEAUTY OUT OF THE SHADOWS

THE INDIGENOUS TURN IN A FILIPINA NARRATIVE
LENY MENDOZA STROBEL

Dalit karing Núnû (Homage to the ancient Kapampangan gods):
Bápû Indûng Láut (Hail to the Ocean Mother)
Bápû Ibpâng Banua (Hail to the Sky Father)
Bápung Aldó a Sínukuan (Hail to the Victorious Sun)
Bápûng Búlan a Maliári (Hail to the Omnipotent Moon)
Makiágum kó pû sána kékami ngan (We beg you to become One with Us)
Bang yang misaplálâ ing Indû ming Tibûan (So that our Earth Mother becomes abundant)

My name is Elenita Fe Luna Mendoza Strobel. My ancestral roots are in Pampanga, a province in the center of Luzon in the Philippines. This Kapampangan chant was taught to me by a young culture-bearer, Mike Pangilinan. When he told me that the chant is sung to the tune of the *pasyon*,[1] I told him that I am not Catholic and I do not do the *pasyon*. He then said that the *pasyon* is actually an indigenous form of Kapampangan chanting and it was the Spanish colonizers who appropriated it as they went about their missionizing work.

I have reclaimed this chant.

I left Pampanga 30 years ago to come to Turtle Island. In truth, my family left our roots even earlier as my paternal grandparents were claimed by Protestant Christianity at the turn of the twentieth century after the US bought the Philippines from Spain for $20 million, and thus began the American colonial period. My maternal grandparents were Catholicized by centuries of Spanish colonization marked in history books by the landing of Ferdinand Magellan in 1521. Almost four centuries of colonial history's (unintended) consequences brought me to this huge continent—an island girl from a beautiful archipelago in the shape of a dancing woman that was called the "Pearl of the Orient Seas." Such orientalist labeling notwithstanding, it provides a conceptual bridge for me to the rest of the islands of the vast Pacific Ocean. Even though the Philippines is not included in the discourse on Oceania,[2] I am wondering: why not? What accident of history excludes us?

Not much has been handed down by way of oral tradition about my ancient ancestors. I know that there was once a town in Pampanga named Sulipan[3] that was the five-star resort of the royals in Asia and the Spanish conquerors. The place is blessed by an abundant ecology along the banks of the great Pampanga River. This is how Kapampangans became famous as good cooks. And before then, there were Islamic traders and Chinese traders on our shores. In one history book I learned that the Muslims that reached Southeast Asia were Sufis.[4]

I like imagining that I have Sufi ancestors. Is this why I have always resonated with Rumi's poetry and tales about Sham of Tabriz? Is this why the devotions of the dervishes touch my heart deeply? Who knows.

In earlier times, before the Malay settling (or is it colonizing?) of the islands, there were the indigenous Aetas in Pampanga living in the shadow of Apu Mallari, the mountain god. They are still there. In fact, there are over 150 indigenous communities throughout the Philippines. Their attempts to retain their ancestral domain and their cultural survival are an ongoing struggle with the development policies of the imagined nation-state that succumbs to the pressure of corporate globalization. When I was growing up, as "good" colonial subjects, we were taught to look down on the Aetas and other indigenous Filipinos as "primitives." The civilizing mission wasn't subtle.

Now I am here. A postcolonial and diasporic subject of empire. A settler on Turtle Island. However, I no longer find these labels accurate.

They were useful, though, for the deconstruction of the twentieth century's imperial and colonial narratives. Today, the more I reclaim my indigenous consciousness, the more I realize that the West and its civilizing discourse do not define me. I may have found utility in the theories of hybridity, postcoloniality, and postmodernity during the phase of "strategic essentialism"[5] when I was trying to find a toe-hold for my burgeoning academic understanding of critical and cultural studies theories. But the discourses felt disembodied to me in their abstraction and rationality.

However, I also found other intellectuals who wrote in a manner that felt more sensuous and embodied—writers who didn't eschew the important role of emotions in shaping the intellect. Since I started my decolonization journey in the mid-90s, the road has been marked by encounters with special individuals, like Virgilio Enriquez, NVM Gonzalez, Albert Alejo, Paulo Freire, Gloria Anzaldúa, David Abram, and many other scholars and researchers, whose style of writing gave me permission to write in a language that was accessible by people outside of the ivory tower.[6]

A few years ago, in an encounter with the writings of Martin Prechtel,[7] a shaman in the Tzutujil Maya tradition, and the beautiful Mayan language and world that he translated into English, I was entranced and invited back to the world of orality and to the world of a people that didn't have the verb *to be*. I was drawn into a world that I have been lost to by my modern education. And like Linda Hogan,[8] another Native American writer, I wanted my language to heal, to touch the soul and heart the way I have been touched and transformed. I haven't written an academic paper since. Instead I am learning to chant, dance, and do ritual.

The Call of the Indigenous

During the years of doing research on the Filipino indigenous and shamanic traditions and practices, specifically on the babaylan,[9] I returned many times to the Philippines in search of connection. I attended conferences on Filipino Indigenous Knowledge Systems and Practices (IKSP) and talked to researchers of the babaylan, but in the end it wasn't the research findings that changed me.[10] It was the dance; it was the gongs and bamboo instruments; it was the young indigenous people at Pamulaan College[11] (the first and only indigenous college in the Philippines), who sang about fulfilling the dreams of their ancestors, that drew me in.

Then there is the Land. I had a hard time falling in love with the Land where I am from (Pampanga), for it is now paved over and overcome with shopping malls. In Mindanao/Southern Philippines, in Lake Sebu, I was introduced to the Schools of Living Traditions, to the living myths of the indigenous peoples of Mindanao. I had a glimpse of their tenuous and fragile relationships with outsiders like me who come and go. The brief glimpses of indigenous Mindanao are what finally taught me how to return my body to the home of my ancestors in Pampanga: the body that felt drowned in grief over what has been lost through the centuries and the body that finds peace now, in whatever small ways, in seeing that there are still people in Pampanga who are keeping the indigenous culture alive, albeit in transformed and revitalized ways by indigenous cosmopolitans.[12]

But what does this have to do with being in the diaspora? Can the uprooted body learn how to dwell in another place? How does having a sense of connection to a homeland keep us grounded even while being displaced? And what of our sense of place in the land where we have settled, which belongs to the first indigenous peoples? How do we make meaning when the modern concepts of nation-state and other master narratives begin to fray under the weight of corporate globalization? When postmodern paradigms do not quite provide a sufficient sense of "Home"?

In grappling with these questions, I reach for intellectual frameworks in articulating my experiences. As English is not my first language and as I've tuned in more to my body and my senses in these last few years, it has become more difficult to theorize in an academic language. So I am thankful for the work of James Clifford, for example, as he writes about becoming indigenous in the twenty-first century.[13] Many Native academics today, like Taiaiake Alfred, Devon Abbott Mihesuah, and Angela Cavender Wilson, are writing about indigenizing the academy.[14]

Clifford offers articulation, performance, and translation as concepts for describing the multi-faceted negotiations that indigenous and indigenizing people are engaged in.[15] Very often, when I read the theoretical work of these authors, I realize that the work that I do today has always been guided by these embodied practices. I feel validated. My intuition, which responded to the call of the indigenous, is confirmed.

Another colleague, Jurgen Kremer, has coined the term "ethnoautobiography" to talk about indigenization as the practice of radical presence and developing a participatory sense of self that is connected to ancestry, place, community, nature, history, dream, myths, spirituality, stories, and storytelling.[16] In this work, the privileging of indigenous perspectives displaces the modern identity that is "masterful but empty" as a way to decolonize Eurocentric/white/colonial thinking. It is a critique of modern identities characterized by fragmentation, cognitive dissonance, individualism, separation from nature and place, and ancestral roots; hierarchy and patriarchy; gender and racialized identities. It is a decolonization tool that de-centers Eurocentric colonial thinking.

For several years, Kremer and I collaborated on using the conceptual framework and pedagogical tools of "ethnoautobiography" in undergraduate courses in Ethnic Studies, with tremendous success. As a transformative learning framework, we are witnesses to the way the students are able to develop a larger participatory sense of self and a willingness to unlearn racial, class, and gender privileges. We think of this work as the missing link in multicultural studies and indigenous studies. The indigenous turn in the academe is a welcome move, but it should also behoove academics to address the more critical question: what would it take for the Euro-centered/colonial mind to turn loose of its modern worldview? What process and framework can we utilize in higher-education settings to help our students decolonize? I believe the answer is ethnoautobiography.

In de-centering colonial thinking I found in Filipino indigenous psychology the concept of Kapwa;[17] in postmodern discourse this could be translated as intersubjectivity. When I first encountered the concept of "intersubjectivity" in critical theory I thought to myself: "But this is the way we Filipinos have always been." This was the beginning of my attempts to center Filipino indigenous psychology and indigenous knowledge in my scholarly work.[18] I realized that my narratives of decolonization have always included the elements of ethnoautobiography, even before I knew about this conceptual framework.

My body of work privileges the Filipino indigenous research method of *pakapakapa* (literally, it means groping your way to the answer)—it resonates with the theories about improvisation and jazz as metaphors for the sort of creative and open-ended trajectory of narratives that recognize the limits of theorizing. Uncertainty, openness, and elaboration as aspects of improvisation call forth our community's well developed sense of *pakikiramdam*, of deep empathy through listening and sensing and understanding of indirect cues in high context cultures.

So I make work that calls me to be accountable to my ancestors and to my future descendants.

I have not been alone on this path. The Center for Babaylan Studies (CFBS)[19] exists because there are individuals who have heard the call of the indigenous and who wanted to become part of both the invisible and visible flow of indigenous spirit and activism that has been part of our Filipino history of resistance and survivance.[20]

In its current form in the diaspora, the babaylan-inspired community is a virtual community with local communities in Los Angeles, New York, Chicago, Toronto, Vancouver, and affiliated communities in the Philippines. In 2010, the core team and a cohort of volunteers organized the first International Babaylan Conference. This was inspired by the experience of a group of us from the US who attended the Kapwa 2 Conference at the University of the Philippines in Iloilo; we wanted to bring back the experience to California. A convergence of vision, inspiration, and availability of folks willing to organize resulted in the first conference at my university. As an initial endeavor, we thought maybe one hundred would come. On the day of the conference, over 250 came.

A huge buzz circulated in the community about this unique conference—the perfect integration of academe-creative, arts-healing, arts-social, and political activism—as our manifested desire to decolonize and re-indigenize. We were tapping into a deep silence that has found its voice. We tapped into the wellspring of beauty contained in our Philippine indigenous practices.

In 2011, we organized an invitational retreat/symposium to deepen and strengthen the foundation of babaylan-inspired work in the diaspora. We focused on naming our grief, and the power of our dreams and storytelling. We brought in the Philippine National Commission on Culture and the Arts Chairman, Felipe de Leon Jr, who taught us beyond-the-basics understanding of Kapwa psychology.[21] During our closing ritual, each participant was gifted with a bamboo pendant carved with Filipino indigenous motifs done by one of our healers and tribal tattoo artist, Lane Wilcken.[22] To each participant, Lane explained the meaning of the symbol and why he sensed that it belonged to the person receiving it.

To Will, an intersex, Lane told a Cordillera story about the deity who, when putting together bodies that have been dismembered in a fight, put the body of the woman of top of the male body. Lane said that the body that was both male and female is sacred and whole. When Lane placed the pendant around Will's neck, there wasn't a dry eye in the circle. Even as I write this I am teary-eyed.

There is a depth to ritual that words alone cannot reach. No wonder our ancestors danced rather than theorized.

At the same retreat, our attention was called to the "No to Mining in Palawan" movement.[23] In solidarity with the indigenous peoples in Palawan, the participants mobilized and formed a caucus on how best to participate in homeland concerns around indigenous peoples' rights.

When we are not organizing our own CFBS events, our volunteers are invited to participate at festivals like the Festival of Philippine Arts and Culture (FPAC) in Los Angeles, the Filipino American Book Festival in San Francisco, and at the Asian Art Museum's Filipino American History celebrations. The core group and volunteer cohort are often engaged in their respective communities as culture-bearing artists, ritualists, healers, activists, and teachers.

In 2012, a group of us went to the Kapwa 3 Conference[24] at the University of the Philippines in Baguio. We went to learn from the indigenous elders and their Schools of Living Traditions; we went to engage the academics in dialogue on how to bridge local and global knowledge and how to privilege indigenous knowledge systems and practices in the Philippine academe. In addition to these conversations, many of the Filipino Americans and Filipino Canadians reconnected with their own tribal ancestries or developed new and now ongoing relationships with indigenous peoples and communities.[25]

In 2013, we organized the Second International Babaylan Conference. We felt that during this time of civilizational crisis, a time of great turning and transformation, our own Filipino Kapwa psychology and indigenous knowledge systems and practices have much to offer to our communities. If we can find our way out of colonial and modernist thinking, if we can achieve a clarity of vision in drawing a map to a sustainable future, it will also heal our imperial trauma and cultural amnesia. In healing ourselves, we will be contributing to the global healing movement through a return to ancient wisdom and indigenous ways of being.

This is the work that calls me. I am here today because of this call.

Doing Grief Work

Recently I was reading a long manuscript on mental health and climate change, and after all the scientific data quantifying the increase in mental illness as people face the effects of climate change, I couldn't help but feel sad for the poverty of the modern imagination.[26] If the DSM 5 is already putting grief as a mental disorder, think about the impact of untended grief that erupts in violence and wars. I compare this to the work of healing grief through indigenous ceremony or ritual because we are never meant to grieve in solitude; we need witnesses and we need our communities.

Indigenous paradigms have a much better understanding of the role of grief and suffering as part of the human experience. Grief is balanced by a cosmic vision that doesn't put human species as the be-all and end-all of creation. When we take our place as one of the beautiful beings among millions of other beings, human and non-human, then our grief is released from the individualistic isolation that marks the modern experience. In so doing, grief can be a work of love and compassion; a work of restoring balance and harmony—all of which are done in the context of community. In my personal grief work, I found blessing in the recovery of a tribal myth that spoke to me.

In the Manobo story about the first babaylan, Mungan, the epic heroine,[27] talks of a woman who leads her people away from the coast where the invaders have landed and begun to pillage. Mungan leads the way to the mountain, where she and her people seek refuge. In working with Mungan's story, it solidified my need to learn how myth, when read through an indigenous lens, can lend meaning to our contemporary whereabouts. Below is a brief recap of her story:

Dear Mungan,
To the people of Bukidnon, you are the first babaylan. You are the true heroine of their beloved epic, Ulaging, even though the honor goes to Agyu and his brothers.
Your husband shunned you because of your leprosy but your brothers-in-law were kind to you.
They took turns carrying you on their backs on the long journey from the sea to the mountain top of Mt Kitanglad.
Conflict has come to the shore so your people had to flee to the mountains.

One day you told your brothers-in-law that you didn't want to slow them down anymore.
So they built you a hut and went on their journeys, returning on occasion to bring you food and gifts.

In truth, they returned for instructions from you because you alone knew where they should go and how they can find food for their bodies and souls.

You taught them the virtue of sharing food. You told them that even if the meat is no bigger than a baby's fingernail, that they must share it.

You taught them that they can achieve immortality without first experiencing death.

You taught them that they can attain the highest state of spirituality by abstaining from material wants.

You taught them that they will lose their fear of famine and starvation.

You taught them that their bodies will shine like gold in the end carried on a magic flying ship to the world beyond the skies.

One day, just before dawn, you began to beat your gong. Slowly at first, then building up to a rhythmic trance.

It soon became light and just before the sun rose, you looked up with amazement...
The sky in the east looked like polished metal

You kept on beating your gong while never taking your eyes off the Sun
Gazing at it without blinking.

You were amazed that the sound of the gong now sounds like laughter and it became so loud
When you took your gaze off the sun to look around you, all the weeds and wild plants around your hut have turned to gold
And the leprosy slowly left your body.

The Sun—source of magical power
The blinding light heals the leprous body of the gong-playing maiden
Your eyes became the conduit for the energy that would humanize the gong with the gift of laughter
Having conquered disease and death, now your scabs have turned into mountain rice birds; they flew away but one of the birds returned to you with a vial of coconut oil, a gold striped betel nut, and pinipig from the first rice harvest.

Mungan, all around you shines with golden light.
In rapture and spiritual ecstasy, your body is radiant with transcen-
dent light.

To Lena, the first brother, you gave the first betel nut of immor-
tality
And as he chewed, his speech became different
He began to speak in the words of ancient poetry

Dear Mungan, your quest for a safe homeland for your people
In the time of war and violence
Your desire to lead them to paradise
To found a new community
To lead people in times of trouble
Is hiding in the words of the ancient epic

In these millennial dreams
At the heart of it is the desire for Oneness
People of all creeds, ethnicities belong to one extended family
Who will attain immortality without passing through death

Dear Mungan,
I beseech you now to shine your light upon us
Teach us how to gaze at the Sun without blinking
So, too, may our bodies shine like gold
So, too, may everything around us shine like gold

We are your descendants in the here and now
Flying ships carried us not quite to the world beyond the skies
But to this continent
Where we are tracing your steps
Where we are building our huts
Where we are forging Oneness
Where we are forging Wholeness
Shine your light upon us, Mungan.
Shine your light upon us.

The story of Mungan lives among the Talaandig, Matigsalugs, Kirintekens, Ilianen-Manobo, Kulamanen, Bukidnons, Higaunon, and Livunganen-Arumanen Manobo of Central, Northern and parts of Western Mindanao. Her story lives within the bigger story of Agyu, the epic's hero. As a sacred chant, the ulahing is believed to be never ending as long as there are storytellers and singers/chanters. I want to keep Mungan alive in each of us so I tell her story whenever I can.

It is because of this belief in the power of indigenous myths that I named our 2013 conference *"Katutubong Binhi*/Native Seeds: Myths and Stories that Feed our Indigenous Soul."[28]

We gathered to feed our indigenous soul with myths and stories as a way of reconnecting with our indigenous roots as Filipinos. All of us have ancestors who, once upon a time, were indigenous to the Land. Our separation from the Land and our subsequent distancing from our indigenous consciousness is a historical event that began about 10,000 years ago. What we are calling our ecological crisis, climate change, global warming, economic recession—all tell us of the consequences of having lost our sense of indigeneity, this sense of knowing why rooted-ness in the Land is the way to our future.

Our Filipino experience is particularly unique in the history of colonized peoples because the colonization of our islands by the US stands at the center of the narrative of empire building in the late nineteenth century. More than a century of denial by the US of its colonial enterprise in the Philippines and its denial of itself as an empire complicates and shapes the Filipino experience. "Benevolent assimilation" and "manifest destiny" came to be called "white love,"[29] thus denying the psychic and epistemic violence of colonization. Filipinos, in turn, internalized our oppression by believing ourselves to be "little brown brothers and sisters."

It is now time to tell a different story.

We are people in the diaspora and we are settlers on Turtle Island. Today I dwell on Pomo and Coast Miwok land. Many of the Filipino settlers on Turtle Island now live in places called Home by the Ohlone, Anishinabe, Luiseno, Mohawk, and other indigenous communities. How do we learn to dwell on someone else's land without thinking like a colonizer? How do we dwell on someone else's land without taking over and imposing what we modernized/undecolonized folks think is best? How do we dwell in full awareness that the Earth is dreaming and alive?

Guided by these questions, we chose our conference theme of "mythic stories as seeds that feed our indigenous soul" because we needed to reach back into our indigenous history and memory to know and love ourselves as island peoples. Additionally, we are natural storytellers. We never tire of telling stories about ghosts and spirit encounters, about our faith and religious devotion, about community, about our dreams, about our travels to places around the planet in search for a sense of belonging. And we always surround ourselves with food as we tell stories. In all of these stories, there are bigger myths also waiting to be remembered, danced, sung, or chanted. It is my hope that we will continue to find some of these seeds that we can nurture to fruition.

The opening of the conference was on the power of storytelling by Greg Sarris, Tribal Chair of the Federated Indians of Graton Rancheria, who is Filipino and Pomo. As tribal chairman for the past two decades, Greg led the campaign to get his tribe federally recognized in 2000. He is also leading his tribe in keeping their myths and stories alive. As a beautiful and prolific writer, Greg writes about Coyote trickster stories in *How a Mountain Was Made*; in *Mabel McKay: Weaving the Dream* he writes about Mabel McKay, the Pomo medicine woman; he includes stories about the Filipino Manongs of Sonoma County in his novels *Grand Avenue* and *Watermelon Nights*.

In these glimpses of what the Center for Babaylan Studies does, I am offering a testimony of how my personal journey of decolonization and indigenization started as a solo adventure to deal with personal, cultural, racial, and ethnic identity issues. However, it soon became a decolonization movement and an indigenizing community that is making its way around our communities in the diaspora. We are also beginning to nurture cross-cultural relationships with Filipinos who are also part Native (e.g., Filipino and Pomo, Filipino and Native Hawaiian).

More recently I've been having "oceanic dreams" where I am questioning why the Philippines is not part of Oceania; why, in spite of our myths and stories that connect us to Oceania, there is no awareness of our interconnectedness in our respective communities. I have been questioning maps and their making during colonial and imperial times. How do we claim, for example, as Epeli Hau'ofa does, that "We are the Ocean."[30]

This, too, signals a new and shifting awareness about water. All of the discourses that have shaped me as an organic intellectual have been based on maps made by colonial geography of continents (Land). As I keep track of the ways that Pacific Island nations are reclaiming their voyaging and star navigational traditions, rebuilding canoes and reviving cultural practices, I am meditating on the archipelago of 7,000 islands that came to be called by colonizers "the Philippines." Is it time to revisit this history and re-draw the maps and ask new questions?[31]

As I think about "edges of transformation" I go back to the processes (internal and external) that enable me to be a servant-leader. I remember my father saying, "you will make a good teacher" when I was a child. I remember the dreams about my grandmother as I reached back into the well of memory for stories that would become my stories of taking off the colonial jacket that we were made to wear for five centuries. I had many archetypal dreams and revelatory dreams that became my inner compass as I made my decision to follow the path of decolonization—a path which was then without a map, as far as I can tell, for someone like me. The inner promptings led me to seek mentors who encouraged the path I was on. My mentor/friend, Roshni,[32] told me that the myth of Inanna belongs to me—she who went to the underworld to meet her dark sister, Ereshkigal, and then was re-born to rule her world.

The Filipino concept of *Loob*, the core of the inner self, is connected to the outer dimensions of the self through the concept of *Kapwa* (or intersubjectivity) via the affective dimension of *Pakikiramdam*. Thus, the Self is always in the Other or "You and I are One." So, as I describe the transformative process of the last two decades, what becomes evident is the interplay of the internal and external dimensions of the journey. The inner work of the psyche via dreams, self-reflection, and critical thinking, and the external input from mentors, books, events, friendships, retreats, and conferences, co-mingles and connects with the work of others who are also called to the path of decolonization and indigenization.

Together we create projects and events that manifest our deep desire for healing and in so doing nurture our beloved communities.

May it always be so.

Notes

1 http://en.wikipedia.org/wiki/Pasyon (accessed 29 June 2014). When we were growing up in San Fernando, Pampanga, one of the Holy Week Rituals is the recitation of the life of Christ through the *pasyon* and it is broadcast through a loudspeaker 24/7 for 3–5 days so that the entire barrio can listen. For those of us who were not Catholics, this was more than a nuisance. My father once tried to get the barrio captain to order the removal of the loudspeaker, but to no avail.

2 Hau'ofa, E. *We Are the Ocean: Selected Works.*

3 Gonzalez, *Cocina Sulipena: Culinary Gems from Old Pampanga.*

4 Ansary, *Destiny Disrupted: A History of the World Through Islamic Eyes.*

5 "Spivak coined the term 'strategic essentialism,' which refers to a sort of temporary solidarity for the purpose of social action. For example, the attitude that women's groups have many different agendas makes it difficult for feminists to work for common causes. 'Strategic essentialism' is about the need to accept temporarily an 'essentialist' position to be able to act." Available online at http://en.wikipedia.org/wiki/Gayatri_Chakravorty_Spivak (accessed 15 October 2014).

6 Enriquez, *From Colonial to Liberation Psychology*; Gonzalez, "Even as the Mountain Speaks;" Alejo, *Tao Po! Tuloy!: Isang Landas ng Pag-unawa sa Loob ng Tao*; Freire, *Pedagogy of the Oppressed; The Politics of Education; Pedagogy of Hope. Reliving Pedagogy of the Oppressed*; Anzaldúa, *Borderland: La Frontera, the New Mestiza*; Abram, *The Spell of the Sensuous: Perception and Language in a More-Than-Human World; Becoming Animal: An Earthly Cosmology.*

7 Martin Prechtel, www.floweringmountain.com/. See links to books and CD, Bolad's Kitchen, and other events.

8 Hogan, *The Woman Who Watches Over the World.*

9 Strobel, *Babaylan: Filipinos and the Call of the Indigenous; A Book of Her Own: Words and Images to Honor the Babaylan.*

10 In 2006 and 2008, I went on two Fulbright-Hays grants with groups of K-12 California teachers as Project Director and we immersed ourselves in learning about multicultural education in the Philippines with focus on indigenous people's education. I also attended conferences on the Babaylan at the Women's Studies Center, St. Scholastica College in Manila in 2005 and the KAPWA Conferences on Filipino Indigenous Knowledge Systems and Practices at the University of the Philippines in Iloilo and Baguio in 2008 and 2012, respectively. These conferences are co-hosted and sponsored by the Heritage and Arts Academies of the Philippines (HAPI) and the National Commission on Culture and the Arts (NCCA).

11 The Pamulaan Center for Indigenous People's Education is located within the University of Southeastern Mindanao. Indigenous Communities send their chosen students to college and the students are required to return to their communities to help maintain and sustain their cultural practices.

12 Forte, *Indigenous Cosmopolitans: Transnational and Transcultural Indigeneity in the 21ˢᵗ Century.*

13 Clifford, *Returns: Becoming Indigenous in the 21ˢᵗ Century.*

14 Alfred, *Peace Power and Righteousness: An Indigenous Manifesto*; Mihesuah and Wilson, *Indigenizing the Academe: Transforming Scholarship and Empowering Communities.*

15   Clifford, *Returns: Becoming Indigenous in the 21ˢᵗ Century*, 44–48.

16   Kremer and Jackson-Paton, *Ethnoautobiography: Stories and Practices for Unlearning Whiteness, Decolonization, and Uncovering Ethnicities.*

17   In Filipino indigenous psychology, Kapwa means "the self is in the other" and this self is connected to our innermost being (Loob). Our capacity to feel and sense (Damdam) our deep interconnectedness is a holistic way of being. See the work of Virgilio Enriquez, *From Colonial to Liberation Psychology.*

18   Strobel, *Babaylan: Filipinos and the Call of the Indigenous*; *A Book of Her Own: Words and Images to Honor the Babaylan*; *Coming Full Circle: The Process of Decolonization among Post-1965 Filipino Americans.*

19   Center for Babaylan Studies, www.babaylan.net. Also check out our Facebook page: www.facebook.com/groups/CenterforBabaylanStudies/?ref=br_tf.

20   The word "survivance" was coined by Gerald Vizenor, Native American author, as the fusion of two words, survival and resistance, in connection with Native Americans. See Vizenor, *Survivance: Narratives of Native Presence.*

21   Kapwa psychology is another term used to refer to Filipino indigenous psychology, or Sikolohiyang Pilipino. See Pe-Pua and Protacio-Marcelino, "Sikolohiyang Pilipino (Filipino Psychology): A Legacy of Virgilio G. Enriquez."

22   Wilcken, *Filipino Tattoos Ancient to Modern.*

23   "No to Mining in Palawan" is a grassroots movement to try to stop new mining contracts on the island. See Facebook page: www.facebook.com/no2mininginpalawan/timeline.

24   The KAPWA Conferences are organized by Heritage and Arts Academies of the Philippines, Inc. (HAPI), led by Kidlat Tahimik, Father of Philippine Independent Cinema, and Katrin de Guia, PhD, Philippine Studies, and author of *Kapwa: The Self in the Other* (Manila: Anvil Publishing, 2005), a key text in Filipino indigenous psychology (also known as Kapwa Psychology). The KAPWA conference, held every two or three years, is an academic conference and cultural exchange and gathering of indigenous leaders and youth, scholars, artists, and culture-bearers. Since 2008, the KAPWA organizers have welcomed the attendance and participation of Filipinos in the diaspora. This began the collaboration between HAPI and the Center for Babaylan Studies.

25   For example, the Kapwa Collective in Toronto created the Tiboli Exchange program. Many of the CfBS core group members and volunteers and event attendees go on ancestral journeys to the homeland, connect with indigenous communities, and collaborate on cultural projects.

26   Coyle and Van Susteren, "The Psychological Effects of Global Warming on the United States: And Why the U.S. Mental Health System is Not Adequately Prepared."

27   The version of Mungan's story here was taken from Herminia Menez' *Verbal Arts in Philippine Indigenous Communities: Poetics, Society, History.*

28   Strobel, "Summary Report: Second International Babaylan Conference."

29   Rafael, *White Love and Other Encounters in Filipino History.*

30   Hau'ofa, E., *We are the Ocean.*

31   There are ongoing Facebook and email discussions with Filipino scholars and culture-bearers who are interested in these questions. We are currently brainstorming of the possibility of organizing a conference around the interconnection (through myths and folkstories, canoe traditions, star navigation) between the Philippines and Pacific Island nations.

32   Sonoma State University Professor Emeritus, Roshni Rustomji, was my mentor during my graduate studies. She introduced me to the myth of Inanna and guided my process of decolonization. We eventually collaborated on many writing projects and presentations at academic conferences.

Bibliography

Abram, David. *The Spell of the Sensuous: Perception and Language in a More-Than-Human World*. New York: Vintage Books, 1997.

____. *Becoming Animal: An Earthly Cosmology*. New York: Pantheon Books, 2010.

Alejo, Albert, S.J. *Tao Po! Tuloy!: Isang Landas ng Pag-unawa sa Loob ng Tao*. Quezon City: Office of Research and Publication, Ateneo de Manila University, 1990.

Alfred, Taiaiake. *Peace Power and Righteousness: An Indigenous Manifesto*. Ontario, Canada: Oxford University Press, 1999.

Ansary, Tamim. *Destiny Disrupted: A History of the World Through Islamic Eyes*. New York: Public Affairs, Inc., 2009.

Anzaldúa, Gloria. *Borderland: La Frontera, the New Mestiza*. San Francisco, CA: Aunt Lute Press, 1987.

Clifford, James. *Returns: Becoming Indigenous in the 21ˢᵗ Century*. Cambridge and London: Harvard University Press, 2013.

Coyle, Kevin J. and Lise Van Susteren. "The Psychological Effects of Global Warming on the United States: And Why the U.S. Mental Health System is Not Adequately Prepared." National Wildlife Federation, 2011. Available online at www.christiansforthemountains .org/site/Topics/Issues/Climate/NWF%20Pyschological%20Effects%20Climate%20 Change.pdf (accessed 18 March 2016).

de Guia, Katrin. *Kapwa: The Self in the Other*. Manila: Anvil Publishing, 2005.

Enriquez, Virgilio (ed.). *Indigeonus Psychology: A Book of Readings*. Quezon City: Philippine Psychology Research and Training House, 1990.

____. *From Colonial to Liberation Psychology*. Manila: DeLa Salle University Press, 1994.

Forte, Maxmillian C. *Indigenous Cosmopolitans: Transnational and Transcultural Indigeneity in the 21ˢᵗ Century*. New York: Peter Lang Publishers, 2010.

Freire, Paulo. *Pedagogy of the Oppressed*. New York: Seabury Press, 1970.

____. *The Politics of Education*. Boston, MA: Bergin and Garvey, 1985.

____. *Pedagogy of Hope. Reliving Pedagogy of the Oppressed*. New York: Continuum Press, 1994.

Gonzalez, Gene R. *Cocina Sulipena: Culinary Gems from Old Pampanga*. Manila: Bookmark, Inc., 1993.

Gonzalez, NVM. "Even as the Mountain Speaks." *Amerasia Journal* 18, 3 (1992): 55–67.

Hau'ofa, Epeli. *We Are the Ocean: Selected Works*. Honolulu: University of Hawaii Press, 2008.

Hogan, Linda. *The Woman Who Watches Over the World*. New York: W.W. Norton, 2001.

Kremer, Jurgen W. and Robert Jackson-Paton. *Ethnoautobiography: Stories and Practices for Unlearning Whiteness, Decolonization, and Uncovering Ethnicities*. Sebastopol, CA: ReVision Publishing, 2014.

Menez, Herminia. *Verbal Arts in Philippine Indigenous Communities: Poetics, Society, History*. Manila: Ateneo de Manila University Press, 2010.

Mihesuah, Devon Abbott and Angela Cavender Wilson. *Indigenizing the Academe: Transforming Scholarship and Empowering Communities*. Lincoln and London: University of Nebraska Press, 2004.

Pe-Pua, Rogelia and Elizabeth Protacio-Marcelino. "Sikolohiyang Pilipino (Filipino Psychology): A Legacy of Virgilio G. Enriquez." *Asian Journal of Social Psychology* 3, 1 (2000): 49–71.

Prechtel, Martin. *Secrets of the Talking Jaguar*. New York: Jeremy P. Tarcher, 1999.

____. *The Disobedience of the Daughter of the Sun*. Berkeley, CA: North Atlantic Books, 2005.

____. *The Unlikely Peace at Cuchumaquic: The Parallel Lives of People as Plants; Keeping the Seeds Alive*. Berkeley: North Atlantic Books, 2012.

Rafael, Vicente. *White Love and Other Encounters in Filipino History*. Durham: Duke University Press, 2000.

Sarris, Greg. *Grand Avenue: A Novel in Stories*. London: Penguin Books, 1994.

___. *Mabel McKay: Weaving the Dream*. Berkeley: University of California Press, 1994.

___. *Watermelon Nights*. London: Penguin Books, 1998.

___. *How a Mountain Was Made*. 2012. Available online at http://greg-sarris.com/wp-content/uploads/2013/07/How-a-Mountain-Was-Made1.pdf (accessed 18 March 2016).

Strobel, Leny Mendoza. *Coming Full Circle: The Process of Decolonization among Post-1965 Filipino Americans*. Quezon City: Giraffe Books, 2001.

___. *A Book of Her Own: Words and Images to Honor the Babaylan*. San Francisco, CA: Tiboli Press, 2005.

___ (ed.). *Babaylan: Filipinos and the Call of the Indigenous*. Santa Rosa, CA: Center for Babaylan Studies, 2010.

___. "Summary Report: Second International Babaylan Conference." Available online at www.babaylan.net/events/2013-conference/summary-report/ (accessed 18 March 2016).

___. (ed. with Mendoza, Lily). *Back from the Crocodile's Belly: Philippines Babaylan Studies and the Struggle for Indigenous Memory*. Santa Rosa, CA: Center for Babaylan Studies, 2013.

Vizenor, Gerald. *Survivance: Narratives of Native Presence*. Lincoln: University of Nebraska Press, 2008.

Wilcken, Lane. *Filipino Tattoos Ancient to Modern*. Atglen, PA: Schiffer Publishing, Ltd., 2010.

HEALING

Recently Uncovered, Prescott National Forest by M. Jennifer Chandler

Healing
Our waters
Our selves; inside out
                    —Rachel Bagby

9

NAVAJO YOUTH

CULTIVATING HEALTHY RELATIONSHIPS THROUGH TRADITIONAL RECIPROCITY
MOLLY BIGKNIFE ANTONIO

Each individual participates in many relationships throughout life's journey. Reciprocity transpires between these relationships through the flow of giving and receiving. Whether a relationship occurs within one's own body, among humans, between humans and nature, or within nature itself, it has been my personal experience that Navajo (Diné) traditional teachings and practices dictate that reciprocal acts are sacred and essential for cultivating and maintaining balance and harmony within any relationship.

Navajo cultural teachings of reciprocity, which I refer to as "traditional reciprocity," are rooted in the Navajo creation and historical narrative.[1] The importance of the role of reciprocal relationships in promoting beauty and harmony is taught, reinforced, and "remembered"[2] through intergenerational sharing of these sacred narratives, through ceremonies,[3] and through what I describe as "right ways" of thinking, living, and connecting, which includes fostering healthy reciprocal relationships. Dr Gregory Cajete, a Native scholar from Santa Clara Pueblo and Dean of Native American Studies at the University of New Mexico, teaches that relationships from an Indigenous perspective are vast, and can include environment, guidance, kinship, diversity, special status, ethical models, clear roles, customs and practices, recognition, unique ways of learning, community work, and spirit, to name a few.[4] Thus, from an Indigenous point of view, nurturing a relationship through reciprocity positively affects and includes human and nonhuman relationships.

The Navajo believe that positive relationships promote healthy individuals, families, communities, and environments; therefore, traditional cultural teachings and values imparted to children, adolescents, and adults advocate that coherence within relationships must be maintained through reciprocal actions.[5] Sprinkling corn pollen towards the eastern horizon at dawn, giving corn pollen, white corn meal, or tobacco to the spirit of the plants before collecting their medicines, or providing food and drink to a guest are examples of personal offerings that can be presented as an exchange for the gifts that the day, the plant medicine, and the company are bringing to the individual. These seemingly simple acts of acknowledgment and giving stimulate positive energetic motion that promotes and nurtures harmony for humanity and our natural world.

I believe that Diné traditional teachings and practices of reciprocity help Navajo youth facilitate a state of balance and harmony, resulting in healthier relationships. To demonstrate this belief, this essay will present cultural teachings that inform the Navajo practice of traditional reciprocity in nurturing relationships, both human and nonhuman. Within this construct, I will share how Navajo reciprocity is anchored to a spiritual belief system that all things are connected and interrelated; thus, reciprocal action produces multidimensional effects that honor the past, encompass the present, and inform the future. I will also show that traditional reciprocity contains inherent qualities of gratitude and altruism that inform positive relationships. Finally, I will demonstrate through the experiential learning activity of bow making how traditional reciprocity emerges and guides Navajo youth in making decisions that benefit the self, the family, and the extended human and nonhuman communities.

As I introduce the reader to Navajo concepts and beliefs pertaining to reciprocity and its role in forming and reinforcing positive relationships, understand that many Navajo youth are learning these same concepts explicitly, experientially, and implicitly as they are submersed in their traditional cultural teachings and values from birth. To begin, a description of the ancestral homelands of the Navajo will now be presented, followed by samples of Diné cultural teachings that emphasize the value of positive interrelationships and the importance of reciprocity between these relationships.

All Things are Connected and Interrelated

I am a Shawnee woman who has lived on the Navajo Nation for over 20 years. My husband is Navajo and together we have raised our three children within this beautiful culture and landscape. It has been my experience living within the Navajo Nation that a correct name for the Navajo People is Nihokaa' Diyin Dine'é, which translates into "Earth Surface Holy People." They also refer to themselves as Diné and Navajo; I will use the two latter terms in this essay. The modern homelands of the Diné, called the Navajo Nation, are roughly located in the southwestern United States near the "four corners" area: where Colorado, New Mexico, Arizona, and Utah converge.[6] However, their ancestral landscape is called Dinétah and extends far beyond assigned Navajo Nation boundaries. Bordered by four sacred mountains that are located in Colorado, New Mexico, and Arizona, Dinétah is still recognized by the Diné as the current and true land base for the Navajo People.[7] The Navajo are intricately connected to this land and their traditional teachings express a belief that everything is alive and capable of conscious thought and interaction.[8] The late scholar and philosopher Vine Deloria, Jr., Standing Rock tribal member, concurs with this Indigenous belief in his book *God is Red: A Native View of Religion*. He states, "All inanimate entities have spirit and personality so that the mountains, rivers, waterfalls, even the continents of the earth itself have intelligence, knowledge, and the ability to communicate ideas."[9] Since relationships with both people and nature are conscious and interactive, Navajo traditional practices provide guidelines for thinking and living in ways intended to positively benefit all relationships, including guidelines for reciprocal interaction.[10] As I begin to examine the practice of traditional reciprocity, I will first explore the deep concept of "relationship" within Navajo cultural beliefs.

The traditional Navajo belief system teaches that humans, nature, and spirit are connected to each other.[11] When Indigenous Peoples assert that all things are connected, they definitively mean *everything*: people, all aspects of nature including animals, plants, wind, rocks, temperature, etc., and even a realm beyond the five senses: that of spirit, thought, and potential.[12] This multifaceted belief system can be summarized into the statement that human beings are intricately connected to all things through a complex web of interrelationships.[13] Evidence of complex interrelatedness within the natural systems of the world, including human dimensions and even spiritual connections, is also supported by the theories and research produced by physicist and ecological advocate Fritjof Capra[14] and his collaborative work with natural scientist Pier Luisi.[15] In their book *The Systems View of Life: A Unifying Vision* they state, "The systems view of life is an ecological view that is grounded, ultimately, in spiritual awareness. Connectedness, relationship, and community are fundamental concepts of ecology; and…are the essence of spiritual experience."[16] Traditional Diné beliefs support interrelatedness; therefore, I believe that knowledge of these human and nonhuman communal connections, as taught in Navajo culture, naturally promotes a sense of responsibility aimed at honoring and protecting the integrity of these relationships.[17] To demonstrate interrelatedness from a Diné perspective, I will explore the relationship humans have with nature. So intimate is the Diné perspective of our relationship to nature that traditional teachings reveal that human beings are not separate from nature: they *are* nature.[18] Traditional Diné practitioner, Annie Kahn, also known as "Flower That Speaks in a Pollen Way,"[19] teaches that "self is nature, is harmonious with the universe."[20] This embodiment of nature within the Navajo belief system, as expressed by Ms Kahn, will be expanded upon below using the following reflections: The first example is from a Beauty Way Curriculum handout and describes a Diné person as being "of nature," as well as "dressed with nature;" the second example, presented by Navajo traditional practitioner Harrison Jim, summarizes a traditional prayer that portrays a Diné person "becoming nature," physically, mentally, and spiritually. Both point to interrelationship and kinship between humans and the natural world.

For traditional Navajo people, nature is in intimate relationship within and around the individual. One selection describing this concept is revealed in a handout from the Navajo Department of Diné Education, Beauty Way Curriculum, which states:

> Our physical body is made of the four sacred elements: Mother Earth, air, water and fire. The blanket we wrap around us is Dawn. The moccasins we wear represent Dawn and Mother Earth. Our clothing is of dark clouds, our sash belts represent sunrays, our hair is of the "dark cascading rainfall" and is tied with a rainbow. This is our spiritual identity, our status as a child of divine nature.[21]

This passage shows a belief of spiritual connectedness, as well as kinship and lineage between humans, the earth, and the cosmos as its title states that the human being is the "Child of Mother Earth and Father Sky." Kinship between humans and nature is further emphasized in this example as it describes how humans are made of earthly elements—earth, fire, air, and water; and dressed in various attributes of earth and sky. This example from the Beauty Way Curriculum, which is still used in some classrooms on the Navajo Nation, implies that these connections and relationships are inherent, as well as divine. However, although our connections to all our relations are inherent, it has been my experience that Native people recognize the importance of also remembering and reinforcing these connections in a positive way through prayer, ceremony, and living in a good way. Traditional beliefs and practices suggest that connections and relationships can and need to be developed and nurtured.[22] The late Trudy Griffin-Pierce, an anthropologist who was allowed by several Diné traditional practitioners to study intimate ceremonial aspects of the Diné, wrote that the Navajo believe "no state of being is permanently fixed. Thus, beauty, balance, and orderliness are conditions that must be continuously recreated...[and] continually renewed."[23] Prayer and ceremony is one avenue used by the Diné to accomplish the renewal of balance and beauty while also reminding each participant that he or she is intimately connected to their natural and spiritual world. The next example provides a summary of a traditional Diné prayer, where the words in the prayer describe an individual intentionally embodying or "becoming" nature. I infer from this prayer that the physical, mental, and spiritual merging with nature positively acknowledges our inherent connection to nature, encouraging us to treat our relationships and the gifts they provide reverently and respectfully.

The words in the Diné prayer presented by Navajo traditional practitioner Harrison Jim describe a process where sacred corn pollen is "becoming" aspects of the individual saying the prayer. Mr Jim explains that the Diné words in this prayer translate as "corn pollen is becoming" the individual's feet, legs, torso, hands, face, voice, and mental plume emanating into the universe.[24] These words show me that through this prayer, corn pollen is becoming infused within the individual reciting the prayer. I will now reflect on the deeper cultural meaning behind corn pollen to show how the above example of humans and nature becoming fused together is significant to the importance of reciprocity and healthy relationships.

Traditional Reciprocity, Interrelationships, Lineage

Corn pollen, or tádidíín, is very sacred to the Diné and represents "hózhǫ́," or balance, health, happiness, and beauty.[25] Corn pollen can also represent light, life, and protection.[26] I suggest that the individual "becoming corn pollen" in the prayer is literally becoming hózhǫ́. I believe that to embody corn pollen physically, mentally, and spiritually, as communicated in the above, implies that this individual is consciously choosing to connect in a beneficial way with the self, with nature, and with the divine. The Navajo call this conscious positive path "walking in beauty"[27] or "hózhǫ́ǫgo naasháadooleeł." The concept of walking in beauty also dictates that reciprocity is being honored, in my opinion, because maintaining healthy relationships is a part of this path of hózhǫ́. Both examples of cultural teachings shared above provide a glimpse into the Navajo's relationship with nature in context with physical and spiritual aspects of Diné thinking and living. Additionally, because the above examples tie in with the traditional concept of hózhǫ́ǫgo naasháadooleeł, and consciously walking in beauty includes "right relationships through reciprocity," I suggest that the above passages directly correlate to the Diné concept of reciprocity. I will now examine the act of reciprocity from a Diné perspective and begin to show how this practice helps support healthy relationships in this culture.

As expressed above, Navajo culture acknowledges that all things are connected and their belief system allows for the embodiment of nature into their being. I believe this intimate connection between humans and nature encourages conscious positive interaction with all things, human and nonhuman. For the Diné, an important form of positive interaction includes the act of reciprocity: presenting an offering in exchange for receiving something in return.[28] Don Denetdeal, Professor of Diné Studies at Diné College on the Navajo Nation, shared with me that the Navajo "word for reciprocity and the word for making an offering are one and the same: that word is yeel." Mr Denetdeal explains that "yeel means giving something of personal value and in return, you receive." Further, "the recipient of an offering can be a person or all species and all nature: an herb, the air, water, Mother Earth, sky, sun, snake, or horned toad, for example. Reciprocity, or yeel, covers it all."[29] The fact that the recipient of this reciprocal act of giving an offering can be human or nonhuman, as shared by Mr Denetdeal, shows that the Navajo concept of maintaining healthy relationships transcends human relationships and includes relationships in nature. Also, a relationship with the divine is implied because the offering being made is a "vehicle," as described by Mr Denetdeal, which connects us to the sacred and to all relations.[30] These reciprocal connections encourage health, wellness, and balance in our relationships. Conversely, disharmony, such as illness or environmental degradation, can emerge when "taking" outweighs "giving back." This belief is reinforced further through Navajo traditional practitioner Emerson Gorman. Mr Gorman explained to me that the main reason we make offerings is because:

> [W]e want to have good health and receive good thought, thinking, planning and have good faith, and structure of ceremony. If we do that our children and grandchildren grow healthy, even amongst negativity and problems. They are protected in a way, connected to spirits, holy beings.[31]

So I deduce from Mr Gorman's and Mr Denetdeal's teachings that making an offering, or reciprocity, positively affects physical and spiritual relationships, human and nonhuman relationships, as well as current and future generations. Both Mr Denetdeal and Mr Gorman agree that any time you receive something from nature or ask for help from a traditional practitioner, an offering has to be made as an exchange. Offerings will now be described further, because examining these "vehicles" can give additional insight to the Navajo concept of complex interrelationships with human and nonhuman relations.

As revealed above by Mr Denetdeal, an offering includes anything of value to an individual; however, both Mr Denetdeal and Mr Gorman shared that different offerings are appropriate for different situations. Depending on the situation, an appropriate offering might be monetary, traditional food, water, or sacred beads such as white shell, turquoise, abalone shell, black jet, or coral. The situation may also call for tobacco or corn pollen. This practice of making an offering, or yeel, is a positive reciprocal action which, according to the Navajo and this author, is an integral part of maintaining balance and promoting positive relationships. I do not give context for identifying the specific offering that is appropriate for each given situation, as my main focus for this essay is to acknowledge that it is the "reciprocal act" that nourishes positive, healthy relationship through conscious connection and exchange. However, I do want to share more information about corn pollen, which is commonly used as an offering in Diné culture. I believe the reciprocal act of offering corn pollen serves as a multifaceted example of how yeel acknowledges the interconnection of all relationships while, at the same time, acknowledging our relationship to "lineage;" simultaneously making a positive connection in the present, while honoring past relations and informing future relationships. I will now demonstrate how kinship and lineage are woven into traditional practices and how the act of offering corn pollen as yeel honors one's relations in Navajo culture.

The Diné consider corn pollen an appropriate offering to humans and to nature in many, but not all, reciprocal situations. For example, it is my experience that it is appropriate to sprinkle a prayer offering of corn pollen into the air towards the morning dawn in exchange for blessings throughout the new day, or when collecting plants for medicine; conversely, it is not appropriate to offer corn pollen into a fire when praying at the fireplace. A more appropriate offering in the latter situation would be juniper or cedar leaves. In either situation, both the offering and its intended purpose are derived from conscious thought and action rooted in traditional reciprocity. The act of making an offering acknowledges relationships, and a Diné cultural teaching that addresses relationships and kinship is called "k'é."[32] The concept of k'é is multigenerational, which includes the past: knowing where you come from; the present: knowing one's relatives and walking in beauty; and the future: honoring one's relationships appropriately so that future generations can benefit from the beauty, balance, and harmony produced when k'é is honored and practiced.[33] Harmonious relationships are extremely important to the Navajo. Anthropologist and professor Dr John R. Farella studied Navajo culture extensively. Dr Farella discussed the concept of relationships with one of his Diné elder consultants, Grey Mustache, who shared: "the questions about these things and all else will ultimately be questions about kinship, how we are related to the beginnings."[34] From this statement and from his extensive work with Grey Mustache, Dr Farella concluded that underlying the Navajo belief system is a "unifying principle…[which is] there is only one type of question to ask about important matters, and that is the question of kinship, or relatedness."[35] Reciprocity is a part of k'é relational teachings and offering corn pollen is a reciprocal act.[36] Drawing from the cultural teachings of "all things are connected and interrelated," I postulate that corn pollen, as well as any offering, has its own k'é relations because it has its own lineage. This is important, as I will explain, because it further solidifies the power that reciprocity has in connecting all relationships and positively affecting the health of those relationships.

The Diné concept of k'é encourages healthy relationships and, as I have explained, k'é relationships occur in the present, reach into the past, and affect the future; thus, relationships have lineage. Given that traditional Navajo relations include human and nonhuman entities, I surmise that nonhuman entities also have lineage. Lineage of a nonhuman entity becomes obvious when you think of a tree releasing a seed and that seed later producing another tree. Corn pollen also has lineage, both historical and biological.

The fact that corn pollen is mentioned in Diné creation narratives indicates that corn and corn pollen have been integral in the culture for a very long time;[37] they have a history and lineage with the culture. There is also the biological lineage for corn pollen: a corn plant grows and releases pollen, which pollinates a corn plant, producing an ear of corn with seeds that can be planted to grow more corn. However, I believe that corn pollen has a less obvious aspect of lineage that demonstrates intricate interrelationships dictated by the Diné belief system around reciprocity, and therefore shows that while making an offering such as corn pollen is a reciprocal act, this action also strengthens healthy relationships on multiple levels.

When a person is making an offering of corn pollen to nature or the divine, a relationship is made between the person and the offering. There is also a lineage leading up to this reciprocal interaction. Exploring the *lineage of the corn pollen* brings to light the vast reality of interconnectedness attached to the corn pollen that the individual is holding in his or her hand. I will describe this stream of lineage, based on my personal experience of being submersed in Navajo culture for over two decades. Before the birth of the corn pollen, corn had to be grown from corn seed. This corn seed came from a previous harvest, and was dried, cleaned, stored, and eventually planted. Before the corn could be planted, a cornfield had to be identified and prepared. Preparations included songs and prayers, as well as weeding and preparing the soil, then planting, watering, and tending. After the corn pollen was produced within the corn plant tassels, it had to be harvested, dried, and cleaned. Next, it needed to be stored. A traditional container for storing corn pollen is a corn pollen bag sewn from deer hide. The lineage of the corn pollen bag, and how it is traditionally constructed, has its own proper teachings, songs, and prayers. For example, to acquire the hide, first the deer had to be hunted in a way that includes its own traditional lineage of protocols concerning appropriate songs and prayers, preparation, timing, harvesting, and processing. Even the teachings of how a specific offering should be made could be called the "lineage of the process of making an offering."

All of the lineages offered above are guided by their own lineage of cultural protocols rooted in the historical and creation narratives of the Diné. I offer this portrayal of lineage from a Diné perspective to give the reader insight into the complexity of connectedness that all things have to one another. Moreover, by incorporating traditional practices into one's life, an individual is honoring and validating the lineage of these narratives, their ancestors, their culture, and all of the interrelationships therein. Referencing corn pollen shows how an offering reaches many layers of lineage and relationships. I contend that consciously making an offering from this place of interrelationship can release deep feelings of gratitude, and that gratitude and altruism are natural expressions contained within traditional reciprocity. I will explore this statement and reveal how gratitude and altruism emerging from reciprocal action inform Navajo youth in facilitating and promoting healthy relationships.

Navajo Youth, Traditional Reciprocity, and Healthy Relationships

Based on my lived experience with Navajo culture and Navajo youth, and my investigative research into Diné beliefs and practices, it has been my experience that traditional reciprocity contains inherent qualities of gratitude and altruism. I also contend that gratitude and altruism anchored in traditional practices are transformative and help develop personal wellbeing, as well as positive human and nonhuman relationships in the lives of Navajo youth. Before transformation occurs, however, I assert that these beliefs are first internalized and integrated into the self. It is through this internalization that gratitude and altruism arise, which I believe fuel reciprocity as well as promote positive forward thinking for the benefit of future generations. Navajo teachings and western studies support this idea, as I will explain below. First I will look at how Navajo youth are exposed to traditional concepts and practices and how these become embodied, promoting holistic wellness. Then I will present western research pertaining to gratitude and altruism to bridge the two constructs.

Navajo youth exposed to traditional teachings and practices are taught reciprocity within a structure of being connected to all things, as demonstrated above. They learn traditional reciprocity from adults, elders, and peers who engage in traditional practices.

From the time they were small, these young people were exposed to traditional etiquettes, cultural narratives, ceremonies, and traditional daily life practices.[38] They acquired teachings explicitly, as adults, elders, and peers model traditional practices; experientially, by practicing these teachings themselves; and implicitly, as the subtleties of cultural teachings become internalized and seated within the individual: fusing with their being.[39] Cultural teachings, such as those shared in the previous sections, are holistic: they integrate within the self mentally, physically, socially, emotionally, and spiritually, creating balance and harmony within the individual.[40] According to Diné teachings, it is from this integrated place of harmonious being that an individual is more likely to positively affect outward relationships, as this next example will reveal.

A handout titled "Ádaa'áhashyą́" from the Navajo Department of Diné Education Beauty Way Curriculum[41] summarizes the five quadrants of the holistic self mentioned above, emphasizing that mental, physical, social, emotional, and spiritual health all contribute to balance and wholeness while promoting health and harmony within the individual. There is no direct English translation for the title of the handout, Ádaa'áhashyą́; however, it embodies the Navajo teaching for taking care of oneself first so that one can be healthy and in turn help others effectively. I suggest that this example encourages an individual to embody holistic wellness, and in doing so he or she will naturally become an asset to human and nonhuman relationships. In this section, I presented a framework whereby Navajo children and youth exposed to traditional beliefs and practices receive and integrate cultural knowledge holistically into their being. If we reflect back in this essay, we see that traditional reciprocity is informed by these cultural teachings; therefore, it is likely that traditional reciprocity becomes embodied within the holistic individual as well. I believe that when an act of reciprocity is made from this holistic, integrated state of being, connected to all one's relations, feelings of gratitude and altruism emerge. It is also my belief that feelings of gratitude and altruism nurture and promote healthy relationships with the self, the community, and with nature. There is agreement in western research that supports my latter conviction, as I will now explain.

Through their collaborative research on gratitude and wellbeing, Professor of Psychiatry and of Internal Medicine, Dr Randy A. Sansone, and Family Medicine practitioner Dr Lori A. Sansone, present one definition of gratitude as "the appreciation of what is valuable and meaningful to oneself; it is a general state of thankfulness and/or appreciation."[42] They also indicate that studies agree upon "an association between gratitude and a sense of overall well being."[43] JoAnn "Grif" Alspach, RN, MSN, EdD, and editor of *Critical Care Nurse*, investigated gratitude research pertaining to health benefits and also found that "[i]n addition to enhancing one's general sense of well-being, those who engage in practicing gratitude report significantly greater happiness, optimism, and satisfaction with their lives, greater progress in attaining important life goals, [and a] higher frequency of feeling loved."[44] Further, psychologists Jeffrey J. Froh, Giacomo Bono, and Robert Emmons conducted several studies pertaining to gratitude, specifically with adolescents. In their article "Being Grateful is Beyond Good Manners: Gratitude and Motivation to Contribute to Society among Early Adolescents," their findings showed that although more studies were needed on the subject of gratitude and adolescents, "[g]ratitude may help youth foster prosocial relationships, self-esteem and competence, well-being, and purpose in life" and "[g]ratitude...may aid adolescents' development by fostering both a general sense of connectedness to others, the community and society at large."[45] Sansone and Sansone's, and Alspach's, research documents gratitude's effect towards enhancing one's wellbeing; and Froh, Bono, and Emmons' studies found gratitude as a factor for increased positivity in adolescents within the self and towards the human community.[46] The above references support my belief that gratitude promotes healthy relationships, with the self and the human community, though none addressed the effects of gratitude towards nature. However, for the purposes of this essay, since nature *is* considered a part of a Navajo youth's community, I argue that these findings could be extrapolated to include nature as well for this population. As stated previously, these selected studies reveal positive effects of gratitude upon the individual and his or her relationship with others. It was also found that the practice of gratitude advanced an adolescent's "purpose in life."[47] The fact that gratitude created positive effects beyond the self shows altruistic qualities and, because it informed the young person's outlook on the future in a positive way, I infer that gratitude and altruism help adolescents make conscious decisions and actions that positively affect relationships in the present and in the future. Support for this inference comes from Froh, Bono, and Emmons through their statements "Compelling evidence suggests that gratitude evolved to stimulate not only direct reciprocal altruism but also 'upstream reciprocity'"[48] and "Gratitude...may ignite in youth a motivation for 'upstream generativity' whereby its experience contributes to a desire to give back to their neighborhood, community, and world."[49] Recall that traditional reciprocity involves conscious positive thought and action intended to nourish healthy relationships, and relationships from an Indigenous belief system include human and non-human entities, including spirit. Traditional reciprocity was also shown to be multigenerational in its consideration of k'é, and bidirectional in acknowledging the integrated relationship of past, present, and future. Furthermore, gratitude and altruism could be described as byproducts of traditional reciprocal thoughts and actions, positively influencing multigenerational and bidirectional relationships. This information supports my argument that when Navajo youth embody traditional reciprocity, healthy relationships emerge. To demonstrate this belief, I will now share my experience with Navajo youth on the Navajo Nation in the context of an experiential learning setting.

As revealed above, Navajo youth learn cultural teachings and practices explicitly, experientially, and implicitly. It has been my experience that Navajo youth who have been raised with traditional teachings and practices also embody respect and reverence for these traditions. They have seen firsthand that these practices have had positive effects on their human and nonhuman relationships, therefore I believe that through witnessing and experiencing these positive effects, Navajo youth are more likely to engage in traditional reciprocal actions so that relationships remain healthy. I can personally attest to the positive effects of traditional reciprocity upon Navajo youth. For over two decades, I have been engaged with traditional Navajo youth in a multitude of environmental and cultural experiential learning settings. Experiential learning activities included service learning projects geared towards helping elders or the land, as well as cultural enhancement projects such as pressure flaking (a stone shaping technique), medicine plant harvesting, wild horse tracking, and traditional bow making. As the youth engaged in these activities, I observed traditional reciprocal actions that embodied multigenerational and cultural awareness. Although I could give specific examples of youth engaging in traditional reciprocity in all of these past activities, I will use the bow making workshops to demonstrate traditional reciprocity enacted by Navajo youth, and how this practice strengthens their relationships with human and nonhuman relations.

Bow making is a traditional art form within many Indigenous cultures, including the Navajo culture. Not every tribal member knows how to make a bow, so creating a workshop focused on traditional bow making helps youth participants experience and learn this traditional utilitarian art form. On several occasions, I was involved in bringing Navajo youth and bow makers together to learn from one another. Although the bow makers for these events, Lonnie Hamilton and Andrew Bonifazi, were teaching how to make a Muscogee (Creek) style bow, the approach and process were successful in revealing cultural connectedness and reciprocity from a Navajo perspective, as I will explain. Before the youth started working on a bow, offerings were given in the form of prayers, corn pollen, and traditional tobacco. The words emanating from these prayers expressed gratitude to nature for giving the wood for the bow; to the elders for passing on these traditions; for the teachers coming to teach the youth; for the participants and their part in bringing new life to the wood in the form of a bow; and for each participant's intention to use the bow in a respectful way and teach the process of bow making to someone else in the future. The youth were told by the teachers that similar offerings were made when the wood was harvested for bow staves, and when these teachers learned from their teacher, the late Muscogee elder and master bow maker Mike Berryhill. It was expressed that prayers and offerings would also be made prior to using the bow, whether in hunting or ceremonially. Throughout the bow making workshop I saw deep relationships in the form of gratitude, centeredness, care, and personal accomplishment emerge between each young person and his or her bow. Altruism emerged, as well; some of the Navajo youth intended to give the newly constructed bow away to a sibling or elder, and one young man made a bow, which would be used specifically for ceremonies, for his father. All of the youth intended to share what they learned with others, ensuring that traditional knowledge in the form of bow making continued into the future. I share this experience of traditional bow making as an excellent example portraying Navajo youth practicing traditional reciprocity, while honoring their past, present, and future. This example has also brought us full circle as I bring these teachings to a close.

Conclusion

This essay explored Diné teachings and practices of traditional reciprocity and how this author has experienced and witnessed the embodiment of traditional reciprocity by Diné youth on the Navajo Nation in cultivating healthy relationships. I have uncovered how relationships, from an Indigenous cultural perspective, encompass human and nonhuman entities and reach from the present bilaterally: into the past and towards the future. Using the bow making workshop as an example, I shared my experience with Navajo youth nurturing healthy relationships through traditional reciprocal processes. These personal experiences informed my belief that Navajo youth engaging in traditional reciprocity help create and promote balance and harmony for the self, the community, and for the natural world. My findings were supported and informed through direct communication with Diné traditional practitioners, through my literary research of Indigenous and Navajo cultural perspectives and practices, and through my literary research of non-Native pedagogy pertaining to interconnectedness, gratitude, and altruism. Future research related to my presentation could examine how reciprocity is viewed and practiced by Navajo youth who did not grow up exposed to traditional beliefs and practices and the effect of reciprocity on relationships. Gratitude studies, such as the non-Native examples presented in this chapter, could also specifically examine

Indigenous cohorts. Through this composition, it was my intention to provide the reader a glimpse into this truly precious culture and show how Navajo youth, through positive reciprocal action, are creating positive relationships for themselves and future generations. In closing, I want to share that Diné culture and language are beautiful and complex. Translating Diné concepts and words accurately into the English language can be challenging. I hope as a non-Navajo that I preserved the integrity of the Diné teachings and expressions presented in this chapter.

Notes

1   Farella, *The Main Stalk: A Synthesis of Navajo Philosophy*; Griffin-Pierce, *Earth is My Mother, Sky is My Father: Space, Time, and Astronomy in Navajo Sandpaintings*; Zolbrod, *Diné Bahane': The Navajo Creation Story.*

2   Cajete, *Native Science: Natural Laws of Interdependence*, 284.

3   Benally, "Navajo Philosophy of Learning and Pedagogy;" Cajete, *Native Science: Natural Laws of Interdependence*; Griffin-Pierce, *Earth is My Mother, Sky is My Father: Space, Time, and Astronomy in Navajo Sandpaintings*; Mack et al., "Effective Practices for Creating Transformative Informal Science Education Programs Ground in Native Ways of Knowing;" Mehl-Madrona, *Narrative Medicine: The Use of History and Story in the Healing Process.*

4   Cajete, *Native Science: Natural Laws of Interdependence.*

5   Griffin-Pierce, *Earth is My Mother, Sky is My Father: Space, Time, and Astronomy in Navajo Sandpaintings.*

6   Bigknife, *Creating an Indigenous Experiential Learning Model.*

7   Bigknife, *Creating an Indigenous Experiential Learning Model*; Farella, *The Main Stalk: A Synthesis of Navajo Philosophy*; Griffin-Pierce, *Earth is My Mother, Sky is My Father: Space, Time, and Astronomy in Navajo Sandpaintings.*

8   Deloria and Wildcat, *Power and Place: Indian Education in America*; Farella, *The Main Stalk: A Synthesis of Navajo Philosophy*; Griffin-Pierce, *Earth is My Mother, Sky is My Father: Space, Time, and Astronomy in Navajo Sandpaintings.*

9   Deloria, *God is Red: A Native View of Religion*, 151.

10 Benally, "Navajo Philosophy of Learning and Pedagogy;" Cajete, *Native Science: Natural Laws of Interdependence*; Griffin-Pierce, *Earth is My Mother, Sky is My Father: Space, Time, and Astronomy in Navajo Sandpaintings.*

11 Benally, "Navajo Philosophy of Learning and Pedagogy;" Farella, *The Main Stalk: A Synthesis of Navajo Philosophy*; Griffin-Pierce, *Earth is My Mother, Sky is My Father: Space, Time, and Astronomy in Navajo Sandpaintings.*

12 Cajete, *Native Science: Natural Laws of Interdependence*; Deloria, *God is Red: A Native View of Religion.*

13 Cajete, *Native Science: Natural Laws of Interdependence*; Deloria and Wildcat, *Power and Place: Indian Education in America*; Mack et al., "Effective Practices for Creating Transformative Informal Science Education Programs Ground in Native Ways of Knowing."

14 Capra, *The Web of Life.*

15 Capra and Luisi, *The Systems View of Life: A Unifying Vision.*

16 Ibid., 70.

17   Benally, "Navajo Philosophy of Learning and Pedagogy;" Farella, *The Main Stalk: A Synthesis of Navajo Philosophy*; Griffin-Pierce, *Earth is My Mother, Sky is My Father: Space, Time, and Astronomy in Navajo Sandpaintings.*

18   Capra, *The Web of Life*; Farella, *The Main Stalk: A Synthesis of Navajo Philosophy*; Grandbois and Sanders, "The Resilience of Native American Elders;" Perrone et al., *Medicine Women, Curanderas, and Women Doctors.*

19   Perrone et al., *Medicine Women, Curanderas, and Women Doctors*, 29.

20   Ibid., 38.

21   Navajo Department of Diné Education, "I'm a child of Mother Earth and Father Sky," 1.

22   Cajete, *Native Science: Natural Laws of Interdependence*; Griffin-Pierce, *Earth is My Mother, Sky is My Father: Space, Time, and Astronomy in Navajo Sandpaintings*; Mack et al., "Effective Practices for Creating Transformative Informal Science Education Programs Ground in Native Ways of Knowing."

23   Griffin-Pierce, *Earth is My Mother, Sky is My Father: Space, Time, and Astronomy in Navajo Sandpaintings*, 25.

24   Jim, Interviewed by Molly Bigknife Antonio.

25   Benally, "Navajo Philosophy of Learning and Pedagogy."

26   Griffin-Pierce, *Earth is My Mother, Sky is My Father: Space, Time, and Astronomy in Navajo Sandpaintings.*

27   Eason and Robbins, "Walking in Beauty: An American Indian Perspective on Social Justice;" Perrone et al., *Medicine Women, Curanderas, and Women Doctors.*

28   Griffin-Pierce, *Earth is My Mother, Sky is My Father: Space, Time, and Astronomy in Navajo Sandpaintings.*

29   Denetdeal, Interviewed by Molly Bigknife Antonio.

30   Ibid.

31   Gorman, Interviewed by Molly Bigknife Antonio.

32   Benally, "Navajo Philosophy of Learning and Pedagogy;" Griffin-Pierce, *Earth is My Mother, Sky is My Father: Space, Time, and Astronomy in Navajo Sandpaintings.*

33   Benally, "Navajo Philosophy of Learning and Pedagogy."

34   Farella, *The Main Stalk: A Synthesis of Navajo Philosophy*, 178.

35   Ibid., 178.

36   Raitt, "The Ritual Meaning of Corn Pollen among the Navajo Indians."

37   Capelin, Emily Fay. "Source of the Sacred: Navajo Corn Pollen, Hanne' Baadahoste'igii (Very Sacred Story);" Wyman, *Blessingway*; Zolbrod, *Diné Bahane': The Navajo Creation Story.*

38   Cajete, *Look to the Mountain: An Ecology of Indigenous Education*; Cajete, *Native Science: Natural Laws of Interdependence.*

39   Bigknife, *Creating an Indigenous Experiential Learning Model*; Cajete, *Native Science: Natural Laws of Interdependence*; Deloria and Wildcat, *Power and Place: Indian Education in America.*

40   Bigknife, *Creating an Indigenous Experiential Learning Model.*

41   Navajo Department of Diné Education, "Ádaa'áhashyá."

42   Sansone and Sansone, "Gratitude and Well Being: The Benefits of Appreciation," 18.

43   Ibid., 18.

44   Alspach, "Extending the Tradition of Giving Thanks: Recognizing the Health Benefits of Gratitude," 13.

45   Froh et al., "Being Grateful is Beyond Good Manners: Gratitude and Motivation to Contribute to Society among Early Adolescents," 145.

46   Sansone and Sansone, "Gratitude and Well Being: The Benefits of Appreciation;" Alspach, "Extending the Tradition of Giving Thanks: Recognizing the Health Benefits of Gratitude;" Froh et al., "Being Grateful is Beyond Good Manners: Gratitude and Motivation to Contribute to Society among Early Adolescents."

47   Froh, et al, "Being Grateful is Beyond Good Manners: Gratitude and Motivation to Contribute to Society among Early Adolescents," 145.

48   Ibid., 147.

49   Ibid., 144.

References

Alspach, Grif. "Extending the Tradition of Giving Thanks: Recognizing the Health Benefits of Gratitude." *Critical Care Nurse*, 29, 6 (2009): 12–18.

Benally, Herbert J. "Navajo Philosophy of Learning and Pedagogy." *Journal of Navajo Education*, 12, 1 (1994): 23–31.

Bigknife Antonio, Molly. *Creating an Indigenous Experiential Learning Model*. Master's Thesis, Prescott College, 2006.

Cajete, Gregory. *Look to the Mountain: An Ecology of Indigenous Education*. Skyland, NC: Kivaki Press, Inc., 1994.

Cajete, Gregory. *Native Science: Natural Laws of Interdependence*. Santa Fe, NM: Clear Light Publishers, 2000.

Capelin, Emily Fay. "Source of the Sacred: Navajo Corn Pollen, Hanne' Baadahoste'igii (Very Sacred Story)." Master's Thesis, Colorado College, 2009.

Capra, Fritjof. *The Web of Life*. New York: Anchor Books, 1996.

Capra, Fritjof and Pier Luigi Luisi. *The Systems View of Life: A Unifying Vision*. Cambridge, England: Cambridge University Press, 2014.

Deloria, Vine, Jr. *God is Red: A Native View of Religion*. Golden, CO: Fulcrum Resources, 1994.

Deloria, Vine, Jr. and Daniel Wildcat. *Power and Place: Indian Education in America*. Golden, CO: Fulcrum Resources, 2001.

Denetdeal, Don. Interviewed by Molly Bigknife Antonio. Window Rock, AZ, 2014.

Eason, Evan Allen and Rockey Robbins. "Walking in Beauty: An American Indian Perspective on Social Justice." *Counseling and Values*, 57, 1 (2012): 18–23.

Farella, John R. *The Main Stalk: A Synthesis of Navajo Philosophy*. Tucson: University of Arizona Press, 1990.

Froh, Jeffrey J., Giacomo Bono, and Robert Emmons. "Being Grateful is Beyond Good Manners: Gratitude and Motivation to Contribute to Society among Early Adolescents." *Motivation and Emotion*, 34, 2 (2010): 144–157.

Gorman, Emerson. Interviewed by Molly Bigknife Antonio. Window Rock, AZ, 2014.

Grandbois, Donna M. and Greg F. Sanders. "The Resilience of Native American Elders." *Issues of Mental Health Nursing*, 30, 9 (2009): 569–580.

Griffin-Pierce, Trudy. *Earth is My Mother, Sky is My Father: Space, Time, and Astronomy in Navajo Sandpaintings*. Albuquerque, NM: University of New Mexico Press, 1995.

Jim, Harrison. Interviewed by Molly Bigknife Antonio. Fort Defiance, AZ, 2009.

Mack, Elizabeth, Helen Augare, Linda Different Cloud-Jones, et al. "Effective Practices for Creating Transformative Informal Science Education Programs Grounded in Native Ways of Knowing." *Cultural Studies of Science Education*, 7, 1 (2012): 49–70.

Mehl-Madrona, Lewis. *Narrative Medicine: The Use of History and Story in the Healing Process*. Rochester, VT: Bear & Company, 2007.

Navajo Department of Diné Education. "Ádaa'áhashyá" (handout courtesy of the Beauty Way Curriculum). Window Rock, AZ: Navajo Department of Diné Education, 1990.

Navajo Department of Diné Education. "I'm a Child of Mother Earth and Father Sky" (handout courtesy of the Beauty Way Curriculum). Window Rock, AZ: Navajo Department of Diné Education, 1990.

Perrone, Bobette, Henrietta Stockel, and Victoria Krueger. *Medicine Women, Curanderas, and Women Doctors*. Norman, OK: University of Oklahoma Press, 1989.

Raitt, Thomas M. "The Ritual Meaning of Corn Pollen among the Navajo Indians." *Religious Studies* 23, 44 (1987): 523–530.

Sansone, Randy A. and Lori A. Sansone. "Gratitude and Well Being: The Benefits of Appreciation." *Psychiatry* 7, 11 (2010): 18–22.

Wyman, Leland C. *Blessingway.* Tucson: University of Arizona Press, 1970.

Zolbrod, Paul G. *Diné Bahane': The Navajo Creation Story.* Albuquerque: University of New Mexico Press, 1987.

10

A Yinyang, Ecocritical Fabulation On *Doctor Who*

Ju-Pong Lin

I stand at the edge where earth touches ocean
where the two overlap
a gentle coming together
at other times and places a violent clash.

—Gloria Anzaldúa[1]

Anzaldúa was one of the "women on the edge of transformation" I
met as a young, anti-racist activist organizing the national conference,
"Parallels and Intersections: Racism and Other Forms of Oppression"
with the Women Against Racism Committee in Iowa City, Iowa.
These few lines from the opening poem in *Borderlands/La Frontera*
weave a world view in which the healing from wounds of social injustice and of environmental damage are intertwined. An immigrant from
Taiwan, perpetual migrant (more than 25 relocations in 53 years) and
inhabiter of marginal spaces myself, I found my own voice by listening
to the courageous voice of Anzaldúa and many other voices gathered in
the seminal text she co-edited, *This Bridge Called My Back* and *Making
Face, Making Soul: Haciendo Caras: Creative and Critical Perspectives by
Feminists of Color.*[2] I invoke these feminists of color to stand with me,
as I "stand on the edge where earth touches ocean," in the struggle

for global justice and the healing of self and earth. I will argue for bridging—or *a*bridging—the academic–activist debate and for *doing* ecocriticism as praxis and advocacy. I investigate the potential for a decolonial, ecocritical practice grounded in a non-Western epistemology (specifically Daoism), theorized from the borderlands between cultures and embodied in the margins between spiritual, rational, emotional, and ethical spaces. In solidarity with the global indigenous resurgence movement and the earth on which we all depend, drawing on the collective wisdom of the "blessed unrest,"[3] I join the movement for ethical responsibility to transform the destructive force that humans have become to the planet.

My fabulation[4] circles around "The Beast Below," the opening episode of Season 8 of the BBC series, *Doctor Who*.[5] The Doctor, a space traveler in his ninth incarnation as a Time Lord, breathlessly encapsulates the situation at the beginning of the show—the flight of the human race from earth. "It's the 29th century, solar flares roast the earth and the entire human race packs its bags and moves out – whole nations migrating to the stars, searching the stars for a new home."[6] Not only does the whole race flee the planet, but they flee by way of a post-WWII construction of nationhood seemingly untouched by the ravages of time. The episode opens with a starry sky through which the British Empire, ensconced in a metropolis-sized starship emblazoned with the Union Jack, aimlessly floats. The Doctor and his companion arrive on the starship to find the nation in the grips of a collective, perpetual amnesia; what is the horror they keep electing to forget? (And elect they do, via a video-voting booth in which adults of age are made to see the truth, and make a choice, the "forget" button or the "protest.")

The whole of imperial Britain in space, wrapped in parasitic relationships with a living, non-human body, bio-techno-interspecies mash up? This episode provokes all kinds of questions about power, complicity, coloniality, what it means to be human or alien—an ideal text with which to examine the intersection of questions that have haunted me for the past few years.

Before diving into the unpacking of this particular episode of *Doctor Who*, I want to "place" myself and name the brambly margins whence

I come to this work. My younger son, a big fan of *Doctor Who*, would entice me away from my study of postcolonial ecocriticism to watch the new series. Naturally, I began to look at the Doctor through the framework of postcolonialism and ecological issues. For many so called Third World and indigenous communities, colonialism, the despoliation of homelands, cultural theft, and economic confiscation are inextricably linked. "Environmentalism of the poor," as Rob Nixon has called it,[7] does not separate subjugation of humans; they are profoundly entwined. "Given the ample body of scholarship on nature and empire, we must ask, why are environmental concerns often understood as separate from postcolonial ones?" wrote the editors of *Postcolonial Ecologies: Literatures of the Environment*.[8]

In the United States, all of us who are not indigenous to this land suffer from amnesia of the conquest by which our privilege was seized. We are blind to the present deplorable conditions suffered by indigenous people, while we appropriate traditional knowledge to heal our bodies. In this climate, I take up ecocriticism as an act of resistance, and imagination as a practice of creative healing. As for my approach of synthesizing theoretical, critical, and creative methodologies, I will borrow the phrase of ecocritic Patrick Murphy and call myself a "playful fabulist" in this endeavor.

> I must also embrace my role as a playful fabulist who critiques literature and weaves ecocritical theory and criticism into fabulations of how society might embrace the wild knowledge of this world's multitudinous contingencies to become ecologically literate and do justice to each other and the world in which we live and die.[9]

I draw from the Third World feminist insights of Chandra Mohanty, Gloria Anzaldúa, Chela Sandoval, Papusa Molina, and many others, as well as the work of Linda Tuhiwai Smith and other indigenous scholars and activists. These scholars understood the naming of decentered places, and the narrating of particular journeys, to be an integral part of an anti-colonial process. Through telling our stories, making new theory, seeing correspondences between our stories, we build coalitions and we re-claim the world from Western eyes.

I came to learn about postcolonialism first as an activist, then as an artist–educator, and most recently as a scholar. Pregnancy and mother-hood led me into the most generative period of my life, then marriage sent my activist–artist–radical self underground, and I found that I had allowed a soccer-mom persona to possess me. Now undergoing an exor-cism, I am joining my students in critical learning, reflecting critically on my own personal history, and what I have inherited of the colonial history of Taiwan. In the process, I am developing a critical–creative–decolonial practice and working in solidarity with indigenous commu-nities for sovereignty and ecological and cultural health.

Who am I?

> I was born on an island
> my family called *taipuk*,
> the place my body knew as "home,"
> an ocean's width away from the place i now
> call home—
> eldest daughter of a farmer become scientist,
> first of 3 who came through my mother,
> and she through hers, 7 generations
> of island dwellers.

> i learned to walk in the fertile dirt
> of taiwan, at the feet of my amah—
> one who birthed my father alone
> near the peanut field, the other
> a widow whose brick factory held her
> family together; warehouse become hospital
> when the Japanese dropped bombs.

> i know these stories from my mom,
> reluctant mother become career-woman,
> reluctant child witness

who escaped from hiding too soon, whose
eyes widened at the sight of bloody limbs
the **wound** of conquest seared into her child's heart.

i know from her telling;
i know from listening—love
lost between mother and daughter and
daughter and father…love lost between
generations was confiscated, stories buried
when our mother tongue was disallowed.

I am an artist. listener. learner. writer.
recovering lost stories,
lost love.[10]

In my early days as an anti-oppression activist and educator, I began
to examine the effects of assimilation on my identity and my view of
the world. At the time I didn't have the language or the framework to
understand that assimilationist immigration policies are bound up with
colonialism.

Iowa City, 1986–1989
In the little yellow bungalow that housed the Women's Center in Iowa City,
wounded women sat in circles and asked each other, "how were you hurt?" We
listened to each other's stories and told each other that we mattered. "You don't
have to relive your family's trauma. You're strong, and you can heal." I stumbled
into this house after burrowing myself in a tiny studio apartment for a year of
writing bad checks and battling an unshakeable depression. Tiny as it was, the
apartment had a luxuriously spacious bathroom with a claw foot tub just my
size. I got through the year canvassing for Greenpeace. I got through the long
days of getting pummeled by righteous anti-environmentalists by thinking
about the long soak in the tub awaiting me. On one of my canvassing days, the
little yellow house beckoned me inside, where a circle of wild women motioned
me to sit. They were holding each other, black, Chicano, white, Asian, mixed
race, straight and queer. "The master's tools will never dismantle the master's
house," they said, quoting Audre Lorde.[11] "You are not alone."

At the height of the debates about identity politics, some of us were talking weekly in this little house, about the intersection of the various forms of oppression we experienced. We realized that similar conversations were happening at lots of kitchen tables and community rooms across the country, so we *organized* a national conference called "Parallels and Intersections: Racism and Other Forms of Oppression" in 1989. "Intersectionality" is now a hot buzz word with this generation's feminists, attributed to Kimberle Crenshaw.[12] I do not want to dispute the origins of the term, but I feel it's only the feminist thing to do to link that story with another, parallel story. When I co-coordinated that conference with Papusa Molina, I was still using the English name given to me by my kindergarten teacher—Polly. Since then I've reclaimed my Taiwanese name, Ju-Pong (spelled the way my father spelled it, without any respect to conventional systems of transliteration), and am learning about the colonial history of Taiwan. Many decades later, I am learning to understand more clearly how racism, colonialism, and heteronormativity intersect with the domination of nature.

Unpacking Colonialism, Postcolonialism, and Decolonial Theory

In my work with environmental activists and advocates for sustainable living, I often rub up against the ivory-toweredness of academic language. When I say I'm studying postcolonial ecocriticism, I'm apt to get a look of "What the…?!?" I have learned to see this look as an opportunity to open up conversation about the amnesia of North Americans— the denial of our settler colonial history and our colonial present. When I first attempted to learn about postcolonialism in a graduate degree, I was overwhelmed by the obscure language and forms of argumentation endemic to the field. I could not see myself as "subaltern," nor feel moved to discover my voice as a subaltern. I have been moved by eminent indigenous scholar Linda Tuhiwai Smith, who, in *Decolonizing Methodologies: Research and Indigenous Peoples*,[13] called for indigenous scholars to articulate their own theory. Smith's framing of theory motivates me as an educator to build clear pathways towards understanding complex ideas and theories.

> Theory enables us to deal with contradictions and uncertainties. Perhaps more significantly, it gives us space to plan, to strategize, to take greater control over our resistances...Theory can also protect us because it contains within it the way of putting reality into perspective. If it is good theory it also allows for new ideas and ways of looking at things to be incorporated constantly without the need to search constantly for new theories.[14]

What is colonialism? As Pramod Nayar clearly articulates, colonialism was based on the systematic study and suppression of colonized cultures: "Colonization was a violent appropriation and sustained exploitation of native races and spaces by European cultures...New systems of schooling, architecture and even agriculture forced the colonized natives to acquire new skills and methods."[15] A necessary revision to this definition would underscore the point she makes later that there are many forms of colonialism. Japan's colonization of Taiwan was based on a rigorous study of European techniques, but they prided themselves on "improving" on previous practices.[16] Nayar's definition also highlights the often quoted, concise words of anthropologist Patrick Wolfe: "invasion is a structure, not an event."[17] Nayar expands on this idea clearly.

> Colonialism was never just as an exploitative political or economic process, it was also a *cultural conquest* of the native whereby the native's forms of knowledge, art, cultural practices and religious beliefs were studied, classified, policed, judged and altered by the European.[18]

Colonialism also needs to be seen as *one* expression of imperialism, as Smith asserted. Nayar succinctly defines the relationship: "Imperialism is the theory and colonialism is the practice, where both are based on racial difference."[19] Smith elaborates on other aspects of imperialism: economic expansion, the subjugation of "others," the spirit of imperialism (related to the spirit of Enlightenment), and imperialism as discourse: "a discursive field of knowledge,"[20] as in the case of Japanese use of modern medicine to persuade Taiwanese to succumb to imperial rule.[21]

If imperialism is the theory of colonialism, what is the theory of anti-colonization? Postcolonial scholars such as Frantz Fanon, Edward Said, and Gayatri Spivak[22] developed theoretical frameworks and methods of critical analysis. Following on Wolfe's idea that "invasion is a structure," many activists, artists, and scholars argue that the "post" is an inaccurate prefix when colonialism still persists. Smith quotes Aborigine activist Bobbi Sykes, "what? Post-colonialism? Have they left?"[23] Again, I will refer to Nayar's definition:

> *Decolonization* is the process whereby non-white nations and ethnic groups in Asia, Africa and South America strive to secure freedom (economic, political, intellectual) from their European masters. "Postcoloniality" and "decolonization" are used, especially in postcolonial theory to describe resistance, particularly against class, race and gender oppression.[24]

Now to return to the "undisciplined" collage of *Doctor Who* and Taiwan, I will attempt to theorize and perform a decolonial ecocriticism from a decentered place, with all due respect to bell hooks and the historic significance of *Feminist Theory: From Margin to Center*.[25] From this place of displacement, I will dive back into my proposal for potential uses of *Doctor Who* and other examples of popular culture to entice the public to reflect on the coloniality of North America.

A Postcolonial Ecocritical Take on *Doctor Who*

As mentioned previously, my introduction to *Doctor Who* came through my son. I hesitate to make any generalizations about young people across the range of cultural differences in those who I anticipate might read this essay. However, I think I would be safe to assume that electronic media are fairly omnipresent among the English-speaking youth. My teenage son is fairly typical of North American youth in his attachment to electronic devices. I love Patrick Murphy's description of his daughter, and find it fitting for my son as well.

> For the sake of the possibility for an ecologically sustainable future,
> I must hope that my multitasking mixed realist mode daughter,
> who shifts from textual reading to multimodal reading, from biog-
> raphy to fantasy, to documentary, from playing the emergency vet
> computer game to volunteering on weekends with the local pet
> rescue and adoption organization and donating money to save the
> manatees, will use digital technology in ecologically beneficial and
> productive ways.[26]

Murphy expresses the balance of urgency, despair, love, and hope that
I share in regards to how I might galvanize my professional work as an
educator and public artist to act now, to shift the paradigm with which
we as communities, peoples, and even as nations (with all the baggage
and complexity that word holds) regard and respond to the crisis of
our existence on the planet. This is why I choose to focus my inquiry
through *Doctor Who*.

The method I'm playfully fabulating, to borrow Murphy's phrase
again, is a mash up of postcolonial ecocriticism, "green media citizenship," and an emergent study of Daoism and the principles of
yinyang. Green media citizenship comes from the work of Antonio
López on greening media literacy.[27] López has created a handout on
greening media literacy education which states, "Ecomedia literacy is
understanding how everyday media practice impacts our ability to live
sustainably within earth's ecological parameters for the present and
future."[28] He has developed an ecomedia wheel, a heuristic or hands-on,
problem-solving tool, to scaffold the teaching and learning of ecomedia
literacy. In my study of postcolonial ecocriticism and ecofeminist perspectives, I have puzzled over the critique of hierarchical binary that Val
Plumwood theorized undergirds Western thinking and how to resist
or transform the "system of ideas that takes a radically separated reason to be the essential characteristic of humans and situates human life
outside and above an inferiorised and manipulable nature."[29] Murphy
and many other ecocritics advocate for "biophilia," or a love of nature,
to disrupt the rationalism that Plumwood and other ecofeminists have

identified as a destructive force, not only to the natural world and more-than-human beings, but to humans viewed by colonizers as less rational (more primitive).

Both my community performance and teaching practice has revolved around working with powerful questions, which dovetails well with my philosophy of education. My teaching praxis is grounded in a co-learning, learner-centered approach which I have honed at The Evergreen State College and now at Goddard College. So, out of this dance with López and ecofeminist thinkers, I've fabulated this question: What if we could approach media ecocriticism from a non-rationalistic, non-hierarchical tradition of thought and culture? What if we approached media ecocriticism through a Daoist framework?

From Robin Wang's thorough study of yinyang, I understand that "Yinyang is a particular term, but it also represents an underlying structure in an enduring tradition...we can consider yinyang as a thinking paradigm. Thomas Kuhn...argues that paradigms precede and shape all the operations of rational thinking."[30] So a paradigm is more than a way of thinking, but encompasses how we think and how we perceive. Wang goes on to write:

> Yinyang in Chinese culture fits this description. At the same time, yinyang can also be seen as a constellation of lay beliefs and practices, functioning explicitly and implicitly in activities ranging from philosophy to health care and from warfare to a way of life.[31]

This range of applications, from the earthy work of making a wheel to the understanding of heavenly cycles to predictions of dynastic turnover, feeds my optimism for the possibility of crafting an ecocritical framework guided by yinyang, which "functioned as the warp and woof of Chinese thought and culture."[32]

How might a yinyang paradigm intersect with postcolonial ecocritical practice? A full discussion of yinyang is beyond the scope of this essay. I will just riff on three key aspects that Wang discusses.

> Xiangyi 相依: interdependence. One side of the opposition can-
> not exist without the other...According to yinyang thinking, how-
> ever, interdependence of opposites does not simply refer to the
> relativity of our concepts, but also to how things themselves exist,
> grow, and function.[33]

The colonized being of "The Beast Below"[34] is the Star Whale, a creature drawn to the dying civilization by the cries of suffering children.
The story of "The Beast Below" is structured somewhat like a whodunit,
with the Doctor and his companion, Amy, sleuthing to understand the
mystery of Starship UK. How does this behemoth fly? What keeps it
going? The Doctor notices the palpable fear in the air, underneath a
veneer of normalcy. A child crying to herself, as if to hide her tearful-
ness. The Doctor also goes around placing glasses of water on the floor,
a method by which he deduces that there is no motor. We learn that the
Starship UK was constructed so that the entire surviving population of
British citizens could ride atop the Star Whale. We later learn that not
only is the whole of England dependent on and living off the life-blood
of this Star Whale, the poor creature is being tortured under the delusion that keeping the creature imprisoned under constant pain is the
only way to control its energy towards powering the ship.

The story can be seen as a response to ecological disaster, as told
by the Doctor, a civilization responding to "solar flares" or a dying sun
by seeking to escape their devastated planet. The Doctor rattles off his
prognosis: "society on the brink of collapse, a police state."[35] The society's
response fuses technology and biocolonialism into one solution—build
a ship on a living creature and escape the devastation we have probably
created. Their solution is a floating testimony to what Val Plumwood
called a Techno-fix solution.[36]

> Techno-fix solutions make no attempt to rethink human culture,
> dominant lifestyles and demands on nature, indeed they tend to
> assume that these are unchangeable. They aim rather to meet these
> demands more efficiently through smarter technology, deliberately

bracketing political and cultural reflection and admissions of failure.[37]

Applying yinyang thinking, we could consider how the idea of interdependence and of change and transformation might produce a different kind of narrative and vision of the world. While yinyang is based on a dynamic of binary opposition, binaries are not understood in the sense of static categories, nor is there a hierarchical sense of one opposing element dominating another. Instead, according to Wang, yinyang sees the world as a continuous flow of "[c]hange and transformation. One becomes the other in an endless cycle. Yinyang thought is fundamentally dynamic and centers on change."[38] In this futuristic Britain, a living being becomes technologized to serve the needs of human beings. Some humans are also technologized in the form of Winders, cyborg versions of the Smilers who police the mechanized way of life which the citizens continue to "choose." Yet the lifestyle they sustain is chilling and raises questions about what it means to be alive.

The yinyang concept of interdependence can be related to an ecological ethics, as distinguished from the androcentric ethics on which Western science has been based. Before they embark on the Starship UK, the Doctor articulates an ethics of twentieth-century anthropology, reminiscent of the Prime Directive of Star Trek. "Thing one. We are observers only," he says. While viewing on the monitor the goings-on of the Starship, Amy shows that she understands this ethos: "sooo we're like a wildlife documentary, yeah?" She plays out a scenario: "if they come across a wounded cub, they can't save it. They just have to keep filming and let it die…don't you find it hard to be all detached and cold?" Meanwhile, the Doctor has already boarded the ship. The next scene cleverly instructs the audience, as the Doctor instructs Amy, on the methodology of close, but detached, observation. The story takes an interesting turn in its resolution. As the Doctor is about to zap the beast's brain, thus numbing the pain of being hooked up to the Starship UK and allowing the humans to continue extracting its life, Amy suddenly realizes through a montage of flashbacks that they've got it all wrong. The Star Whale didn't come to attack the humans, but came because she couldn't stand to hear the children suffer. Amy stops the Doctor and saves the creature, opening up the potential for humans to evolve a new kind of relationship with the Star Whale.[39]

A generative question can be framed to bring yinyang thinking into closer correspondence with popular representations of humans' relationship with "nature." Reflecting on the relationships that unfold in "The Beast Below," between human and machine, non-human and animal, the earth, the sun, and the universe, it seems fruitful to consider the whole of the world of Starship UK as a complex system.

> Yinyang thought appeals to integrated processes rather than divided dualisms. It addresses what we could call a state of complexity, a term widely invoked in the field of contemporary science, particularly in relation to biological systems. The idea of complexity shows "the whole being formed of numerous parts in nonrandom organization."[40]

Wang's articulation of yinyang parallels the ideas of ecologists and scientists advancing the theory of panarchy and complex systems. As we search for ways to adapt to climate change, to build resilient communities, to live within planetary limits, and to live by an ecocentric ethics of care, I propose one avenue for playful fabulation might lie in the Dao. What if we worked with different sorts of questions? What is the element of yin in our yang? How can we transform our culture from an egocentric to an ecocentric one? Who is the animal within us?

Viewing "The Beast Below" through a decolonial ecocritical lens, we can see the show as posing the questions "what if we woke up one day and discovered that our normal life was so very, very wrong? What if we woke up from our amnesia, woke up to the truth that our comfort and survival was being extracted, literally, from the backs of others?" We can look to *culture* as an expression of our collective dreams, nightmares, aspirations, and wildest imaginings for a more ethical, loving world. Some may see popular culture as more a reflection of the nightmarish side of civilization; if so, a yinyang approach to ecomedia might hold an answer. Ecomedia literacy engages us to talk back to the movies, to borrow from bell hooks, to work with the questions with which popular culture troubles us. "Whether we like it or not, cinema assumes a peda-gogical role in the lives of many people."[41] Seeing the world in terms of dynamic relationships, of opposites in a constant, inter-transformational flow, offers hope for a necessary culture shift if we are to save ourselves from our own extinction.

Providence, Rhode Island, 2013
This last time I moved house, while re-shelving my huge book collection once again, my copy of Making Face, Making Soul: Haciendo Caras *fell open to a place at the back marked by a postcard. On the front was a print of two geese entwined at the neck; on the back, the art was identified as "Mating Geese," the artist Kavavaow Mannomee. The handwritten note read, "Dear Ju-Pong, Enjoy the book! It's now a gift for you to keep or pass on as you wish."*
It was signed, "Gloria."
Gloria, I'm so sorry that our meeting lapsed into amnesia. We met in Iowa City, where a community of women of color changed my life; where I worked and argued with and loved women committed to the struggle against rac-ism, across race and class and sexual orientation and reclaimed my Taiwanese name. Gloria, I want you to know that there's a Wikipedia entry for you. And it reads, "Gloria Anzaldúa. Scholar."

Notes

1   Anzaldúa, *Borderlands/La Frontera: The New Mestiza*, 1.
2   Moraga and Anzaldúa, *This Bridge Called My Back: Writings by Radical Women of Color*; Anzaldúa, *Making Face, Making Soul: Haciendo Caras: Creative and Critical Perspectives by Feminists of Color*.
3   Hawken, *Blessed Unrest: How the Largest Social Movement in History is Restoring Grace, Justice, and Beauty to the World*.
4   Scholes, *Structural Fabulation: An Essay on Fiction of the Future*.
5   Moffat, "The Beast Below."
6   Ibid.
7   Nixon, *Slow Violence and the Environmentalism of the Poor*.
8   DeLoughrey and Handley, *Postcolonial Ecologies: Literatures of the Environment*, 387–388.
9   Murphy, *Ecocritical Explorations in Literary and Cultural Studies: Fences, Boundaries, and Fields*, 919–923.
10 Unpublished poem by Ju-Pong Lin.
11 Lorde, "The Master's Tools Will Never Dismantle the Master's House."

12 Crenshaw, "Mapping the Margins: Intersectionality, Identity Politics, and Violence Against Women of Color."
13 Tuhiwai Smith, *Decolonizing Methodologies: Research and Indigenous Peoples.*
14 Ibid., 38.
15 Nayar, *Postcolonialism: A Guide for the Perplexed*, 1.
16 Shiyung Liu, *Prescribing Colonization: The Role of Medical Practices and Policies in Japan-Ruled Taiwan, 1895-1945.*
17 Wolfe, *Settler Colonialism and the Transformation of Anthropology: The Politics and Poetics of an Ethnographic Event*, 3.
18 Nayar, *Postcolonialism: A Guide for the Perplexed*, 2.
19 Ibid., 2.
20 Tuhiwai Smith, *Decolonizing Methodologies: Research and Indigenous Peoples*, 21.
21 Shiyung Liu, *Prescribing Colonization: The Role of Medical Practices and Policies in Japan-Ruled Taiwan, 1895-1945.*
22 Fanon, *Black Skin, White Masks*; Said, *Orientalism*; Spivak and Harasym, *The Post-Colonial Critic: Interviews, Strategies, Dialogues.*
23 Ibid., 24.
24 Nayar, *Postcolonialism: A Guide for the Perplexed*, 3.
25 hooks, *Feminist Theory: From Margin to Center.*
26 Murphy, *Ecocritical Explorations in Literary and Cultural Studies: Fences, Boundaries, and Fields*, 919–923.
27 López, *Greening Media Education: Bridging Media Literacy with Green Cultural Citizenship.*
28 López, "Greening Media Literacy Education," 4.
29 Plumwood, *Environmental Culture: The Ecological Crisis of Reason*, 4.
30 Wang, *Yinyang: The Way of Heaven and Earth in Chinese Thought and Culture*, 210–212.
31 Ibid., 215–217.
32 Ibid., 226–227.
33 Ibid., 226–227.
34 Moffat, "The Beast Below."
35 Ibid.
36 Plumwood, *Environmental Culture: The Ecological Crisis of Reason*, 8.
37 Ibid., 8 [citing Pusey, Michael. *Economic Rationalism in Canberra: A Nation-building State Changes Its Mind.* New York: Cambridge University Press, 1989].
38 Wang, *Yinyang: The Way of Heaven and Earth in Chinese Thought and Culture*, 336.
39 Moffat, "The Beast Below."
40 Wang, *Yinyang: The Way of Heaven and Earth in Chinese Thought and Culture*, 14.
41 hooks, *Reel to Real: Race, Sex, and Class at the Movies*, 2.

References

Anzaldúa, Gloria. *Making Face, Making Soul: Haciendo Caras: Creative and Critical Perspectives by Feminists of Color.* San Francisco: Aunt Lute Foundation Books, 1990.
Anzaldúa, Gloria. *Borderlands/La Frontera: The New Mestiza.* San Francisco: Aunt Lute Books, 2012.
Crenshaw, Kimberle. "Mapping the Margins: Intersectionality, Identity Politics, and Violence Against Women of Color." *Stanford Law Review*, 43, 6 (July 1991): 1241–1299.
DeLoughrey, Elizabeth M. and George B. Handley, editors. *Postcolonial Ecologies: Literatures of the Environment.* New York: Oxford University Press, 2011.
Fanon, Frantz. *Black Skin, White Masks.* Get Political. London: Pluto, 2008.

Hawken, Paul. *Blessed Unrest: How the Largest Social Movement in History Is Restoring Grace, Justice, and Beauty to the World*. New York: Penguin Books, 2008.

hooks, bell. *Feminist Theory: From Margin to Center*. Cambridge, MA: South End Press, 1984.

hooks, bell. *Reel to Real: Race, Sex, and Class at the Movies*. New York, NY: Routledge, 1996.

López, Antonio. *Greening Media Education: Bridging Media Literacy with Green Cultural Citizenship (Minding the Media: Critical Issues for Learning and Teaching)*. New York: Peter Lang Publishing, 2014.

López, Antonio. "Greening Media Literacy Education." 2014. Available online at http://ecomedialit.com/wp-content/uploads/2014/03/handout.pdf (accessed 3 April 2016).

Lorde, Audre. "The Master's Tools Will Never Dismantle the Master's House." *Sister Outsider: Essays and Speeches*, 110–114. New York: Crown Publishing Group, 2007.

Moffat, Steve. "The Beast Below." In Dr. Who [Television]. Directed by Andrew Gunn and Euros Lyn. UK: BBC Productions, 2010.

Moraga, Cherríe and Gloria Anzaldúa, *This Bridge Called My Back: Writings by Radical Women of Color*. New York: Kitchen Table/Women of Color Press, 1984.

Murphy, Patrick D. *Ecocritical Explorations in Literary and Cultural Studies: Fences, Boundaries, and Fields*. Lanham, MD: Lexington Books, 2010.

Nayar, Pramod K. *Postcolonialism: A Guide for the Perplexed (Guides for the Perplexed)*. London: Continuum, 2010.

Nixon, Rob. *Slow Violence and the Environmentalism of the Poor*. Cambridge, Mass.: Harvard University Press, 2011.

Plumwood, Val. *Environmental Culture: The Ecological Crisis of Reason (Environmental Philosophies)*. New York: Routledge, 2002.

Said, Edward W. *Orientalism*. New York: Vintage Books, 1994.

Scholes, Robert E. *Structural Fabulation: An Essay on Fiction of the Future*. Notre Dame, IN: University of Notre Dame Press, 1975.

Shiyung Liu, Michael. *Prescribing Colonization: The Role of Medical Practices and Policies in Japan-Ruled Taiwan, 1895-1945*. Ann Arbor: Association for Asian Studies, 2009.

Spivak, Gayatri Chakravorty and Sarah Harasym. *The Post-Colonial Critic: Interviews, Strategies, Dialogues*. New York: Routledge, 1990.

Tuhiwai Smith, Linda. *Decolonizing Methodologies: Research and Indigenous Peoples*. New York: Zed Books, 1999.

Wang, Robin R. *Yinyang: The Way of Heaven and Earth in Chinese Thought and Culture (New Approaches to Asian History)*. New York: Cambridge University Press, 2012.

Wolfe, Patrick. *Settler Colonialism and the Transformation of Anthropology: The Politics and Poetics of an Ethnographic Event (Writing Past Colonialism)*. London: Cassell, 1999.

11

PIERCING THE SHELL OF PRIVILEGE

HOW MY COMMITMENTS TO
ENVIRONMENTAL AND GENDER JUSTICE
MOVED FROM MY HEAD TO MY HEART
NINA SIMONS

This chapter is dedicated to anyone who has ever felt powerless,
experienced being the dissenting or minority voice,
or felt unfairly judged, devalued or dismissed for being different.
It is offered for anyone who has experienced a culture
that elevates some while denigrating others,
or who is awakening to having had privileges that
afford them opportunities others do not receive,
while denying them access to other forms of community.

I might seem an unlikely person to contribute to this book, as I was first called to work in the arts, then found my way to working on environmental issues, and only later awakened to my own relatively privileged position and my need to look deeply at—and engage with—my relationship with gender, environmental and racial justice. One throughline that has permeated all of the varied paths I have traveled is a deep desire to contribute—to whatever extent I can—to personal, ecological and collective healing.

I have come to believe that the wounds that plague our relationships with our selves, with each other and with our Mother Earth are related—that they're fractals of the same societal imbalance and relational amnesia. As many have noted, the way Western cultures have treated the natural world is profoundly connected to the damage they have inflicted on women, Indigenous nations, people of color and the poor. In my view it seems to begin, at its core, with a false sense of separation and a subsequent pattern of ranking and "othering" encouraged by an over-emphasis on the mind and an undervaluing of the emotional, physical and spiritual spheres of life. In the spirit of Gandhi's suggestion that "social change occurs when deeply felt private experiences are given public legitimacy,"[1] and to share context about my learning, I offer a brief overview of the arc of my efforts to clarify my own sense of purpose and calling.

My path toward healing had to begin with a broken heart. My largely unconscious sense of privilege and separateness had to be shattered, in processes that have been punctuated by shame, fear and uncertainty. These feelings have diminished over time and with practice, as I've realized the deep personal and social benefits of facing into cultural healing work. And, since my journey also involves overcoming internalized gender oppressions while noting their relatedness to racial justice, awakening to the fullness of what having privilege means continues throwing up new challenges and pitfalls today, and probably will for the rest of my life.

That increasing awareness continues to open new doors, precipitates some of the most deeply valued experiences I've ever had and permits me to forge life-changing relationships, for which I am deeply grateful. Though the fear that arises as a White person considering entering this realm may be widely apparent, few have written of the breakthrough benefits and joys that are possible from encountering that fear and facing it fully, in the interest of beloved community. For the sake of a just, diverse and verdant future, and the exquisite beauty and mystery of the web of life on Earth, may enough of us choose to awaken to the deep, insidious wounds of false separation, our ability to lean into relatedness and our own capacity to transform ourselves to increasingly act as agents of healing and transformation.

I grew up in a huge city filled with people of every nationality and ethnicity. I identified myself as being progressive and valuing difference, but I understood those things conceptually, as if from a distance. I was aware of some systemic inequities that occurred due to race and class, and was sure I stood on the right side of the equation, toward justice, as my parents had taught me I should. But my heart wasn't engaged. The problems of racial and class and gender-based injustice were ethical realities I had wrapped my mind around intellectually. My unconscious distance prevented me from feeling it in my heart, and from truly grasping the profound pain that these social contradictions inflict on so many people each minute of every day.

What first began to expand my awareness was my exposure to the extraordinary power and beauty of nature's diversity. I visited a biodiversity garden in southern New Mexico in 1989, and experienced for the first time the fertile vitality, the dazzling array of colors, textures and shapes, and the sensual wonder of the tastes and smells of hundreds of endangered heirloom and traditional varieties of food and herb plants. Being in that garden, I felt ecstatic, as if my senses were dancing. The lush beauty and sensuality of it filled me with joy. I felt enlivened by its abundant diversity, and wondered whether the Garden of Eden might have been modeled after just such a place.

Then I learned about the purpose of this diverse seed garden. I discovered the urgent threat to our food supply posed by the loss of biodiversity in our food system and the centralization of seed companies. I began learning about the real value of diversity, as nature's best strategy for survival. That garden was an ark of endangered varieties and species being grown out for seed, to preserve their unique traits from which we could ensure future options for nourishment in a rapidly changing global environment. I learned that having many options for adaptation is how nature ensures resilience and guards against extinction. I discovered that ecosystems rich in diversity rebound toward health far faster after trauma, while systems with fewer species are much slower to recover and heal. As I left that garden, I felt as though the spirit of the natural world tapped me on the shoulder and said "You're working for me, now." I quit my job in the arts to embark upon the steepest learning curve of my life: going to work for what became a mission-driven entrepreneurial company called Seeds of Change.

The next year, as we worked to grow the seed company, my partner and husband Kenny Ausubel asked me to help produce a conference, which he called Bioneers.[2] It was a gathering of ecological and social innovators, people who had peered deep into the heart of nature to understand how to reinvent human civilization, how to live in harmony with the Earth and each other. They included people of every race, discipline, age and orientation, with a strong emphasis on Indigenous wisdom and a particular focus on traditional ecological knowledge, or TEK.

The visions, stories and values of the people we featured as "Bioneers" deeply inspired me. These were the kinds of leaders and visionaries I wished to support with my communication skills, and Kenny and I entered a partnership to produce the Bioneers Conference that continues to this day. We loved the work and felt committed to delivering it as medicine to an ailing world. We saw ecological and social change-makers and leaders as lacking connectivity to each other and to the whole living system, and thought that more cross-pollination could strengthen all their efforts. We sensed that bringing people together across disparate but related fields of endeavor would help accelerate innovation and movement building. We believed that the more people knew about these inspiring solutions, the more it would inspire greater engagement. We learned over time that by honoring their many different issues and perspectives in a pluralistic and deeply respectful way, it was often possible, despite the great varieties of people and fields of endeavor represented, to evoke a unifying field of shared hope and future vision.

Informed by many of the remarkable visionaries who spoke from the Bioneers' stage each year, my understanding about the central role of diversity to any living system continued to deepen. I began to see that just as diversity affects adaptation and survival in the natural world, so too it enhances the health and resilience of our organizations, movements and social systems. The most diverse human communities are also the most likely to survive and thrive, the ones most likely to keep generating imaginative new solutions to their most pressing challenges.

Valuing diversity became an internal process as well as an external approach to life for me. I realized that I needed to learn to respect and listen to a much wider array of the voices within myself, including the wisdom of my body, heart and spirit, as well as my mind. I needed to exercise my own capacity to consider conflicting views within my own internal sphere, and resolve them in ways that were not damaging to me. This has meant trying to honor the analytical and metaphoric, linear and artistic, focused and diffuse, "masculine" and "feminine," and everything in between. I've been learning to not exclude, belittle or censor any species in the ecosystem of my inner landscape.

In 1997, a new sense of purpose arose for me, as issues of gender justice and the burning need for women's leadership to arise far more extensively in all areas of life began to increasingly call to me. The need to restore the long-neglected and chronically underappreciated feminine qualities in our culture and within each of us (male and female alike) became a core passion. I was startled to realize that I'd navigated most of my professional life until then by relying heavily on my more "masculine" attributes. I yearned to appreciate and integrate those parts of myself that I had previously unconsciously undervalued, and that I had therefore kept largely hidden. I started to question the qualities and behaviors I associated with each gender, and I began exploring practices to achieve greater inner equilibrium. I began to see the imbalance I perceived within myself reflected everywhere in the world around me, within our culture, politics, economics and institutions.

As a child, my parents had brought me to the nation's capital to march for desegregation and racial equity, to end the Vietnam War, and for women's rights. After college, for years I believed the feminist movement had largely accomplished its goals, and that I was stepping onto a level playing field. That same naiveté, mixed with idealism and a hefty dose of cultural blindness, also had me imagining that the Civil Rights Movement had largely ended racial bias and injustice in this country. It wasn't until much later—after years of being the only woman in business settings, of negotiating biased gender dynamics personally, professionally and politically—that I began to realize how much gender roles and related power dynamics were impacting my experience, and how painful and damaging those impacts were. And it wasn't until several years later, as I began peeling back the layers of my own defensiveness and denial, that I began to register how deeply racialized our society still is, and to awaken to my own personal and cultural complicity in it as a White woman.

I started bringing women's issues and restoring gender balance to the heart of Bioneers' programming. At first, I was concerned about focusing on women's issues, as my years of producing Bioneers conferences had taught me to design for inclusive frameworks, not to leave *anyone* out. Over time, however, I came to see these ideas as relevant to everyone, regardless of gender, both individually and collectively.

Many writers and social scientists have explored the impacts of these social and psychological imbalances throughout the arenas of culture, business and governance. I started to see the same imbalances reflected in so many of our systems: in farming, land and resource use; in technology and science; in the financial world; in how we practice medicine, raise our children and feed ourselves. It seemed to me that this bias we'd all inherited and internalized was likely as damaging to men as to women. In a related way, I was coming to understand racial bias as being profoundly harmful to all people, not only as destructive for people of color and Indigenous peoples. I saw that gender-based biases—like racial biases—are especially insidious and pervasive because they are often implicit and deeply unconscious, and I recognized how difficult it can be for those who benefit from the biases to be able to see them. I came to see restoring balance and equity to all of our humanity as an endeavor that affects us all. I believe that the wounds that have accrued through that imbalance must be aired, understood and acknowledged in order to transform and heal our living system.

I began convening groups of women to explore differences and commonalities, and to learn what we could about what women might uniquely bring to the reinvention of leadership at this time. I'd learned from the living system of Bioneers to listen and watch for patterns. Within myself, I found deep internalized conditioning that had been previously invisible to me, related to gender bias. This included voices I heard in my head whenever I started to reach or stretch toward something new or challenging, telling me I wasn't good enough, smart enough, linear or rational enough, experienced or eloquent enough. Many of the women I shared this with, I discovered, heard similar self-limiting voices. Those voices began to seem like pillars holding up an inner story I carried, one that perpetuated a sense of myself as victimized and "less than." Within my work sphere and professional partnership, I saw myself as "the woman behind the man," though no one else saw me that way.

Although I was appalled to discover that I carried such a demeaning story, I was also elated to realize that I held the keys to my own liberation. I began to rewrite my own narrative, and developed daily meditations, rituals and practices to improve my own self-esteem, and to appreciate a fuller spectrum of my own contributions. I noticed that some of this internalized oppression was a result of living in a culture that denigrates many of the human qualities I value, relegating them to a solely "feminine" purview. In the news media, I saw how rarely intelligent women were featured, and how infrequently women were protagonists in movies, television shows or plays. I recognized how often qualities like intuition, relational intelligence, nurturing, tenderness and empathy were devalued or attributed to the sole interest of women, and not to the larger sphere of humanity or leadership. I began to realize how many layers of false beliefs, habits and biases I would need to shed to repair my self-esteem, retire my victimhood orientation and develop a healthy sense of my own wholeness and agency.

When I shared my discoveries with other women—regardless of their color, age or orientation—many nodded their heads in agreement. I began to see that while our experience as women created a unifying field of empathic resonance, it was also necessary to recognize and appreciate the vast differences among our individual experiences. I realized that while we all shared internalized impacts from gender-based biases, many among us had faced other intense and oppressive biases that shaped their lived realities, in addition. I began to see how the experiences of trauma and oppression had not only limited our options or expression, but had often also served to strengthen women's visions, resilience and commitments.

As I continued to explore the many layers of unconsciously accumulated crap I needed to shed to reclaim my health and wholeness, I became appalled that women who were not White might have so

NINA SIMONS

many additional and complex layers to deal with. The more tangible that reality became for me, the more committed I became to trying my best—despite the challenges and pitfalls involved and all the blind spots I surely still had—to stand in solidarity with diverse women in their own struggles. The first step in liberating the full capacity of any woman's leadership is an inside job, but we will need a deep solidarity among the widest array of women (and as many enlightened male allies as possible) to turn our civilization around.

Although gender bias and racial bias manifest differently in our culture, with differing dynamics, I think all women share an empathic window on injustice, a potentially unifying experience of feeling "less than" in our society. I hope that relational window might offer a great many White women an emotional entry point into becoming allies for racial justice.

In an anti-racism training class for White facilitators, I learned about Dr Martin Luther King's vision of "Beloved Community." He envisioned a kinship among people of all ethnicities, classes, spiritual beliefs and tribes, a deeply compelling vision that has inspired me to want to stand in alliance with women (and men) of all colors, nationalities, ages, orientations, faiths and classes, and to learn from our differences and our commonalities.

This led me to collaborate with Toby Herzlich and Akaya Windwood, two highly experienced and skillful facilitators, to co-create *Cultivating Women's Leadership*, a six-day residential, experiential immersion intensive which we began offering for diverse groups of women in 2006. Our primary goals included: clarifying each woman's particular "calling," purpose or assignment; exploring what women are uniquely contributing to the reinvention of leadership; seeking to connect across the differences that often divide us; and experiencing how powerfully women in intentional alliance can accelerate each other's learning, all while acquiring tools and practices to continue to cultivate leadership in themselves. We seek to help women achieve their full potential to lead change joyfully and effectively within their communities, sectors and disciplines.

Since then, each group of twenty has been selected to optimize diversity—not only ethnically, but also in terms of age, orientation and

discipline or issue area. Toby Herzlich and I have refined and co-evolved
the training over the past ten years, and feedback reveals it is delivering strong results. When we learned about research that found that 30
percent was the minimum percentage of minority members required
in a group for most to feel adequately "flanked" to speak up fully,[3] we
determined to establish a minimum of 30 percent women of color and
Indigenous women in each intensive. Our facilitation teams increasingly included skillful leaders who were not White.

Piercings and Crackings

An incident that felt as though it pierced the shell of my privilege
occurred during one of these Cultivating Women's Leadership workshops, one I co-facilitated in a rural retreat site in Northern New Mexico. Our time together included a collective dive into the pain of racial
wounding. We heard about the Chinese grandmother whose bound
feet hurt so much she had to be carried, the great uncle who had been
lynched in the South, the Peruvian Indigenous grandmother who had
been forced to leave her ancestral lands, the woman of mixed ancestry
who had grown up ashamed and targeted because she was the darkest
of her siblings. A White woman spoke of her slave-owner lineage, and
acknowledged the shame and guilt she feels, alongside of her privilege.
We listened deeply, and held each other tenderly. We noted how darkness is widely demonized. We named positive associations for Black
and darkness, to reclaim their value. We collaborated to create and enact
embodied healing rituals.

On the last night, Toby and I were awakened at 3am. One of the
women was having an asthma attack, and she had forgotten to bring
her inhaler. We rushed to her room, uncertain what to do. We were in
a rural setting at high altitude, hours away from a hospital or medical
care. Arriving, I sensed the woman's panic, heard her gasping desper-
ately for breath, trying to fill her lungs. I saw the terror in her eyes.
My mind had no previous experience, and was of no help at all. I
dropped into a place where I could receive my body's instructions.
With her permission, I held her head against my chest. I breathed
slowly and deeply, hoping she might entrain her breathing with mine.

As I stroked her head, I began to rock, rocking her in time with my breath. To comfort her, I began humming a wordless tune, like a lullaby. I had come to love and admire this woman, and to care deeply about her leadership. She was doing environmental justice work, and her asthma was likely a product of environmental injustice. Every particle of my being willed her to live, and I poured my love and desire for her wellness into her, hoping she would relax, yearning for her to recover and be able to breathe. I don't have any illusion that I healed her. But thankfully, after what seemed an endless time, her breathing steadied and slowed.

As she calmed, I laid her head back down on the pillows. I sat beside her, stroking her head and face. When she'd closed her eyes and was breathing normally, I sank down to the floor beside her bed. Tears were streaming down my cheeks. Wondering about the source of my sadness, I knew this was about more than relief. I knew that the shell of my separateness had cracked open.

I sensed that the barrier that my privilege had created between my head and heart had been pierced. I felt the pain of this woman's asthma and the profound injustice of her having to live with it acutely. I knew that it was caused due to racial bias, redlining and corporate malfeasance, and my heart ached even as my anger was kindled to change it. In that instant, I also knew my own complicity and accountability for it.

No matter how many years I'd known about the most toxic industries being sited in poor inner-city neighborhoods, no matter how long I'd known about the elevated rates of asthma and diabetes, of heart disease and cancer in these communities, I had known them from the distance my privilege afforded me. I had known them as statistics that shocked and saddened me, but I had never before felt so personally the direct impacts of that injustice the way I did that night.

After holding her in my arms, rocking her and breathing with her, summoning every bit of love and will I could muster, I'd felt no difference between us. The mother bear within me had been whole-heartedly engaged, and my desire to stand with her fully, to see her live and thrive, had broken my heart wide open. Ever since, I have a new and deepened commitment to environmental justice, and a greater sense of the suffering that results from the toxic inequities, corruption and corporate abuses of our current systems.

That same woman came as my guest to participate in a Bioneers Conference the following year, and I was humbled again to realize how much I don't see, consider or know. A Black woman, she'd driven to the conference in Marin County, California, and had been stopped by a cop for no apparent reason (other than racial profiling) on the highway. She arrived shaken and angry, and I saw and felt again how blinded I had been to the prevalence of that kind of injustice in her daily, lived experience.

Two years later, I became friends with a young woman of Lakota descent who participated in another intensive. She was a young mother, a businesswoman, community organizer and a cancer survivor who had created innovative opportunities to help women from her nation to come together for healing. I was deeply impressed by her courage and creativity, found her wise well beyond her years, and admired her greatly. Months after the retreat, I learned she was going through a difficult time, though I knew nothing of the details. I called her, to offer my support and express my concern on her behalf. She told me that she'd recently learned that her two nieces—aged 8 and 12— had been raped. Sobbing uncontrollably, she told me their names, and about what loving, innocent and tender young girls they'd been. She explained that the perpetrator lived within their family house, and that there were no counseling resources available to them. The girls were not willing to leave their home. I listened to her express her pain, frustration and grief for more than an hour. When I hung up the phone, I felt shattered.

Again, I had known about horrific rates of rape and sexual abuse of women in Indian Country,[4] but I had known about them from afar. I had read articles and seen news reports on the systemic challenges of jurisdiction on reservations, on the increased incidence of rape and sex trafficking in oil and gas drilling camps and on reservation lands, and had felt an affronted indignation at the failures of our systems to protect Native American women and girls. Hearing this beloved friend wail her grief and frustration with the names and descriptions of her young kin brought the truth of that epidemic home to my heart, in a way I had not known before.

Both of these experiences changed me, as others have continued to, since. They not only widened the scope of what—and who—I feel in service to, they deepened my compassion and commitment toward justice in ways I could not previously have imagined.

Justice has become personal, for me. Dr Cornel West says that "justice is what love looks like in public."[5] These experiences remind me to invest in my heart's experience when hearing another's suffering, and to focus on *feeling* injustice, not just thinking about it. They remind me to encourage others to deepen their own capacity for empathy.

Beloved Community

My own vision of beloved community extends beyond people—it includes whales, sea turtles and salmon, egrets, crows, otters and bears. It encompasses jaguars and cougars, bees, elephants, antelope and giraffes. The beloved community I yearn for extends to all the creatures and plants, the oceans, mountains, rivers and fungi, all of which are needed—the whole web of life I consider sacred.

Terry Tempest Williams, in her book *Finding Beauty in a Broken World*, speaks for such a diverse and wide-ranging community. She has studied prairie dogs, keystone creatures upon whom many more depend, and among the most likely North American mammals to face extinction rapidly, as they are being widely exterminated across the southwest. Hundreds are killed daily, shot for sport or fumigated in their burrows. They live in community, with mothers sometimes suckling each other's young. Prairie dogs have one of the most complex language systems of any animal yet studied, and a disarming habit of greeting each sunrise and sunset standing upright and stock still, their paws held together in a position like prayer.

Native peoples understood these creatures' place in relation to the land. When government agents proposed getting rid of the prairie dogs from parts of the Navajo Reservation, the elders objected, saying "If you kill all the prairie dogs, there will be no one to cry for the rain."[6] Where their burrows disappeared, the desert became a virtual wasteland. The ground became hard-packed, unable to accept rain. What ensued were flash floods, desertification and erosion. No one was surprised but the officials. Terry writes:

> [T]he story of the Utah prairie dogs is the story of the range of our compassion. If we can extend our idea of community to include the lowliest of creatures, call them "the untouchables," then we will indeed be closer to a path of peace and tolerance. If we cannot accommodate "the other," the shadow we will see on our own home ground will be the forecast of our own species' extended winter of the soul.[7]

We're all indigenous to someplace, and have community embedded in our cellular and ancestral memory. In some deep corner of our hearts, don't we all yearn for it? But in a quest for certainty, seeking an illusion of "safety," criticism and judgments reinforce our separateness. The invisible stories embedded throughout our culture and the biases they codify lead us to ruthlessly rank ourselves and judge each other. They've led us to commodify the sacred web of life, to assault Mother Earth as if she were not a living system. They've led us to devalue and denigrate women, Indigenous and people of color, and the poor. They've encouraged a polarizing perspective that emphasizes either/or, win/lose approaches, rather than a deep embrace of pluralism and diversity. They've hardened our hearts to experiencing oneness and empathic connection.

"Arrogance is arrogance, and cruelty committed to a person or an animal is cruelty. I believe it is time in the evolution of our imagination," Terry writes, "to make a strong case for the extension of our empathy toward the Other."[8]

> To regard any animal as something lesser than we are, not equal to our own vitality and adaptation as a species, is to begin a deadly descent into the dark abyss of arrogance where cruelty is nurtured in the corners of certitude. Daily acts of destruction and brutality are committed because we fail to see the dignity of the Other.[9]

Since I believe that intention precedes all change, and that there are energies poised to support our transformation, but that they need to hear us ask for their help, I offer, in closing, a prayer:

> May the soil of our souls be sown with seeds that expand our capacity for compassion, watered with the grief that strengthens our commitment and fired by the outrage that fortifies our will.

> May our roots entwine in the Earth like aspen trees or seven sisters oaks, whose underground networks of connection offer them the fortitude and resilience to weather hurricanes and storms.

> May we carry stories of renewal and healing, stories of the depth and endurance of our love, of the marriage of future and present visions with our ancestors' wisdom. May we carry them like seeds in our feathers, to sow fertility to regenerate wholeness, relatedness and community.

> May we savor together some visceral taste of beloved community by falling in love with an "other"—a love so nourishing, so enlivening and so deliciously desirable that our hearts and hands have to embrace it, so the flaming light of our unified purpose, bundled and brilliant in its solidarity, cannot be quenched.

Notes

1   Simons, "Cultivating Connection and Capacity through Story," 11.
2   www.bioneers.org/.
3   Tarr-Whelan, "Why the U.S. Needs More Women in the Government."
4   Futures without Violence, "The Facts on Violence Against American Indian/Native Alaskan Women."
5   West, "A Love Supreme."
6   Williams, "In The Shadow of Extinction."
7   Williams, *Finding Beauty in a Broken World*, 89.
8   Ibid., 90.
9   Ibid., 127.

References

Futures without Violence. "The Facts on Violence Against American Indian/Native Alaskan Women." Available online at www.futureswithoutviolence.org/userfiles/file/Violence%20 Against%20AI%20AN%20Women%20Fact%20Sheet.pdf (accessed 26 March 2016).

Simons, Nina. "Cultivating Connection and Capacity through Story." In *Moonrise: The Power of Women Leading from the Heart*, edited by Nina Simons with Anneke Campbell, 1–15. Rochester, VT: Park Street Press, 2010.

Tarr-Whelan, Linda. "Why the U.S. Needs More Women in the Government." *SF Gate*, December 18, 2009. Available online at www.sfgate.com/opinion/article/Why-the-U-S-needs-more-women-in-government-3278079.php (accessed 26 March 2016).

West, Cornel. "A Love Supreme." *The Occupied Wall Street Journal*, November 18, 2011. Available online at http://occupiedmedia.us/2011/11/a-love-supreme/ (accessed 26 March 2016).

Williams, Terry Tempest. "In the Shadow of Extinction." *The New York Times*, February 2, 2003. Available online at www.nytimes.com/2003/02/02/opinion/in-the-shadow-of-extinction.html (accessed 26 March 2016).

Williams, Terry Tempest. *Finding Beauty in a Broken World*. New York: Vintage Books, 2008.

12

OUR DIFFERENTIATED UNITY

AN EVOLUTIONARY PERSPECTIVE ON HEALING THE WOUNDS OF SLAVERY AND THE PLANET
BELVIE ROOKS

> The great discovery of contemporary cosmology is that the Universe for 14 billion years has been working to bring forth vibrant human communities. Our human role in this process is the healing of personal and collective wounds so that we might revel, even more deeply, in the magnificence of our differentiated unity!
> —Brian Swimme, co-author, *The Universe Story*[1]

Telling the Whole Story: Expanding Our Frames of Reference

We all have stories and they are all important. There is our individual story, as well as our collectively shared story. The Earth has a story, and there is the story of the Universe. In *Liberation and the Cosmos*, Amy Shuman says that storytelling allows us "to make meaning out of raw experiences; to transcend suffering; to offer advice and guidance; to provide a means of traveling beyond the personal; to provide inspiration and new frames of reference to both tellers and listeners."[2] Furthermore, in *The Dream of the Earth*, cultural historian Thomas Berry sums up both the hopes and the challenges confronting our species and the planet with the observation that "we are in between stories."[3] He means we are currently in a space between an old, reductionist, western, scientific paradigm based on compartmentalization and separation, and an emerging "new story" rooted in a more cosmic and indigenous world-view based on interdependence and interrelatedness.

How does the tension embedded in and flowing from this paradox impact how we see ourselves, our communities? How does it impact how we see and understand the planet and our place in it? In order to answer those questions, we need an expanded frame of reference. We need to embody a shift in consciousness that privileges the whole of who we are.

To tell a whole, complete and true story, we will need to expand our frames of reference to embody a shift in consciousness that privileges a whole spectrum from the individual being to the whole cosmos, and that encompasses everything in between. When we tell this story as close to its entirety, we will be ready to acknowledge the relationship of our present to our past and our individual self to our definition, understanding and relationship to "the other," or those who are not us, but actually are. We need to understand how such an expansion might impact our definition, understanding, and relationship to "the other." This is particularly important when those relationships, like enslavement, are rooted in a history of violence, lynching and terrorism.

We all have stories. Here are a few of my stories that reflect on a personal history of both the enslaved and slave-holding ancestors. When viewed from the evolutionary perspective of social healing, it is an emerging "new story" of race, racial identity, intergenerational trauma and collective wounding. I offer these as a meditation on the power of healing the wounds of the past in our present, and as an affirmation of the possibility for creating a sustainable future for the generations to come.

Reflections on the Journey
Journal Entry
   March 7, 2011
   Selma, Alabama
   A few hours ago, I was standing in the Live Oak Confederate Cemetery in Selma, looking down at the gravesite of a 17-year-old "Confederate" soldier

killed in 1862 during the height of the Civil War. As I stood there, the question of wholeness and relatedness in relationship to "the other" was very much on my mind. As I write this, I am also mindful of the fact that for the next four years, until 2015, the nation will be engaged in a commemoration of the 150th anniversary of that tragic war. I stood there holding a long-leaf pine sapling which I had been reading a lot about since we arrived. "It is time for both the uniqueness and plight of the long-leaf pine to come to national attention," said Edward O. Wilson, Pulitzer-Prize winning author and Harvard University Professor Emeritus. According to Professor Wilson, "a substantial part of America's environmental future is tied to this one species."[4]

Traveling across town, from yesterday's Bridge Crossing tree planting ceremony in the Black part of town, I found myself reflecting on the historical moment, the upcoming commemoration and all of the lives lost. It was also hard not to reflect on the fact that most of the planned Civil War commemorative activities consisted mainly of the reenactment of various battles won and lost. Whether won or lost, it felt like a celebration and commemoration of death!

As a lone African American woman, I had entered the Live Oak Cemetery with a great deal of trepidation. The inscription on the Confederate Monument that stands in the center of the cemetery reads, "There is Glory in the Graves." Reading it, I was stunned by the sentiment and needed to read it several times. The very name "Confederate," like the flags fluttering on the nearby gravestones, is for millions of Americans of African ancestry a visceral reminder of the auction block; of rape, random murders and lynchings, and night riding hooded Klansmen bearing crosses. For me, these symbols of the Confederacy are NOT reminders of glory!

I had accepted the invitation to come to Selma, knowing that for over 100 years Selma had been at the very heart of two divergent and contending views of historical possibility: Civil War and Civil Rights! During the Civil War, Selma was one of the Confederacy's main military arsenal and manufacturing centers. *The Battle of Selma* in 1865 was one of the last and hardest fought battles of the Civil War; all of the arsenals and half the town were destroyed.[5] By 1965, exactly 100 years later, Selma would be at the very center of the emerging Civil Rights movement and

Figure 12.1   *Sanofka Bird* by Sue Hammond West.

the site of "Bloody Sunday" and Dr King's historic march from Selma to Montgomery.

As I placed the small long-leaf pine sapling next to the gravesite before leaving the cemetery and walking past the Confederate monument for the last time, I was very much aware of the fact that my own personal journey to this place and to this particular moment began with tears, anger, despair and rage in the depths of a women's holding cell in a West African slave dungeon. It had also ended in that same place informed by a powerfully transformative question.

Journal Entry
September, 2007
El Mina Slave Dungeon
Cape Coast Ghana
The Sankofa Bird in the Akan wisdom tradition of West Africa portrays the image of a bird walking forward while looking back. In some of the images there is an egg in her beak which symbolizes what's being birthed for future generations. The image is a reminder of how important it is, as we move forward, to integrate the wisdom and knowledge of the past into the present, for the welfare of the future and future generations.[6]

The spirit and image of the Sankofa Bird would become the symbol for how we processed and integrated our African Journey. In fact, the Sankofa Bird image was very much on my mind as I stood at the Door-of-No-Return at El Mina slave dungeon on Ghana's Cape Coast, looking out at the vast magnificence of the Atlantic Ocean. There is beauty everywhere, even in the midst of heartbreak, tears and despair. El Mina is referred to as either a "castle" or a "dungeon" depending on whether you were one of the enslaved, inhabiting the damp, dark, crowded underground holdings cells awaiting shipment across the "great water" or whether you were one of the enslavers, attending Mass and dancing until dawn in the courtyard above. As I stood looking out at the vast ocean beyond, I tried hard to imagine what reaching this spot, this "Door-of-No-Return," the last point of physical contact with the African continent, must have felt like for some long-ago, unremembered and forgotten African ancestor as she stood trembling on the precipice of a terrifyingly unknown and uncertain future.

During the height of the slave trade there were so many dead and dying bodies tossed into the sea, at this particular spot, the frenzied feeding opportunity resulted in a change in the shark migration pattern for this entire stretch of coast.[7] Glancing at the brilliant blue ocean a few feet below, the tears flowed uncontrollably. It was hard to process the fact that for nearly 400 years, without interruption, millions of African men, women and children had begun the long journey into slavery from this very spot.

The numerous slave dungeons on the West African Coast, in places like Elmina on the Cape Coast of Ghana and Goree Island in Senegal, are living monuments and stark reminders of our inhumane lapses. The names of the people passing through this "Door-of-No-Return" have all been erased from our historical memory: the names of the mothers and the fathers, the children, the sisters, the brothers, the aunts, the uncles, the babies, the potters, the weavers, the farmers, the healers... Ancestors, all, to the "tribe-of-the-middle-passage" from which I was one of the returned descendants.

For days after visiting the women's dungeon at El Mina, I was immobilized by grief, despair and rage, and shed tears uncontrollably. The "wound of erasure" is, for me, one of slavery's most enduring and heart-breaking legacies. Who were these women? What were their names? What were their stories? The curators shared stories of randomly selected young virgins who were required periodically to ascend the back stairs from the women's dungeon to the governor's bedchamber above. We heard stories of how, when the governor had had his pleasure, the young woman was turned over to his elite guards and raped by each of them in turn before being returned to the women's dungeon. I had sat in tearful silence in the women's dungeon, trying to image what it would have been like to welcome this broken and battered spirit back into the community of women. What were the healing songs that the women sang as they held and caressed this broken woman back into the community? I especially tried to imagine the healing songs that the women sang across the divides of language and tribe. Were the songs and the tears their common language of grief, across the various tribal barriers that separated them?

Sitting in the depths of the women's dungeon, I spent a lot of time thinking about the enslaved women in my own lineage, unknown, unacknowledged and long forgotten, many of whom had come through one of the more than 100 slave dungeons along the West African Coast.[8]

After several days of bearing witness to the depth of my grief and despair, my Beloved, Dedan, asked what has turned out to be a life-altering question: "What would healing look like?" According to cultural anthropologist Angeles Arrien, "In contemplative practices of any kind, questions provoke inquiry, reflection, and conscious awareness of what we are learning or what is being revealed to us about our current inner and outer work."[9] In the context of inner and outer work, The Social Healing Project, funded in part by the Fetzer Institute, posits the need for an evolutionary paradigm shift; one that "seeks to transcend the repetitive cycle of wounding and the focus on right and wrong and shift the focus and the narrative to one having to do with wounding and healing."[10] The social healing paradigm is also evolutionary in the sense that it asks that we rethink our identity in the context of an expanded consciousness of relatedness and our relational selves.

This brings us back to the need for stories. While healing certainly involves justice, reparations and forgiveness, to truly heal we must recognize our inseparability. We must be able to tell and to understand these individual and collective stories—of our ancestors—both the African enslaved woman and the Confederate soldier, as well as the demise of the long-leaf pine, as part of an interconnected tapestry of wounding.

Notes

1 Swimme, *The Universe Story: From the Primordial Flaring Forth to the Ecozoic Era—A Celebration of the Unfolding of the Cosmos*. [The quote used is personal correspondence with Belvie Rooks, 2013.]
2 Holmes, *Liberation and the Cosmos*, 1.
3 Berry, *The Dream of the Earth*, 1.
4 National Wildlife Federation, "Standing Tall: How Restoring the Long Leaf Pine Can Help Prepare the Southeast for Global Warming."
5 The Selma-Dallas County Historic Preservation Society, "Brochure Commemorating the 150th Anniversary of the Battle of Selma."
6 DeWolf, *Inheriting the Trade: A Northern Family Confronts Its Legacy as the Largest Slave-Trading Dynasty in U.S. History*, 38
7 Hartman, *Lose Your Mother: A Journey Along the Atlantic Slave Route*.
8 Ibid.
9 Arrien, *Living in Gratitude*, 196.
10 O'Dea and Thompson, "A Summary Report to the Fetzer Institute: Social Healing for a Fractured World."

References

Arrien, Angeles. *Living in Gratitude*. Boulder, CO: Sounds True, Inc., 2011.

Berry, Thomas. *The Dream of the Earth*. San Francisco: Sierra Club Books, 1988.

DeWolf, Thomas N. *Inheriting the Trade: A Northern Family Confronts its Legacy as the Largest Slave-Trading Dynasty in U.S. History*. Boston: Beacon Press, 2009.

Hartman, Saidiya. *Lose Your Mother: A Journey Along the Atlantic Slave Route*. New York: Farrar, Straus and Giroux, 2008.

Holmes, Barbara A. *Liberation and the Cosmos*. Minneapolis: Fortress Press, 2008.

National Wildlife Federation. "Standing Tall: How Restoring the Long Leaf Pine Can Help Prepare the Southeast for Global Warming." December 10, 2009. Available online at www.nwf.org/~/media/PDFs/Global-Warming/Reports/LongleafPineReport .ashx (accessed 27 March 2016).

O'Dea, James and Judith Thompson. "A Summary Report to the Fetzer Institute: Social Healing for a Fractured World." *Shift: At the Frontiers of Consciousness*, 7 (June–August 2005): 10–13.

Swimme, Brian. *The Universe Story: From the Primordial Flaring Forth to the Ecozoic Era—A Celebration of the Unfolding of the Cosmos*. New York: HarperOne, 1994.

The Selma-Dallas County Historic Preservation Society. "Brochure Commemorating the 150th Anniversary of the Battle of Selma." Selma, AL, April 2, 2015.

ACKNOWLEDGMENTS

This book emerged out of the ashes of another project and, as soon as its seeds were planted, seemed to take on a life of its own. There are so, so many people that helped to shape and support its creation. First, I must thank my dearest mentor, Belvie Rooks, who told me I needed to create this book, and to do it with people I love. Similarly, my beloved friend and colleague, Nina Simons, instantly gave me encouragement and connected me to two of the contributors. Along with Belvie and Nina, my fellow Unreasonable Women for the Earth, Rachel Bagby, Susan Griffin and Melissa Nelson, were invaluable sources of support. Thank you to all of the additional contributors—Molly Bigknife Antonio, Ana Baptista, Mei Mei Evans, Ju-Pong Lin, Nina Roberts, Anita Sanchez, Leny Mendoza Strobel and Nícola Wagenberg. Your visions and stories inspire me and it has been an honor to do this work with you.

I have the utmost gratitude to give to my dear, dear friend, Jennifer Weaver, for her editing eyes on several of the chapters. Thank you to Chuck Lief for introducing me to my future publisher. Thank you to Dean Birkenkamp and Amanda Yee at Routledge for guiding and sticking with this project and for the initial support from Megan McClure. My dear colleague and friend Vicky Young has been such an instrumental source of support. Thank you to Raina Gentry for your beautiful art; to M. Jennifer Chandler for your amazing photographs; and a big thank you to both Sue Hammond West and Patty Dean for your last minute help with images! I must of course extend my deep, deep gratitude toward my parents, Carol-Ann and Joseph Canty, for always supporting my work and well-being, and thank my godfather, Billy Nowell, for always checking in on me.

The following folks helped in both big and small ways with the creation and foundation of this book whether they know it or not: Suzanne Benally, Urusa Fahim, Noël Cox Cañiglia, Jesse Giles, Rachel Peters, Joni Adamson, Michelle Gabrieloff-Parish, Ramon Parish, Joanna Macy, Michelle DePass, Rev. angel Kyodo williams, Anne Waldman, Jason Gerhardt, Anne Parker, Jason Appt, Jeremy Lowry, Paul Burkhardt, Ellen Greenblum, Margery Goldman, Gaylon Ferguson, Lee Worley, Frank Berliner, Elizabeth Bumgarner, Amy Brummer, Alison Holmes, Carl Anthony, Noliwe Rooks, the late and beloved Dedan Gills, Brandon Lott, Stephan Snider, Drew Dellinger, David Christopher, Luisa Maffi, Christine Arpita, Barb Catbagan, Kate Mulheron and Paloma Pavel. I know there are so many others I have omitted and do know your support is greatly appreciated. Most importantly, thank you to Mother Earth for your continued love and patience and to all of the ancestors and spirits.

LIST OF CONTRIBUTORS

Molly Bigknife Antonio, MA (Shawnee, Munsee Delaware, Cherokee) is co-founder and Executive Director of Pollen Circles, Inc., a youth organization that provides culturally based holistic wellness camps and activities in and around the Navajo Nation in northeastern Arizona. She has over twenty years of experience working with youth and the environment. She is an associate faculty and a doctoral student at Prescott College.

Rachel Bagby, JD, is devoted to helping people hear and heed women's wisdom. An award-winning social artist who integrates the power of singing and creative, contemplative practices into her leadership trainings, she is the creator of the poetic form Dekaaz Facilitation® and author of *Divine Daughters: Liberating the Power and Passion of Women's Voices*. http://rachelbagby.com/

Ana I. Baptista, PhD, is an Assistant Professor of Professional Practice at The New School's Environmental Policy & Sustainability Management program in the Milano School. She is also Associate Director for the Tishman Environment & Design Center at the New School. She is the former Director of Environmental Programs for the Ironbound Community Corporation (ICC), where she now serves on the Board. She is also a founding member of the New Jersey Environmental Justice Alliance.

Jeanine M. Canty, PhD, is a professor at Naropa University in Boulder, CO. A lover of nature, justice and contemplative practice, her teaching intersects issues of social and ecological justice and the process individuals go through to reach heightened awareness and translating this to positive change. Selected works have been featured in *The Wiley Handbook of Transpersonal Psychology*, *International Journal of Transpersonal Studies*, *Sustainability: The Journal of Record* and *World Futures: Journal of New Paradigm Research*.

M. Jennifer Chandler, MA, (photographs) is a photographer and graphic designer who explores themes of identity, environment and change. She has taught photography in the visual arts department at Prescott College and works in areas of arts administration, grant writing, art installation, nonprofit leadership and making the arts accessible to all.

Mei Mei Evans, PhD, is the author of the novel *Oil and Water* (2013, University of Alaska Press), a PEN/Bellwether finalist, and co-editor (with Joni Adamson and Rachel Stein) of *The Environmental Justice Reader* (2002, University of Arizona Press). A 2009 recipient of an Individual Artist's Award from the Rasmuson Foundation, she teaches full time in the Liberal Studies department at Alaska Pacific University, and lives in Anchorage, Alaska, with her teenage daughter.

Raina Gentry (cover art) is an artist who incorporates printmaking, life drawing, collage and painting. She holds a BA with honors in studio art from the University of Arizona and another in Environmental Studies from Prescott College. She views each canvas as a playground for her psyche with each work of art evolving naturally and intuitively.

Susan Griffin has written over twenty books, including non-fiction, poetry and plays. Her work addresses many social and political issues, social justice, the oppression of women, ecology, war and peace, economic inequities and democracy. Her book *Woman and Nature* is credited with inspiring the eco-feminist movement. She and her work have been given many awards, among them a Guggenheim Foundation Award, an

Emmy, the Northern California Book Award, as well as being a finalist for a Pulitzer Prize.

Ju-Pong Lin, MFA, A Taiwanese immigrant, works at the edges of art and activism. She is a core member of "Wicked Questions: A Global Conversation on Climate," an artist-led intervention that invites *all* people to respond to climate change by transforming isolation and fear into creative and collaborative action. She directs the MFA in Interdisciplinary Arts at Goddard College.

Melissa K. Nelson, PhD, is an ecologist, writer, media-maker and indigenous scholar–activist. She is an associate professor of American Indian Studies at San Francisco State University and president of The Cultural Conservancy. She is the editor of and contributor to *Original Instructions – Indigenous Teachings for a Sustainable Future* and co-producer of the award-winning documentary film, *The Salt Song Trail: Bringing Creation Back Together*. Melissa is Anishinaabe/Métis/Norwegian and an enrolled member of the Turtle Mountain Band of Chippewa Indians.

Nina S. Roberts, PhD, is a professor at San Francisco State University in the department of Recreation, Parks, and Tourism, a Fulbright scholar and Director of the Pacific Leadership Institute. Her research regarding race, class, gender and visiting national parks and other public lands provides managers in outdoor recreation, natural resource management and environmental education with the ideas and resources needed to respond more effectively to changing demographics, cultural shifts and population trends across the US.

Belvie Rooks, MA, is co-founder of Growing a Global Heart as well as a writer, educator and producer who weaves the worlds of spirituality, feminism, ecology and social justice. Her published works have appeared in: *Global Chorus: 365 Voices on the Future of the Planet*, *The Same River Twice: Honoring the Difficult*, *My Soul is a Witness: African American Women's Spirituality*, *Life Notes: Personal Writings by Black Women* and *Paris Connections: African American Artists in Paris*.

Anita L. Sanchez, PhD, is an international consultant, trainer, speaker and coach who is passionate about visionary leadership and the empowerment of women and people around the world. Her work focuses on cultural transformation, organization development and diversity. A member of the Transformational Leadership Council, she is the best-selling co-author of *Success University for Women*. Her forthcoming book, *The Four Gifts: Indigenous Wisdom for Modern Times*, will be published by Simon & Schuster in March 2017.

Nina Simons, President and co-founder of Bioneers, is a social entrepreneur passionate about reinventing leadership, restoring the feminine and co-creating an equitable and healthy world for all. Nina directs Bioneers' Everywoman's Leadership program, is co-editor of *Moonrise: The Power of Women Leading from the Heart*, and is the recipient of a Robert Rodale Award, the Rainforest Action Network REVEL Award, the Green Cross Millennium Award for Community Environmental Leadership and Technica's Top 10 Women of Sustainability.

Leny Mendoza Strobel, EdD, is professor of American Multicultural Studies at Sonoma State University. She is the author of *Coming Full Circle: The Process of Decolonization Among Post-1965 Filipino Americans*, *A Book of Her Own: Words and Images to Honor the Babaylan* and the editor of *Babaylan: Filipinos and the Call of the Indigenous*. She is also the Director of The Center for Babaylan Studies.

Nicola Wagenberg, PhD, is vice president of The Cultural Conservancy. Her work includes directing media projects, developing and implementing arts and cultural health programs and helping with operations and development. Nicola is a clinical psychologist working with diverse communities and organizations using media, the arts and psychology toward personal and cultural transformation. She is co-producer of Traditional Foodways of Native America and The Salt Song Trail and is director of the Native Youth Guardians of the Waters project.

INDEX

Made in United States
Troutdale, OR
01/11/2025

27847342R00130